# Sheltered Content Instruction

## Teaching English-Language Learners with Diverse Abilities

### SECOND EDITION

**Jana Echevarria**

*California State University, Long Beach*

**Anne Graves**

*San Diego State University*

Boston   New York   San Francisco
Mexico City   Montreal   Toronto   London   Madrid   Munich   Paris
Hong Kong   Singapore   Tokyo   Cape Town   Sydney

**Series Editor:** *Aurora Martínez Ramos*
**Editorial Assistant:** *Beth Slater*
**Senior Marketing Manager:** *Elizabeth Fogarty*
**Production Administrator:** *Annette Joseph*
**Editorial-Production Service:** *Susan Freese, Communicáto, Ltd.*
**Electronic Composition:** *Peggy Cabot, Cabot Computer Services*
**Composition Buyer:** *Linda Cox*
**Manufacturing Buyer:** *Megan Cochran*
**Cover Administrator:** *Kristina Mose-Libon*
**Cover Designer:** *Jennifer Hart*

For related titles and support materials, visit our online catalog at
www.ablongman.com.

Between the time Website information is gathered and then published, it
is not unusual for some sites to have closed. Also, the transcription of
URLs can result in unintended typographical errors. The publisher would
appreciate notification where these errors occur so that they may be
corrected in subsequent editions.

**Library of Congress Cataloging-in-Publication Data**

Echevarria, Jana
    Sheltered content instruction : teaching English-language learners with
diverse abilities / Jana Echevarria, Anne Graves.—2nd ed.
      p.  cm.
    Includes bibliographical references and index.
    ISBN 0-205-34225-6
    1. English language—Study and teaching—Foreign speakers.
2. Language arts—Correlation with content subjects.  3. Individualized
instruction.  I. Graves, Anne Wooding.  II. Title.

PE1128.A2  E26  2003
428'.007—dc21                      2002027807

Printed in the United States of America

10  9  8  7  6  5          RRD-VA     08  07  06  05  04

**Text Credit:** Pages 153–154: Dialogue reprinted courtesy of Sharon Pritzos (1992) from
*Teacher Communication in Regular and Sheltered Science Classes,* unpublished master's thesis.

**Photo Credits:** Page 1: Robert Harbison; Pages 31 and 77: Will Hart; pages 52, 96, 121,
150, 169: Will Faller.

*For my children, Paige and Dillon Ratleff*

*For John Forren*
*and our daughter, Grace*

# Contents

## 2 *Theoretical and Historical Foundations*  *31*

## 3 *Sheltered Instruction in the Content Areas*  *52*

**4** *Affective Issues   77*

## 6 *Curriculum Adaptations*  *121*

## 7    *Adjusting Discourse to Enhance Learning    150*

## 8    *Self-Evaluation and Collaborative Implementation    169*

# *Preface*

The number of students who are English-language learners (ELLs) that are entering U.S. schools continues to increase, as do the variations in their academic background and skills. Some students come with grade-level academic preparation, while others are underprepared for the high academic standards of school. In this second edition of *Sheltered Content Instruction,* we address the need for standards-based curricula to be presented in a way that is understandable for ELLs so that they can achieve grade-level standards.

School reform efforts have focused the nation's attention on education—specifically, teacher preparation and student learning. We believe that no child should be left behind; however, many textbooks used in teacher preparation—general education and special education—are inadequate for preparing teachers to work effectively with diverse students. This book is designed to prepare teachers to deliver content area instruction to ELLs with diverse abilities using a sheltered instruction approach.

The terms associated with the education of ELLs vary from region to region and have different meanings for different people. Some terms may even ascribe status, however unintended. In this book, the term *sheltered instruction* indicates the teaching of content area knowledge and skills in a more understandable way while also developing students' English-language proficiency. Some similar terms are *content ESL* and *specially designed academic instruction in English (SDAIE).*

One of the goals of this book is to define what a sheltered lesson is and describe how it can be used on a daily basis in the classroom. Little has been written about the challenges caused by the varying levels of educational background and abilities of English-language learners. Teachers frequently report that they struggle to accommodate the diversity of skills and abilities of the students in their classes. These diverse skills and abilities are even more difficult to understand for those teachers who lack training and knowledge about second-language acquisition and related issues. Certain types of difficulties for ELLs are predictable and understandable, given adequate preparation to work with these students. Other students may have needs that require specialized attention, such as those who are undereducated and those who have learning difficulties. Certain types of instruction are appropriate for English-language learners, regardless of whether they are (1) in small groups or large groups, (2) in primarily bilingual or monolingual placements, or (3) identified for special education services.

In preparing to write this book for teachers and for students studying to become teachers, we have reviewed theory, research, and practice in the areas of second-language acquisition, multicultural education, and special education, including updates from our own ongoing research. This new edition provides the most current information available about students who are learning English.

This second edition has been updated to cover a number of new topics. The current emphasis on standards-based education is addressed throughout the book. In addition, the research-based model of sheltered instruction, the SIOP, is discussed in detail in Chapter 3. Finally, each chapter reports the findings of recent research on effective instructional practices for ELLs.

## Organizational Overview

This book begins by laying a foundation in issues surrounding the education of students learning English. Chapter 1 describes the target population for the book and the functional areas used to describe that population. Such functional areas include native-language knowledge, English-language knowledge, academic background, and behavior and learning patterns. This chapter also describes the procedures within each of these functional areas for informal assessment and instructional planning. Programmatic decisions can have a significant impact on instruction, as any teacher with non-English-speaking students and native speakers in the same biology class can attest.

Chapter 2 provides an overview of the historical background and theories that explain and support procedures for the instruction of students learning English in school. It includes information on the history of second-language acquisition in the schools, an overview of learning theories, and theories of second-language acquisition. It also includes a discussion of the factors that affect second-language acquisition and the influences on an individual's rate and level of learning a new language.

Chapters 3 through 8 provide specific information for teaching ELLs more effectively. Each of these chapters includes specific examples of formats and dialogue for teachers. Chapter 3 introduces sheltered instruction and gives specifics for its effective implementation in the content areas, including examples of the design and delivery of such instruction. Chapter 4 includes information and strategies regarding the appropriate affective or emotional responses of students, teachers, and parents. Research on learning strategies, descriptions of those strategies, and specific examples of strategies that are likely to improve school performance are the focus of Chapter 5. Chapter 6 describes curriculum adaptations and specific examples of appropriate modifications for students who are learning English across grade levels and subject areas. Chapter 7 describes research about and procedures for adjusting discourse to enhance English learning and success in school. Chapter 8 is an overview of the material presented in the book and offers examples of processes that promote networking among school personnel. Shared roles, collaborative work, and mutually supportive environments are essential for the appropriate instruction of students who are ELLs.

Most professionals agree that teaching content material to students who are learning English is one of the greatest challenges teachers face today. One of the reasons for this is the range of skills and abilities that these students bring to learning tasks. This practical guide for teachers recommends methods for adapting instruction and curriculum across grade levels and subject areas for students.

## *Acknowledgments*

A book such as this is developed over time, as a result of many discussions, observations, teaching experiences, and interviews. In particular, we owe a debt of gratitude to the many teachers and school personnel, too numerous to mention individually, whose cooperation and generosity contributed to this book being grounded in classroom experiences and practices. The districts represented include Lennox Unified School District as well as Long Beach Unified School District and the teachers and staff at Hill Middle School, Los Angeles Unified School District, Santa Barbara Unified School District, and San Diego City Unified School District.

We thank the following reviewers of the first edition for their comments and suggestions: Jay Richard Fuhriman (Boise State University), Else Hamayan (Illinois Resource Center), Mary E. McGroarty (Northern Arizona University), Carla Meskill (University of Albany, State University of New York), and Teresa Pica (University of Pennsylvania). We also wish to acknowledge the following individuals who provided valuable feedback on earlier drafts of this book: Charlie Crawford, Claude Goldenberg, Jeff Jung, Deborah Smalley, and Terrence Wiley.

# *Teaching English-Language Learners with Diverse Abilities*

- *Sho-Wen* is the only Cantonese-speaking student in the school. How can school personnel be sure of her academic skills and experience?
- *María* has been educated in Mexico but speaks only limited English. Should she be placed in a mainstream class?
- *Sam* was born in the United States. He speaks both his native language and English. Records indicate that he has a history of poor school performance, including low reading and writing ability. What factors may account for his underachievement?
- *Myoung* is having difficulty completing assignments in a sheltered science class. Should she be referred to special education?

*Limited-English-proficient (LEP)*, *bilingual*, and *language-minority students* are among a variety of terms that can be used to refer to students for whom English is not their native language. We prefer the term *English-language learners (ELLs)* because we feel it is the most positive and accurate description of this population. Whatever term is used, one thing is certain: Only a general term can describe students of many different language proficiency and academic levels.

Some students learning English do well in school, while others experience special challenges (Banks & McGee, 2001; Garcia, 2000; Maik, 1999; Ramirez, 1992; Chinn & Hughes, 1987). Rumberger (1995) and others have reported that in the inner cities, 40 percent of Latino students drop out before high school. The cultural and linguistic rift between English-speaking teachers and their students has been well documented and undoubtedly contributes to some students' poor performance in school (Burnette, 2000; Gay, 1993; Harry, Torguson, Katkavich, & Guerrero, 1993; Hill, Carjuzaa, Aramburo, & Baca, 1993). In response, teachers are giving greater attention to the impact that ethnicity, language, culture, and background have on the education of youth (MacSwan, 2000; Garibaldi, 1992).

Clearly, in order to provide an appropriate education to English-language learners, their individual situations must be considered. Are the students' parents professionals or migrant workers? Did the students learn English while living in a refugee camp or through a private tutor? Are the students recent immigrants or U.S. natives? Do the parents support native-language instruction or not? Have the students been educated at grade level, or do they have significant gaps in their education? The answers to these questions may impact programming decisions. While the diverse backgrounds of individuals do not fit neatly into categories, four general profiles emerge: (1) balanced bilingual, (2) monolingual/literate in native language, (3) monolingual/preliterate in native language, and (4) limited bilingual.

*Sonia* is a tenth-grader who was born in Guatemala. She moved to Southern California in the second grade. She was a good student in Guatemala and learned to read and write in Spanish. When she began school in the United States, she was placed in a bilingual classroom where she received native-language support before transitioning into English instruction. Now in high school, she is performing at or above grade level in mainstream classes and has communication and literacy skills in her native language, as well. Because Sonia can speak, read, and write well in both languages, her English teacher is considering referring her to the gifted program at her school.

Sonia and students like her are not the subject of this book, since they have achieved a balanced bilingual status. Indeed, duplicating this experience is the goal of this book: helping individuals who are academically successful in English to maintain their native languages. We have written this book to help teachers in providing a high-quality education to students from a variety of backgrounds who are learning English.

The other three types of students are of concern to us. These students require special attention, knowledge, and strategies from teachers to enhance their opportunities to learn and their success in school. Teachers routinely see these students in their classes, some of whom experience difficulties in school.

*Krishna* is a recent immigrant who attends middle school. He has grade-level academic ability in his native language but speaks very little English. Since he has lived all his 13 years outside the United States, certain cultural knowledge presents difficulties for him. Krishna is quite shy and does not seek help readily. He has excellent social and academic language skills in his primary language and has already studied English for a few years, but his proficiency is quite limited. His history of learning and behavior at school, at home, and in the community is positive. He is described as a good citizen and a student who demonstrates appropriate behavior in most settings.

*Pon* is a fourth-grader who mainly speaks Khmer (Cambodian) and is one of two Cambodians in a rural school district. He is a nonreader in English and struggles with even the simplest words. His spoken English is quite limited when he interacts with students and the teacher in class. The members of his family are not literate and have not been able to provide literacy experiences for him at home. He has behavior problems in school. He often defies the teacher and engages in surreptitious or antisocial activities (fights, stealing, and so forth).

Born in an urban U.S. city, *Luisa* is a friendly 15-year-old who sits quietly in class as if she understands everything. When written assignments are given, she writes down the assignment and begins to work. Her writing, however, is illegible, and her spelling is extremely poor. Spanish is her first language, although her family speaks a mix of English and Spanish at home. She writes in English in a knowledge-telling mode without recognizable structure in her sentences or in her paragraphs. Luisa can converse quite well in both languages but for some reason has not made academic progress in either language. Although she is popular at school, she is at risk for dropping out because of consistent underachievement.

The purpose of this book is to provide information for teaching English-language learners with diverse abilities, such as Krishna, Luisa, and Pon. Learning in and through a new language is a complex endeavor affected by a variety of factors, some of which are shown in Figure 1.1. A systematic approach will address all of these dimensions to ensure a quality education for students learning English.

Because of the tremendous influx of English-language learners into the schools, the need for programs—and for procedures for placing students in programs—has often outstripped program development. As a result, programs and terminology vary from state to state and region to region, and the terms used in this book may differ from school to school.

School personnel must first evaluate English-language learners in each of the following areas: native-language knowledge, English-language knowledge, school experience and academic background, and learning and behavior patterns (see Figure 1.2, page 6). Once an appropriate assessment has been done, instructional plans can be developed that support learners for academic success. When state standards exist, educational plans can be written to include grade-level and English-language standards. Procedures for the design of these assessments and instructional plans are delineated next.

## *Native-Language Knowledge*

Possible levels of native-language knowledge range from low-proficiency to above-grade-level skills in oral language, reading, and writing. Both theory and practice have illuminated the impact of native-language proficiency on learning (Collier, 1995; Ramirez, 1992; Cummins, 1989). We know that students who speak their native language fluently and have developed age-appropriate literacy skills have increased opportunities for developing language and literacy skills in English (Lewelling & Peyton, 1999; *Reading/Language Arts Framework,* 2000; Faltis & Hudelson, 1994; Franklin & Thompson, 1994; Cloud, 1993; Chan, 1990). Further, those who have developed cognitive knowledge and concept comprehension in their native language have better opportunities for learning English (Barratt-Pugh & Rohl, 2001; Cazden, 1992; Krashen, 1982). For youngsters who have not had literacy models, literacy development in another language (in this case, English) is likely to be more difficult (Franklin & Thompson, 1994). An assessment to determine the student's level of native-language proficiency

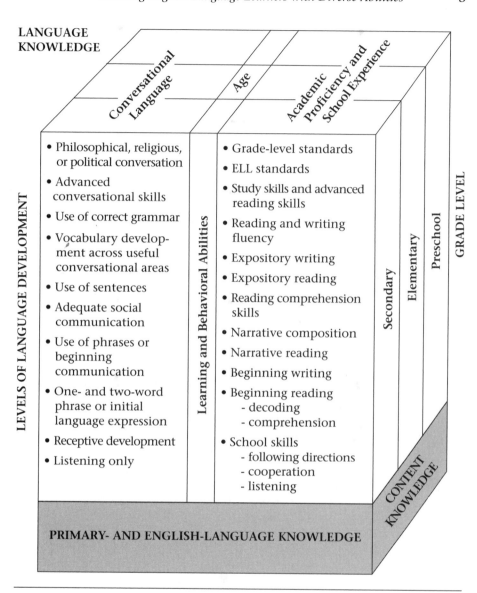

FIGURE 1.1   *Visual Display of Language-Learner Dimensions*

will provide valuable information for making placement and instruction decisions.

## Assessment

In Pon's case, a home language survey should be conducted first to determine his native language, which in his case is Khmer (Figueroa, 1989;

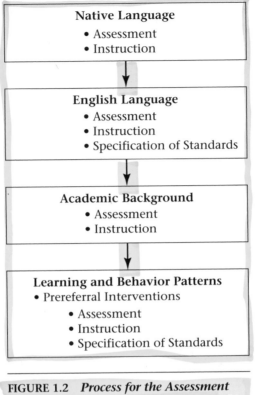

**FIGURE 1.2** *Process for the Assessment and Education of English-Language Learners*

Rueda, 1989; Moll, 1988). Next, a competent speaker of Khmer must assess Pon's native-language knowledge (Ortiz & Wilkinson, 1991; Cloud, Landurand, & Wu, 1989). If native-language professionals are unavailable, personnel from other districts or geographic areas may be hired. Finally, if trained personnel are completely unavailable, community members may be used to ascertain the student's abilities. When this option is exercised, it should be indicated on the record that the student could not be adequately assessed and that valid, reliable judgments about the language and cognitive abilities of the student could not be made (Baca & Almanza, 1991). This is especially important when the student is being considered for special services such as special education. School personnel also benefit from family input and insights into the skills and levels of functioning of the learner (Gonzalez et al., 1993; Chang, 1992; Lynch & Hanson, 1992).

An assessment of Pon's native-language skills includes measuring oral language functioning as well as reading and writing skills (Schiff-Myers,

Djukic, Lawler-McGovern, & Perez, 1994). Once Pon's native-language skills have been assessed, results can be compared to grade-level competencies as much as possible (Perez, 1993; Saville-Troike, 1984). If as a fourth-grader Pon can write a comprehensible 150-word story that is organized and that uses a variety of interesting vocabulary words, then the native-language evaluator will list those skills and determine his approximate grade-level functioning. An approximate determination of third-grade-level writing and reading with good comprehension in the native language would indicate a readiness to begin transferring some of those skills to English.

## Instruction

There are a variety of instructional models for teaching English-language learners: native-language support, English as a second language (ESL) instruction, sheltered instruction, and mainstream classes.

The way *native-language support* is provided is influenced by a host of factors, such as the number of students from the language group and the availability of bilingual personnel. The most effective model is one in which teachers fluent in the students' native language provide instructional support as needed, with beginning speakers requiring more native-language instruction than those with greater English proficiency. Bilingual instructional aides (IAs) are a valuable resource when a certified bilingual teacher is unavailable. In this model, the teacher maintains responsibility for instruction but works as a team with the IA. The teacher plans, monitors, and develops assessment of student progress; the IA works with a group of students, carrying out the lessons in the native language. The IA also documents students' progress and communicates with the teacher. Since IAs are closely involved with the students' education, they assist in developing good working relationships with families. Other options include using peers and members of the community to provide native-language support.

*ESL instruction* (also called *English language development,* or *ELD,* in some states) is a critical component of programs for English-language learners. Language educators trained in second-language acquisition theory and methods provide instruction that focuses on developing oral language, reading, and writing in English so that these students can function effectively in the classroom. Students are trained to use the cognitively complex language of formal education. ELD standards can provide a framework for language development (McKay, 2000).

Traditional language teaching has focused on grammatical aspects of language and vocabulary building. More recently, the communicative purposes of language have been emphasized, often using units or themes from everyday experiences as the curriculum. Students learn names of common objects, interpersonal communication skills, and language necessary for everyday tasks such as taking the bus, going to the store, and using the library. Currently, there is an increased awareness of the importance of integrating academic content areas with language instruction. Rather than introducing a series of isolated units, language instruction is most effective if it teaches language that provides access to subject matter texts, discussions, and class activities (Crandall, 1995; Short, 1991).

*Content-based ESL*, then, teaches English and its components (vocabulary, discourse style, and syntax) using the core curriculum as the means. The components of English being learned are drawn from particular subject areas, thus increasing the relevancy of the curriculum and providing the language teacher with material through which to teach a grammatical point or function (Crandall, 1995). ESL is most often taught by an ESL specialist and is typically provided on either a pull-out basis or as a scheduled class for one or more periods during the day. Table 1.1 provides a brief summary of comparisons between content-based ESL and sheltered content instruction.

Teachers who are certified in content areas (science, mathematics, history, or literature) and have had some sort of training in second-language instruction (preservice or inservice) provide *sheltered instruction*. The primary goal of sheltered instruction is to teach academic subject matter to English-language learners using comprehensible language and context, enabling information to be understood by the learner. Sheltered instruction functions as a support until the student is ready for mainstream classes.

TABLE 1.1 *Comparison of Content-Based ESL and Sheltered Content Instruction*

| *Content-Based ESL* | *Sheltered Content Instruction* |
| --- | --- |
| • English-language development is a goal.<br>• ESL methods are used.<br>• Requisite terminology for content areas is a focus.<br>• Skills and thematic units from a variety of subject areas are integrated.<br>• A teacher certified in ESL theory and methods is in charge. | • Content knowledge and skills as well as English-language development are goals.<br>• Sheltered instruction strategies are used.<br>• Core grade-level curriculum is the foundation.<br>• Content standards and ESL standards drive instruction.<br>• Instruction generally follows the scope and sequence of a mainstream class.<br>• A teacher certified in subject area, with training in teaching English-language learners, is in charge. |

To prepare students for *mainstream classes,* sheltered teachers design lessons that use English in a variety of ways, including reading, discussing, and writing about complex and abstract ideas. This approach integrates natural second-language-acquisition features with direct instruction. Since the emphasis is on meaning, not form, students learning English are able to interact with peers and teachers at their level of English-language proficiency. Students practice using English while participating in discussions centered around content area material, thus increasing language acquisition while developing academic concepts. (Chapter 3 discusses specific sheltered strategies and implementation.)

In practice, the distinction between sheltered instruction and content-based ESL may be blurred, especially in the lower grades. However, a conceptual distinction is important so that the specific characteristics of ESL instruction do not become lost in teaching the core subject area curriculum. Explicit teaching of academic English through ESL techniques is crucial; students will not always pick it up along the way.

A student like Pon would benefit from an instructional program that includes native-language support and comprehensive ESL instruction (Fitzgerald, 1995; Short, 1994; Cloud, 1993; Cummins, 1991). As Pon acquires more English and academic skills, teachers can introduce subject matter teaching in English using sheltered instruction, adapting the instruction to enhance understanding of content material (Pierce, 1988). If Pon's parents support an instructional approach with Pon that focuses on behavioral contracts, special reading and writing instruction, and an adapted curriculum, these techniques can also be used. His behavior and affect should be carefully monitored, along with his academic performance, to determine if he is making progress. Ongoing assessment should indicate improved performance, or an individualized learning plan should be developed.

In summary, for students learning in bilingual settings, the steps for instruction are (1) assess language functions; (2) make an instructional plan that includes ESL, native-language support, and sheltered instruction, as appropriate; and (3) conduct ongoing, informal assessment to determine the student's success in language, academic, and content acquisition (Cloud, 1994; Schiff-Myers, Djukic, Lawler-McGovern, & Perez, 1994; Ortiz & Wilkinson, 1991).

## English-Language Knowledge

For any new language, several possible levels of knowledge exist. Making a distinction between everyday conversational ability and the academic proficiency required for scholastic success was made popular by James Cummins (1994, 1989, 1981). The conversational proficiency needed in everyday situations is termed *basic interpersonal communication skill (BICS),* while the more cognitively demanding language necessary for school success is called *cognitive/academic language proficiency (CALP).* Although the terms BICS and CALP are still widely used, Cummins has more recently used the terms *conversational language* and *academic language* (Cummins, 1994).

Conversational proficiency is relatively easy to acquire. In fact, a person can learn and understand basic words and phrases in a matter of hours, with fluency usually attained in one to three years. In Cummins's conceptualization of bilingual proficiency, conversational proficiency is just "the tip of the iceberg"; below the surface lies the more critical language proficiency required for academic tasks.

The language of school is more complex and more cognitively demanding than everyday language. It is the kind of language needed for tasks such as comprehension of text, analysis, and synthesis of material. If a student speaks little or no English, then the acquisition of new concepts will be expedited when presented in the language the student understands—his or her native language.

Content area instruction, which relies on academic language proficiency, demands more from the student than simple understanding of spoken English. It requires that the student have a good command of the domains of language, such as English phonology (sounds), morphology (basic units of meaning), syntax (grammar), semantics (meaning), and pragmatics (function) across content areas and in each language skill area (see Figure 1.3). Students must understand English syntactic patterns and rules when they read, write, speak, and listen to English. But these skills alone are not sufficient, since each subject area uses a language of its own; for instance, the language of mathematics is different from those of literature and science. Therefore, English-language learners must also learn the specific vocabulary of each subject.

With each succeeding grade level, the ability to learn content material becomes increasingly dependent on interaction with and mastery of the language that is connected to the specific content material. The ability to demonstrate knowledge also requires increasingly sophisticated oral and written forms of language. McKeon (1994) suggests that "careful planning of instruction is needed to help students develop the decontextualized language skills they will need to master the cognitively demanding content in higher grades" (p. 25).

Academic proficiency begins with basic literacy, and the demands increase as a student continues through school. Each academic content area has its own established proficiencies for each grade level. For example, consider the following scenario: A third-grade teacher reads a story aloud to his students. After finishing the story, he asks questions. Students who have had practice listening for important information, main ideas, and drawing

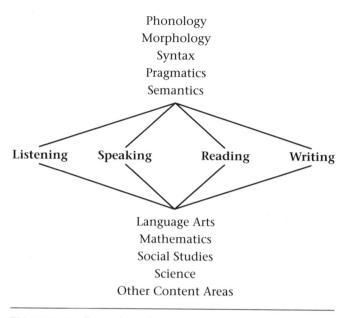

Phonology
Morphology
Syntax
Pragmatics
Semantics

**Listening    Speaking    Reading    Writing**

Language Arts
Mathematics
Social Studies
Science
Other Content Areas

FIGURE 1.3 *Domains of Language*

inferences will be more likely to participate than those who have not. These are the *academic proficiencies* necessary for success at this task. In another example, consider the following scenario: A middle school science teacher tells students, "Read about these marine animals, and write about their common characteristics." Students who are more likely to be able to complete this assignment have analytic skills, grade-level reading skills, and writing skills. In a third scenario, a high school teacher asks tenth-grade students to choose a book and write a book report. Students who are more likely to complete the task successfully can read at an appropriate level, read for understanding and comprehension, make a plan for their report that includes all the important parts of a narrative, and write with the ability to edit and revise. These examples demonstrate that success often depends on the task itself and the amount of contextual support available.

Cummins's conceptualization of language proficiency is not without its critics (Edelsky, 1991; Romaine, 1989; Rivera, 1984; Troike, 1984). Baker (1993) characterizes the limitations of the BICS/CALP distinction as an oversimplification of the reality of how complex and multifaceted language and language competence is. In fact, research indicates that a bilingual student's language competencies are influenced by a number of factors, such as environment and motivation, and are constantly evolving and interacting; they are not simple dichotomies that are easily compartmentalized and unchanging. Further, the notion of distinct levels of language proficiency lacks empirical support.

In spite of its limitations, the notion of everyday language versus academic language (the BICS/CALP distinction) enjoys wide popularity among practitioners, primarily because of its applicability to students in classroom situations. It provides a general understanding of students' language needs and explicitly states that even students who appear to have a good command of spoken English may not yet be ready for academic instruction in English.

It is possible to apply the BICS/CALP iceberg analogy to the case of Luisa, who is a limited-bilingual student. Since she has lived all her life in the United States, teachers are concerned about her low academic levels in English. Records show that initial assessment results of social and academic language skills in Spanish (done in kindergarten) indicate high levels of social language skills and low preliteracy levels (that is, the ability to recognize rhyming words, sound/symbol relationships, and so forth). Although she was in a bilingual kindergarten, the teacher was not a fluent Spanish speaker. Luisa began first grade with a native-Spanish-speaking teacher, but after her family moved, she was placed in an all-English first-grade class at the new school. In second grade, she received limited native-language support from a bilingual paraeducator, but no such assistance was available in third grade and beyond. Report cards and teacher comments reveal that Luisa has performed poorly in school since kindergarten. She is a popular student, has many friends, and has been quite cooperative in school, which may account for her promotion from grade to grade. Now in middle school, Luisa has low academic skills in both English and Spanish.

The iceberg analogy (see Figure 1.4) suggests the following linguistic profile: Luisa has surface features in Spanish and surface features in English, as well. However, she does not fare as well in terms of the more cognitively demanding underlying proficiency. During the critical early developmental period, Luisa did not receive solid, consistent instruction in either language, which restricted her learning. Her conversational proficiency in English does not guarantee academic proficiency.

The iceberg analogy provides a simple but useful profile for teachers. Of course, a more in-depth assessment of levels of language proficiency is essential if students are to be placed in the proper academic program (Garcia & Ortiz, 1988).

## Assessment

After a home language survey reveals that English is not a student's home language, his or her English proficiency is then assessed. School personnel familiar with second-language acquisition conduct the assessment using an instrument such as the *Language Assessment Scales (LAS)* or *Idea Proficiency Test (IPT)* in English. An assessment should also include informal

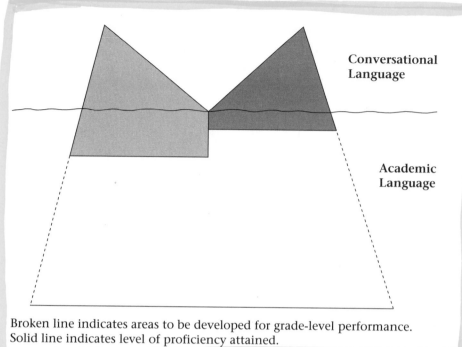

Broken line indicates areas to be developed for grade-level performance.
Solid line indicates level of proficiency attained.

**FIGURE 1.4** *Iceberg Representation of Luisa's Language Proficiency*
*Source:* Based on Cummins, 1994.

assessment of oral language, reading, and writing. Informal assessment may be conducted through observation scales, informal writing samples, and informal reading inventories. Typically, a student who is learning English is assigned a proficiency level for purposes of placement. It is far too simplistic to conclude that all students learning English pass through the same stages of learning and through every level of language development in the same way. However, levels of development are commonly referred to in placing English-language learners in instructional programs.

Informal observation scales, such as the *Student Oral Language Observation Matrix (SOLOM)* (see Figure 1.5, page 14), include levels on which comprehension, fluency, vocabulary, pronunciation, and grammar are points of consideration. For example, a person at Level 1 typically speaks very little English and has limited conversational and academic skills.

## Instruction

As Figure 1.5 illustrates, instructional programs are often based on the *natural approach* (Krashen & Terrell, 1983), which assumes that students acquire a second language in stages, in much the same way that they acquire a first

# FIGURE 1.5   *SOLOM Language Observation Matrix*

**Teacher Observation**
**Student Oral Language Observation Matrix (SOLOM)**

Student's Name: _____   Grade: _____   Examiner: _____
Language Observed: _____                    Date: _____

| LEVEL | 1 | 2 | 3 | 4 | 5 |
|---|---|---|---|---|---|
| (A)<br>Comprehension | Cannot understand even simple conversation. | Has great difficulty following what is said. Can comprehend only "social conversation" spoken slowly and with frequent repetitions. | Understands most of what is said at slower than normal speed with repetitions. | Understands nearly everything at normal speed, although, occasional repetition may be necessary. | Understands every-day conversation and normal classroom discussions without difficulty. |
| (B)<br>Fluency | Speech is so halting and fragmentary as to make conversation virtually impossible. | Usually hesitant; often forced into silence by language limitations. | Speech in everyday conversation and classroom discussions is frequently disrupted by the student's search for the correct manner of expression. | Speech in everyday conversation and classroom discussion is generally fluent, with occasional lapses while searching for the correct manner of expression. | Speech in everyday conversation and classroom discussion is fluent and effortless, approximating that of a native speaker. |
| (C)<br>Vocabulary | Vocabulary limitations so extreme as to make conversation virtually impossible. | Misuse of words and very limited vocabulary make comprehension quite difficult. | Frequently uses the wrong words; conversation somewhat limited because of inadequate vocabulary. | Occasionally uses inappropriate terms and/or must rephrase ideas because of lexical inadequacies. | Use of vocabulary and idioms approximates that of a native speaker. |
| (D)<br>Pronunciation | Pronunciation problems so severe as to make speech virtually unintelligible. | Very hard to understand because of pronunciation problems. Must frequently repeat in order to make him/herself understood. | Pronunciation problems necessitate concentration on the part of the listener and occasionally lead to misunderstanding. | Always intelligible though one is conscious of a definite accent and occasional inappropriate intonation patterns. | Pronunciation and intonation approximates that of a native speaker. |
| (E)<br>Grammar | Errors in grammar and word order so severe as to make speech virtually unintelligible. | Grammar and word order errors make comprehension difficult. Must often rephrase and/or restrict him/herself to basic patterns. | Makes frequent errors of grammar and word order which occasionally obscure meaning. | Occasionally makes grammatical and/or word order errors which do not obscure meaning. | Grammatical usage and word order approximates that of a native speaker. |

The student oral language observation matrix (SOLOM) has five (5) categories on the left: A. Comprehension, B. Fluency, C. Vocabulary, D. Pronunciation, and E. Grammar. It also has five numbers along the top, one (1) being the lowest mark to five (5) being the highest mark. According to your observation, indicate with an (X) across the square in each category which best describes the child's abilities. Those students whose checkmarks (X's) are to the right of the darkened line will be considered for reclassification, if test scores and achievement data also indicate English proficiency.

language. According to the natural approach, students have more receptive ability than expressive ability during the early stages of language learning. These programs therefore attempt to create a nonthreatening and motivating language-learning environment. The stages of the natural approach and their characteristics are shown in Figure 1.6. (For a complete discussion of the natural approach, see Richard-Amato, 1996.)

Once the student's English-language level is determined by formal assessment (using a standardized test such as the LAS or IPT) or by informal assessment (through observation, the use of SOLOM, informal writing samples, or informal reading inventories), this information can be combined with the results of native-language knowledge and skills assessment findings. A comprehensive plan for instruction can then be developed based on the profile of the student. Figure 1.7 (page 16) outlines program options for English-language learners based on their levels of English proficiency.

It is important to note that the model presented assumes the availability of qualified bilingual personnel to provide native-language support.

---

**FIGURE 1.6** *Stages of the Natural Approach*

---

1. *Preproduction.* As the label indicates, students at this stage are not ready to produce language, so they communicate with gestures and actions. They are taking in the new language and developing receptive vocabulary. Lessons focus on listening comprehension to build receptive vocabulary. Total Physical Response (TPR) (Asher, 1982) is an approach that is used during the preproduction phase, since TPR lessons are designed to allow students to demonstrate comprehension through nonverbal means, such as actions and gestures, while developing receptive vocabulary.
2. *Early Production.* Students at this level speak using one or two words or short phrases. Their receptive vocabulary is developing; they understand approximately one thousand words. Students can answer *who, what, where* questions with limited expression. Lessons continue to build receptive vocabulary, and activities encourage students to produce vocabulary they already understand.
3. *Speech Emergence.* Students speak in longer phrases and complete sentences. However, they may experience frustration at not being able to express completely what they know. Although the number of errors they make increases, so does the quantity of speech they produce. Lessons continue to expand receptive vocabulary with activities designed to promote higher levels of language use. Students are able to contribute meaningfully to discussions but in limited form.
4. *Intermediate Fluency.* Students may appear to be fluent; they engage in conversation and produce connected narrative. Errors are usually of style or usage. Lessons continue to expand receptive vocabulary, and activities develop higher levels of language use in content areas. Reading and writing activities are incorporated into lessons to a higher degree. Although spoken language is fairly well developed, contextual support is critical for academic tasks.

---

FIGURE 1.7 *Examples of Subjects and Language Instruction*

| English Proficiency Levels | DISTRICT'S CORE CURRICULUM FOR ENGLISH-LANGUAGE LEARNERS | | | | |
| | Core Curriculum for All Students | | | | Self-Image Cross-cultural LEP 5 |
| | English-Language Development LEP 2 | Native-Language Instruction LEP 3 | Sheltered Instruction LEP 4 | Mainstream Classes | |
| **F E P** — Fluent English Proficient | | | | All Subjects | |
| e. Advanced SOLOM 21–25 | ESL–Advanced* | Language arts or other subject for enrichment *Optimal* | | All Subjects | |
| **L E P** — d. Intermediate SOLOM 17–20 | ESL–4 | Language Arts | Transitional Language Arts, Social Science** | Art, Music, PE, Math, Science, Electives** | *Weave throughout the core curriculum* |
| c. Speech Emergence SOLOM 12–16 | ESL–3 | Language Arts, Social Science | Math, Science | Art, Music, PE, Electives | |
| b. Early Production SOLOM 6–11 | ESL–2 | Language Arts, Math, Social Science, Science (Concepts)** | Math, Science (problems, computation, and experiments)** | Art, Music, PE, Electives | |
| a. Preproduction (non-English) SOLOM 5 | ESL–1 | Language Arts, Math, Social Science, Science** | Art, Music, PE | | |

*May be provided within the transitional or mainstream language arts curriculum with qualified staff, proper planning, material, and training.

**And career/vocational education (applied academics), especially grades 7–12.

*Source:* Adapted from Paramount Unified School District Framework.

In many areas nationwide, this is not the case and students at beginning levels of English are in sheltered content classes. This is especially prevalent at the secondary level and in locations where there are only a small number of students from one language group.

Students learning English receive ESL instruction until they reach fluent English proficiency and are redesignated for enrollment in an all-mainstream program. Ideally, the amount of native-language support and the number of sheltered subject areas and mainstream classes vary with each level of English proficiency. Each individual student is likely to learn English in a unique pattern of development (Garcia, 2000).

*Preproduction Level (Non–English Speaking).*   Students receive as much native-language support as needed in the academic areas. Content-based ESL instruction focuses on developing English while providing the link between the content areas and their associated English vocabulary, oral and written language functions, and structures. Time spent developing skills and knowledge in the native language will theoretically provide a foundation for later learning in English. It has been established that stages such as *preproduction* are not consistent across individuals nor are their durations predictable. Students may very well enter preproduction and early production simultaneously. Students may even begin to develop rudimentary literacy skills during these early stages of language learning.

*Early Production Level.*   Students at this level of English proficiency are still making sense of the new language, developing receptive vocabulary, and using available context clues to understand academic information. They have some degree of basic conversational skills and quite limited academic ability in English.

Pon, the Cambodian student who has exhibited some inappropriate behaviors, is at this level of proficiency. Pon and students like him receive academic development in their native language as needed for context-reduced areas such as language arts, reading, math and science concepts, and social science. Sheltered strategies are utilized to help them with math computation, problem solving, and science labs. They will have increased opportunities for interaction if integrated into classes with native English speakers in art, music, and physical education.

*Speech Emergence Level.*   Students at this level are ready for increased English-language development, including more advanced ESL instruction with academic subjects taught in English in sheltered instruction and mainstream classes. Because of the more contextual nature of science and mathematics classes, which are more visual and hands on, these students are often ready for sheltered instruction in these subject areas. However, once students reach speech emergence, they are likely to continue to demonstrate spiked performance in English production.

Krishna, the recent immigrant who has grade-level academics in his native language, is at the speech emergence stage. Students like Krishna are able to speak in longer phrases and complete sentences, although they may become frustrated by not being able to express completely and correctly what they know. For instance, when talking about a familiar topic, such as food or family, Krishna's English may be at an intermediate or advanced level. Yet in the same hour, when talking about a recent field trip to the Museum of Natural History, Krishna's English may resemble early production. Her prior knowledge and vocabulary in English are not sufficient, in this case, to support confident conversation.

Language arts and the social sciences continue to be taught using native-language support as needed. The social science content area is heavily dependent on language. The terms and concepts used are culturally laden, and lessons often draw on a bank of knowledge that may be unfamiliar to immigrant students, which necessitates native-language support.

***Intermediate Level.***   Students at this level are developing improved conversational skills and increased academic skills, depending on their age and level of literacy in their native language. They are often mistakenly thought to be ready for all-mainstream classes, since their ability to speak and understand English is quite good. However, their ability to understand and complete academic tasks in English may lag behind, especially if they do not have grade-level academic skills in their native language. Therefore, native-language support in language arts continues, providing a strong foundation in literacy, which is necessary for academic success. Sheltered language arts programs are introduced as students begin preparing to transition to the next level.

Although most content areas are taught to these students using sheltered instruction or in mainstream classes, attention to providing them contextual clues must continue to be a priority. Tasks that are cognitively complex need to be modified using sheltered instruction strategies. For many students, an abrupt shift from native-language instruction to all-English instruction is difficult. Effective sheltered instruction facilitates comprehension of content area material; having continued native-language support to clarify concepts and ideas would be ideal.

***Advanced Level.***   For students at this level, instruction focuses on refining and developing advanced uses of academic English. Their conversational English is fairly fluent, and they are able to participate fully in class discussions. However, it is not uncommon for students to be at intermediate or advanced fluency levels while having significant gaps in their academic ability (as was the case with Luisa). Such students need significant intervention, such as specific learning strategies (see Chapter 5), intensive small-group or individualized instruction, or some other environmental adaptations. (See the section titled Learning and Behavior Challenges later in this chapter.)

## Academic Background and School Experience

The number of years students have spent in school, the quality of their school performance, and the consistency of that experience are important data. A student like Krishna, who is monolingual/literate in his native language and who has grade-level school experience and an uninterrupted academic background, requires a different academic focus than a student of the same age who has limited literacy skills. For example, the amount of native-language support is based on student need. For some students, developing basic academic skills, offering native-language support, and concentrating on literacy development are essential.

The importance of the school experience increases with the age of the student. If, like Krishna, a person first enters school in the United States in middle school, prior school experience is a critical factor. But for a child entering school in the United States in preschool, previous school experience is irrelevant. For those who lack school experience, their level of English-language knowledge and their level of academic development may be quite limited and will impact the focus of instruction.

Accurate information about previous school experience, although often difficult to obtain, greatly helps in instructional planning. When records are unavailable, interviews with parents, guardians, and the students themselves are essential. Behavior and learning patterns that appear inappropriate can be due to a lack of school experience. Immigrant students need to be given ample opportunity to adjust to the new setting and to learn school procedures. Modifications and adaptations should be provided when necessary to ease the transition.

### Assessment

Teachers can evaluate academic knowledge in English according to grade-level expectations and standards. Established scope and sequences for grade levels and required literacy skills for specific subject areas, such as science and social studies, are typically available. For example, Krishna's eighth-grade science teacher may discover that he has not acquired certain skills that are emphasized in American schools, such as outlining, specific study skills, or report writing. The teacher can teach those skills to the class at the beginning of the year. (Students who already have these skills might be assigned other tasks.) Krishna's history teacher might establish the practice of giving a background pretest at the beginning of each new unit to assess areas to preteach before introducing the unit, since students like Krishna will not have studied history from an American perspective and may lack the background knowledge upon which the lessons depend.

## Instruction

As Figure 1.7 (page 16) indicates, an instructional plan for maximizing Krishna's potential would include sheltered instruction in the content areas with primary language support as needed. Krishna may move into mainstream classes more quickly than students who do not have as strong an academic background. Goals for his ESL progress and for his performance in content areas that focus on the academic skills he is missing need to be set and an ongoing assessment of his progress made.

Once an instructional program has been developed and his academic background or time in school has been determined, Krishna needs to be taught procedural, organizational, and academic rules and strategies to enhance his school performance. (Chapter 5 includes information on strategy instruction in these areas.)

## *Learning and Behavior Challenges*

Much concern has been voiced in the last 10 years about both the overrepresentation and underrepresentation of minority students in special education classes, especially those who are learning English in school (Baca & Cervantes, 1998; Ruiz, 1995; Gersten, Brengelman, & Jiménez, 1994). Advocates for nonnative students have continuously questioned the quality and appropriateness of special education services for them (MacSwann, 2000; Schiff-Myers, Djukic, McGovern-Lawler, & Perez, 1994; Figueroa, 1989). Many professionals contend that the educational system is insensitive to the issues and stresses surrounding learning English in the public schools and that this situation often creates what may mistakenly be viewed as behavioral or learning disabilities (Baca & Cervantes, 1998; Chang, 1992; Figueroa, 1989). Given that the prevalence estimates of learning disabilities is approximately 10 percent of the school population (U.S. Department of Education, 1993), it is reasonable to assume those estimates would be the same for English-language learners.

Baca and Almanza (1996) estimate that close to 1 million language-minority students have a learning disability. Fradd and Weismantel (1987) indicate that due to a lack of understanding of cultural and language issues, students learning English risk receiving no special services or assistance at all. Trends indicate that students learning English are less likely than other students to receive special services (Cline & Fredrickson, 1999; Gersten, Brengelman, & Jiménez, 1994). It is imperative that teachers in both general education and in special education programs be aware of all of the issues and teaching approaches appropriate for facilitating the progress of students learning English.

## Prereferral Interventions

Students experience difficulties in school for a number of reasons, including language or learning disabilities. Some characteristics of students with learning or behavior problems are as follow:

| | |
|---|---|
| Withdrawn behavior | Memory difficulty |
| Bizarre behavior | Poor motor abilities |
| Aggressive behavior | Poor perceptual abilities |
| Attention problems | Poor language abilities |
| Hyperactivity | Poor academic performance |
| Low motivation | |

When any of these behavior or learning challenges appear, teachers should immediately begin working to help the student meet his or her needs within the regular class setting. A first step is to establish a relationship with the student's parents and gain their support. Individual adaptations require sustained periods of time to facilitate student change.

But students who are learning English often experience learning and behavior difficulties that are more associated with the strain of adapting to a new culture and learning a new language than with some type of disability. In the case of Luisa (limited bilingual), who was born in the United States and began school as a Spanish speaker, inconsistent language instruction at critical developmental stages likely contributed to her current poor performance. High transiency rates, inadequate instruction, and lack of continuity between instructional programs often account for the difficulties experienced by limited bilinguals. However, Luisa and students like her are at risk for referral to special education, because low skills at her advanced age are often assumed to be the result of a learning disability.

What if a student like Pon (monolingual/preliterate) was experiencing difficulties? Assessment results in Khmer indicate excellent social language proficiency and weak academic language. He is at English Level 2 on the SOLOM, although his lack of academic background contributes to the difficulties he is experiencing. In addition, he is a verbal individual (in Khmer) who is unable to communicate effectively with peers in English, perhaps accounting for some of his misbehavior. A certain amount of learning and behavior problems can be expected as part of the normal process of making the significant adjustments required of English-language learners. In Pon's case, the teacher is giving him positive recognition by assigning leadership roles and responsibilities in class, reducing Pon's inappropriate behaviors.

Before referral for special education services is even considered, teachers must first utilize the following interventions:

- Focus on the strengths of the student. Adapt assignments and tasks so that the student can use his or her strengths and experience success (Pease-Alvarez & Winsler, 1994; Gay, 1993; Good & Brophy, 1991; Krashen, 1982).
- Determine that the curricula and instructional materials are effective with other students who are learning English (Hornberger & Michaeu, 1993; Ogbu, 1992; Banks, 1991; Ortiz & Wilkinson, 1991).
- Plan specifically around the linguistic characteristics of the learner (Ortiz & Wilkinson, 1991).
- Identify what the student can and cannot do in academic and linguistic endeavors (Perez, 1993). Start teaching at the appropriate level and with techniques that are known to be effective for students who are learning English so that the student can experience success (Garcia & Ortiz, 1988).
- Confer with parents regularly, and involve the parents in the teaching and learning process (Baca & Cervantes, 1998; Chang, 1992).
- Use alternative approaches to teaching, such as peer teaching, partner sharing, cooperative learning, and cross-age tutoring (Franklin & Thompson, 1994; King, 1990; Slavin, 1990; Schunk & Hanson, 1985).
- Provide emotional security for the student by building a positive supportive relationship while maintaining high expectations (Bandura, 1986). This could include providing both native-language support and community support and showing a genuine interest in the life of the student (Lucas & Katz, 1994; Scarcella & Chin, 1993).
- Encourage goal setting and consistent measurement of academic progress with mechanisms for self-report and regular reports to parents.
- Make directions clear and simple and adjust workload and time requirements (Garcia & Ortiz, 1988).
- Model processes and strategies (Bos, 1995; Chamot & O'Malley, 1994).
- Plan specific written agreements with students that clarify expectations and emphasize self-regulated learning (Bos, 1995; Fradd, 1987).

## Assessment

Typically, interventions will benefit the student, ameliorating any learning or behavior difficulties (Cloud, 1994; Echevarria-Ratleff & Graf, 1988). If the student's behavior or performance does not improve after the teacher implements these classroom interventions, referral to a site-based multidisciplinary team is warranted (Cline & Frederickson, 1999; Lozano-Rodriguez & Castellano, 1999; Baca & Cervantes, 1998). The team, typically comprised of classroom teachers, a school counselor, an administrator, and the school nurse, evaluates the student's situation. The areas examined may include the student's home and family situation, school program and language of instruction, learning style, levels of primary language functioning, English proficiency, attendance patterns, and health issues. By checking records or interviewing the family, the team may discover that the student's academic problems are caused by poor vision or hearing, preoccupation over difficulties at home, or an instructional program that does not meet his or her needs. To ensure appropriate evaluation of the learner, Ortiz and Wilkinson (1991) and Schiff-Myers, Djubic, Lawler-McGovern, and Perez (1994), among others, recommend the following procedural steps when learning or behavioral issues are a challenge:

- Talk to parents and learn as much about the student in both community and school activities as possible, including information previously discussed in this chapter: native-language competence, English-language competence, and prior school experience.
- Ensure that the student who is learning English has teachers who are trained specifically to work in ESL and sheltered instruction.
- Ensure that the curriculum and the adaptations that the teacher uses are those known to be effective for English-language learners.
- Have various school personnel (including several different teachers) document a history of responsive teaching, including accommodations and adaptations over a sustained period of time.
- Create a home and educational record of the student's accomplishments and challenges.
- Document progress, or lack thereof, for all recommendations and accommodations implemented.

If difficulties persist, a formal referral for assessment is made to determine eligibility for special education. The assessment includes use of formal and informal assessments (curriculum based), observations, and interviews. If special education services are to be provided, they must occur in the least restrictive environment, which could be the bilingual, sheltered, or mainstream classroom. The designation ideally provides the student additional support and services with continued and appropriate focus on developing grade-level language and academic competence.

## Instruction

If a special education placement appears warranted and the parent agrees, instruction or behavior management should continue to be adjusted to meet the student's needs in the original classroom environment. A lin-guistically appropriate individualized education plan (IEP) should be de-veloped for the student, including these elements:

1. Assessment in both native- and English-language skills to determine language competence
2. Goals related both to native language and to the development of English
3. Culturally sensitive instructional practices, including those that re-quire the active participation of the learner

The full success of an IEP requires the active involvement of all school personnel and of parents. Accountability is extremely important for designing the best instruction for learners, as is the establishment of a curriculum-based standard of measurement. Goal setting and a careful look at the possibilities for the year as well as for each month are a critical part of good instruction. In setting annual goals, the teacher must assess the learner's current level of knowledge and skills as well as the curriculum to estimate the approximate level of progress that is likely by the end of the year. Short-term objectives require the teacher to break down annual goals into approximately 9 or 10 pieces to make a determination of how much progress a student is likely to make on a monthly basis. The system of measurement must be incorporated into both the goal and objective statements as the teacher describes how progress will be determined. Goal setting is essential both for the learner and for the teacher to maximize progress and the sense of urgency for amelioration. Persistent and contin-ued accommodations for the learner should be undertaken until he or she demonstrates success. An IEP should be adjusted if necessary.

In Luisa's case, after several prereferral interventions were consis-tently implemented, her academic struggles persisted. When the multi-disciplinary team met with her mother, she mentioned that Luisa was referred for special education services by her fifth-grade teacher as a result of persistent difficulties. She was not tested or recommended for place-ment because her parents did not approve of this type of approach. Her family now realized the need for more intensive interventions and ap-proved the formal assessment, qualifying Luisa for special education ser-vices. The IEP delineated an aggressive instructional plan for maximizing Luisa's potential, which included work with a resource specialist in the school three times a week focusing on reading and writing development. Ongoing assessment to determine the success of the instructional plan would be conducted by collecting samples of her work on a regular basis and tracking progress, as in portfolio assessment.

At this point, federal laws regarding IEPs can supercede state laws. For instance, if state laws prohibit native-language instruction, the IEP can be written so as to require it as part of an appropriate education for that student. If a student has been placed in the special education system, the IEP can provide protection and assurances that he or she would not otherwise have had (Baca & Cervantes, 1998).

Many students who do not require or qualify for special education services would benefit from the same process of setting individually designed goals and objectives, involving families and other school personnel in the plan, and consistently measuring progress, making appropriate adjustments as needed.

## *Summary*

Currently, there are students in the schools who represent each of the four types of students mentioned in this chapter. Indeed, students' abilities in a variety of areas—such as native-language levels, English-language levels, school experience, academic background, and learning or behavior problems—create an infinite number of complex, individual profiles for the students often referred to simply as *language minority*. Students may have high levels of performance in English but not in their native language, high levels of performance in both languages (type 1), high levels of performance in their native language but low levels of performance in English (type 2), low levels of performance in all areas due to lack of school experience (type 3), or low levels of performance in all areas due to improper instruction, improper learning, or behavior problems (type 4). Students' abilities can vary within areas and may not fit neatly into types, but this system of analysis assists us in determining how to address the needs of these youngsters.

To best meet the needs of each of these students, it is imperative that a systematic process be followed to program and educate properly all students to their potential. The process discussed in this chapter includes gathering data, conducting assessments, and implementing instruction in the following areas: (1) native-language knowledge, (2) English-language knowledge, (3) academic background and school experience, and (4) learning and behavior patterns. For students who experience persistent problems that are clearly beyond what would normally be expected for English-language learners, a team-based intervention plan, in which ways of alleviating the students' difficulties, is suggested. Such an instructional plan should include criteria for maximizing potential and for an ongoing assessment to determine the success of the instructional plan.

The remainder of this book will provide specific theory and instructional approaches for teaching that can improve the performance of individuals who are learning English. Chapter 2 will provide theoretical background for the instructional approaches presented in Chapters 3 to 8.

## *Activities*

1. Lupe has lived in a large urban U.S. city for 10 years. She was in bilingual classes in elementary school and is now mainstreamed for all subjects, although her English is not completely fluent. She is friendly and cooperative when she is in class but has high absenteeism. She seems to prefer talking with friends to completing assignments. Teachers think she has academic potential but are worried that she will eventually drop out of school because of persistent underachievement. Outline five prereferral interventions that could be implemented with Lupe.

2. Hui came from Vietnam, where he worked with his uncle before immigrating to the United States last year. He had about six years of full-time schooling in Vietnam and two years of intermittent attendance. Now in the tenth grade, he is struggling academically. Draw an "iceberg" representation of Hui's levels of language proficiency, and explain your reasoning.

3. Sara has lived in the United States for six months. She seems withdrawn and does not socialize much with other students. She was educated in her home country and, in fact, studied some English as a foreign language in school. Her teachers are pleased with her work, given the limited time she has been in this country. What type of student is she, and what is an appropriate educational program for her? What do you think the relationship is between an appropriate academic program and her behavior?

## *References*

Asher, J. (1982). *Learning another language through actions: The complete teacher's guidebook*. Los Gatos, CA: Sky Oaks.

Baca, L., & Almanza, E. (1996). *Language minority students with disabilities*. Reston, VA: Council for Exceptional Children.

Baca, L., & Cervantes, H. (1998). *The bilingual special education interface* (2nd ed.). Boston, MA: Merrill.

Baker, C. (1993). *Foundations of bilingual education and bilingualism*. Philadelphia: Multilingual Matters.

Bandura, A. (1986). *Social foundations of thought and action*. Englewood Cliffs, NJ: Prentice-Hall.

Banks, J. A. (1991). A curriculum for empowerment, action, and change. In C. E. Sleeter (Ed.), *Empowerment through multicultural education* (pp. 125–141). Albany, NY: State University of New York Press.

Banks, J. S., & McGee Banks, C. A. (2001). *Multicultural education: Issues and perspectives* (4th ed.). New York: Wiley.

Barratt-Pugh, C., & Rohl, M. (2001). Learning in two languages: A bilingual program in Western Australia. *The Reading Teacher, 54,* 664–676.

Bos, C. (1995). *Accommodations for students with special needs who are learning English*. Paper presented at the First Congress on Disabilities, Mexico City.

Burnette, J. (2000). *Assessment of culturally and linguistically diverse students for special education eligibility* (Report No. EDO-EC-00-13). Arlington, VA: ERIC Clearinghouse on Disabilities and Gifted Education. (ERIC Document Reproduction Service No. ED449637)

Cazden, C. B. (1992). *Language minority education in the United States: Implica-*

*tions of the Ramirez report* (Educational Practice Report: 3). Santa Cruz, CA: National Center for Research on Cultural Diversity and Second Language Learning.

Chamot, A. U., & O'Malley, J. M. (1994). *The CALLA handbook: Implementing the cognitive academic language learning approach.* Reading, MA: Addison-Wesley.

Chan, S. (1990). Early intervention with culturally diverse families of infants and toddlers with disabilities. *Infants and Young Children, 3,* 78–87.

Chang, J. M. (1992). Current programs serving Chinese-American students in learning disabilities resource issues. In *Proceedings of the Third National Research Symposium on Limited English Proficient Issues: Focus on Middle and High School Issues* (pp. 713–736). Washington, DC: U.S. Department of Education, Office of Bilingual Education and Minority Language Affairs.

Chinn, P. C., & Hughes, S. (1987). Representation of minority students in special education classes. *Remedial and Special Education, 8*(4), 41–46.

Cline, T., & Frederickson, N. (1999). Identification and assessment of dyslexia in bi/mutilingual children. *International Journal of Bilingual Education and Bilingualism, 2,* 81–93.

Cloud, N. (1993). Language, culture and disability: Implications for instruction and teacher preparation. *Teacher Education and Special Education, 16,* 60–72.

Cloud, N. (1994). Special education needs of second language students. In F. Genesee (Ed.), *Educating second language children* (pp. 243–277). New York: Cambridge University Press.

Cloud, N. (1994). Special education needs of second language students. In F. Genesee (Ed.), *Educating second language children: The whole child, the whole curriculum, the whole community.* New York: Cambridge University Press.

Cloud, N., Landurand, P. M., & Wu, S. T. (1989). *Multisystem: Systematic instructional planning for exceptional bilingual students.* Reston, VA: Council for Exceptional Children.

Collier, V. (1995). Acquiring a second language for school. *Directions in Language and Education, 1*(4), 1–12.

Crandall, J. (1995). *Developing content-centered language learning: Strategies for classroom instruction and teacher development.* Thailand: Chulalongkorn University.

Cummins, J. (1981). The role of primary language development in promoting educational success for language minority students. In *Schooling and language minority students: A theoretical framework.* Los Angeles: California State University, National Evaluation, Dissemination and Assessment Center.

Cummins, J. (1989). A theoretical framework for bilingual special education. *Exceptional Children, 56,* 111–128.

Cummins, J. (1994). Primary language instruction and the education of language minority students. In *Schooling and language minority students: A theoretical framework* (2nd ed.). Los Angeles: California State University, National Evaluation, Dissemination and Assessment Center.

Echevarria-Ratleff, J., & Graf, V. (1988). California bilingual special education model sites (1984–1986): Programs and research. In A. Ortiz & B. Ramirez (Eds.), *Schools and the culturally diverse student: Promising practices and future directions.* Reston, VA: Council for Exceptional Children.

Edelsky, C. (1991). *With literacy and justice for all: Rethinking the social in language and education.* London: Falmer Press.

Faltis, C. J., & Arias, M. B. (1993). Speakers of languages other than English in the secondary school: Accomplishments and struggles. *Peabody Journal of Education: Trends in Bilingual Education at the Secondary School Level, 69,* 6–29.

Faltis, C. J., & Hudelson, S. (1994). Learning English as an additional language in K–12 schools. *TESOL Quarterly, 28,* 457–468.

Figueroa, R. A. (1989). Psychological testing of linguistic-minority students: Knowledge gaps and regulations. *Exceptional Children, 56*(2), 111–119.

Fitzgerald, J. (1995). English as a second language learners' cognitive reading processes: A review of research in the United States. *Review of Educational Research, 65,* 145–190.

Flores, B., Rueda, R., & Porter, B. (1986). Examining assumptions and instructional practices related to the acquisition of literacy with bilingual special education students. In A. Willig & H. Greenberg (Eds.), *Bilingualism and learning disabilities* (pp. 149–165). New York: American Library.

Fradd, S. H. (1987). Accommodating the needs of limited English proficient students in regular classrooms. In S. Fradd & W. Tikunoff (Eds.), *Bilingual education and special education: A guide for administrators* (pp. 133–182). Boston: Little, Brown.

Franklin, E., & Thompson, J. (1994). Describing students' collected works: Understanding American Indian children. *TESOL Quarterly, 28,* 489–506.

Garcia, E. (1993). *Education of linguistically and culturally diverse students: Effective instructional practices* (Educational Practice Report: 1). Santa Cruz, CA: National Center for Research on Cultural Diversity and Second Language Learning.

Garcia, G. N. (2000). *Lessons from research: What is the length of time it takes limited English proficient students to acquire English and succeed in an all-English classroom? Issue Brief No. 5* (Report No. FL 026 601). Washington, DC: National Clearinghouse for Bilingual Education. (ERIC Document Reproduction Service No. ED450585)

Garcia, S., & Ortiz, A. (June, 1988). Preventing inappropriate referrals of language minority students to special education. *Focus, 5.* The National Clearinghouse for Bilingual Education.

Garibaldi, A. M. (1992). Preparing teachers for culturally diverse classrooms. In M. E. Dilworth (Ed.), *Diversity in teacher education: New expectations* (pp. 23–39). San Francisco: Jossey-Bass.

Gay, G. (1993). Building cultural bridges: A bold proposal for teacher education. *Education and Urban Society, 25,* 285–299.

Gersten, R., Brengelman, S., & Jiménez, R. (1994). Effective instruction for culturally and linguistically diverse students: A reconceptualization. *Focus on Exceptional Children, 27,* 1–16.

Gersten, R., & Jiménez, R. (1994). A delicate balance: Enhancing literature instruction for students of English as a second language. *The Reading Teacher, 47,* 438–449.

Gollnick, D. M., & Chinn, P. C. (1990). *Multicultural education in a pluralistic society.* Columbus, OH: Merrill.

Gonzalez, N., Moll, L. C., Floyd-Tenery, M., Rivera, A., Rendon, P., Gonzales, R., & Amonti, C. (1993). *Teacher research on funds of knowledge: Learning from households* (Educational Practice Report: 6). Santa Cruz, CA: National Center for Research on Cultural Diversity and Second Language Learning.

Good, T. L., & Brophy, J. E. (1991). *Looking in classrooms* (5th ed.). New York: HarperCollins.

Harry, B., Torguson, C., Katkavich, J., & Guerrero, M. (1993). Crossing social class and cultural barriers in working with families: Implications for teacher training. *Teaching Exceptional Children, 26*(1), 48–51.

Hill, R., Carjuzaa, R. H. J., Aramburo, D., & Baca, L. (1993). Culturally and linguistically diverse teachers in special education: Repairing or redesigning the leaky pipeline. *Teacher Education and Special Education, 16,* 258–269.

Hornberger, N., & Michaeu, C. (1993). Getting far enough to like it: Biliteracy in the middle school. *Peabody Journal of Education: Trends in Bilingual Education at the Secondary School Level, 69,* 54–81.

King, A. (1990). Enhancing peer interaction and learning in the classroom through reciprocal questioning. *American Educational Research Journal, 27,* 664–687.

Krashen, S. (1982). *Principles and practice in second language acquisition.* Oxford, England: Pergamon Press.

Krashen, S., & Terrell, T. (1983). *The natural approach: Language acquisition in the classroom.* Englewood Cliffs, NJ: Alemany/Prentice-Hall.

Lewelling, V. W., & Peyton, J. K. (1999). *Spanish for native speakers: Developing dual language proficiency* (Report No. EDOFL-99-02). Washington, DC: ERIC Clearinghouse on Languages and Linguistics. (ERIC Document Reproduction Service No. ED433696)

Lozano-Rodriguez, J. R., & Castellano, J. A. (1999). *Assessing LEP migrant students for special education services* (Report No. EDO-RC-98-10). Washington, DC: ERIC Clearinghouse on Rural Education and Small Schools. (ERIC Document Reproduction Service No. ED425892)

Lucas, T., & Katz, A. (1994). Reframing the debate: The roles of native languages in English-only programs for language minority students. *TESOL Quarterly, 28,* 537–562.

MacSwan, J. (2000). The threshold hypothesis, semilingualism, and other contributions to a deficit view of linguistic minorities. *Hispanic Journal of Behavioral Science, 22,* 3–45.

Maik, M. (1999). *Reducing class size in America's urban schools* (Report No. UD 033-182). Washington, DC: Council of the Great City Schools. (ERIC Document Reproduction Service No. ED435778)

McKay, P. (2000). On ESL standards for school-age learners. *Language Testing 17,* 185–214.

McKeon, D. (1994). When meeting "common" standards is uncommonly difficult. *Educational Leadership, 51,* 45–49.

Moll, L. C. (1988). Some key issues in teaching Latino students. *Language Arts, 65,* 465–472.

Ogbu, J. U. (1992). Understanding cultural diversity and learning. *Educational Researcher, 21,* 5–14.

Ortiz, A., & Wilkinson, C. (1991). Assessment and intervention model for the bilingual exceptional student (AIM for the BESt). *Teacher Education and Special Education, 14,* 35–42.

Pease-Alvarez, L., & Winsler, A. (1994). Cuando el maestro no habla Espanol: Children's bilingual language practices in the classroom. *TESOL Quarterly, 28,* 507–536.

Perez, B. (1993). Biliteracy practices and issues in secondary schools. *Peabody Journal of Education: Trends in Bilingual Education at the Secondary School Level, 69,* 117–135.

Pierce, L. V. (August, 1988). *Facilitating transition to the mainstream: Sheltered English vocabulary development.* Washington, DC: National Clearinghouse for Bilingual Education.

Ramirez, J. D. (1992). Executive summary: Longitudinal study of structured English immersion strategy, early-exit and late-exit transitional bilingual education programs for language-minority children. *Bilingual Research Journal, 16*(1), 1–62.

Ramirez, J. D., & Quezada, M. (1996). *Transition guide.* Long Beach, CA: Center for Language Minority Education and Research.

*Reading/Language arts framework for California public schools: Kindergarten through grade twelve* (2000). Sacramento, CA: California Department of Education.

Richard-Amato, P. (1996). *Making it happen: Interaction in the second language classroom.* New York: Longman.

Rivera, C. (Ed.) (1984). *Language proficiency and academic achievement.* Avon, England: Multilingual Matters.

Romaine, S. (1989). *Bilingualism.* Oxford, England: Blackwell.

Rueda, R. (1989). Defining mild disabilities with language-minority students. *Exceptional Children, 56,* 121–128.

Ruiz, N. (1995). The social construction of ability and disability: I. Profile types of Latino children identified as language learning disabled. *Journal of Learning Disabilities, 28,* 476–490.

Rumberger, R. (1995). Dropping out of middle school: A multilevel analysis of students and schools. *American Educational Research Journal, 32,* 583–626.

Saville-Troike, M. (1984). What really matters in second language learning for academic achievement? *TESOL Quarterly, 18,* 117–131.

Scarcella, R., & Chin, K. (1993). *Literacy practices in two Korean-American communities* (Research Report: 8). Santa Cruz, CA: National Center for Research on Cultural Diversity and Second Language Learning.

Schiff-Myers, N. B., Djukic, J., Lawler-McGovern, J., & Perez, D. (1994). Assessment consideration in the evaluation of second-language learners: A case study. *Exceptional Children, 60,* 237–248.

Schunk, D. H., & Hanson, A. R. (1985). Peer models: Influence on children's self-efficacy and achievement. *Journal of Educational Psychology, 77,* 313–322.

Short, D. (1991). *How to integrate language and content instruction.* Washington, DC: Center for Applied Linguistics.

Short, D. (1994). Expanding middle school horizons: Integrating language, culture, and social studies. *TESOL Quarterly, 28,* 581–608.

Slavin, R. E. (1990). *Cooperative learning.* Englewood Cliffs, NJ: Prentice-Hall.

Troike, R. C. (1984). SCALP: Social and cultural aspects of language proficiency. In C. Rivera (Ed.), *Language proficiency and academic achievement.* Avon, England: Multilingual Matters.

U.S. Department of Education. (1993). Fifteenth annual report to Congress on the implementation of the Individuals with Disabilities Education Act. Washington DC: U.S. Government Printing Office.

Vygotsky, L. S. (1978). *Mind in society: The development of higher psychological processes.* Cambridge, MA: Harvard University Press.

Yates, J. R., & Ortiz, A. A. (1991). Professional development needs of teachers who serve exceptional language minorities in today's schools. *Teacher Education and Special Education, 14,* 11–18.

# 2

## *Theoretical and Historical Foundations*

- An ESL teacher encourages students to talk about their experiences riding the bus and then has them write a letter to the bus company addressing some of their concerns. What makes this different from a grammar-based approach to second-language learning?
- In a math class, the teacher indicates the precise tasks students must perform to be judged successful. The tasks are sequenced from simple to more difficult. The teacher uses verbal praise, stickers, tokens, free time, and other reinforcers that are effective in motivating students. What theory drives this teacher's practices?
- If students learn the curriculum through instruction in their native language, will they need to study the same material again once they are proficient in English?

This chapter presents an overview of the historical background and theories that underlie instruction for students learning English in school. Sheltered instruction involves both learning new concepts and skills and learning a new language. Therefore, this chapter includes a brief discussion of learning theories that address how students learn new material and ideas, followed by a presentation of theoretical perspectives on second-language acquisition. It begins with an overview of the history of education for language-minority students. It is easier to appreciate where we are today by examining where we have been. Thus, an understanding of the theories that support current practice is important in developing effective instructional programs for English-language learners (ELLs).

## History of Education of Students Learning English in School

In 1965, the United States abandoned its quota system, which had sustained the overwhelmingly Northern European make-up of the nation for nearly half a century. Unlike the immigrants who arrived in the so-called Great Wave around the turn of the twentieth century from the Old World, the post–1965 immigrants were from the Third World, mainly Asia and Latin America (Molesky, 1988). By 1980, there were over 16 million Latinos in the United States, many of whom spoke Spanish as their first language. Large numbers of legal and illegal immigrants continued to pour into the United States throughout the 1980s, coming from over one hundred different countries and representing a variety of languages and dialects. In 1980, 11 percent of the U.S. population reported speaking a language other than English at home; by 1990, that percentage had risen to over 13 percent; and in 2000, over 17 percent of Americans reported this preference (U.S. Census Bureau, 2000, 1990, 1980). This trend has been felt acutely in U.S. schools.

In fact, the proportion of English-language learners in U.S. schools continues to grow more rapidly than overall student growth. From 1985–86 to 1994–95, the number of ELLs in the public schools grew 109 percent while total enrollment increased by only 9.5 percent (Olsen, 1997). Not only are large numbers of these students limited English proficient, but they come from a variety of divergent language backgrounds.

Following the Immigration Act of 1965, new legislation was passed to assist the public schools in dealing with the influx of non-English-speaking students. Title VII of the Elementary and Secondary Education Act of 1965 offered assistance to schools in setting up programs to prepare these students for education in American schools. Although bilingual education, as it has come to be known, was not specifically stipulated, funds were provided only for those programs that delivered instruction to low-income students in and through both English and the students' native language (Faltis & Arias, 1993). The Bilingual Education Amendment of 1974 stated that in addition to studying English, subject matter should be taught in the student's primary language to the extent necessary to allow for progress through the education system.

Although bilingual programs have been available since the 1970s and were theoretically designed to facilitate students' successful progress through the education system, minority students from low-income backgrounds who speak a language other than English have continued to experience disproportional underachievement, leading to high dropout rates (Crawford, 1991; Arias, 1986; Orfield, 1986). One reason for the disproportionate underachievement of language-minority students can be traced to the quality of programs for these students. Widespread implementation of effective programs has been hampered by several factors, including a lack of trained bilingual personnel to deliver quality instruction in the primary language and a low level of commitment on the part of school districts to develop and implement quality programs (Gold, 1993). Many bilingual and English as a second language (ESL) programs in the United States teach little more than English, neglecting the importance of content learning. Responsibility for the education of these students is often relegated to second-language specialists and classroom paraeducators. Many English-language learners are not included in the larger school community and often are not integrated into mainstream classes socially or academically (Bunch, Abram, Lotan, & Valdes, 2001; Genesee, 1994).

The dramatic increase in the number of ELL students has resulted in a shortage of teachers qualified to offer ESL instruction or bilingual instruction (NCTAF, 1996) and has moved the teaching of content out of specialized classes and into mainstream classes. In response, some states with large populations of ELL students, such as California, have begun teacher preparation programs that enable all beginning teachers to be effective in teaching students who are "culturally, linguistically and academically diverse" (Olebe, 2001). However, most teacher preparation programs still do not provide teacher candidates with strategies for teaching culturally and linguistically diverse students (Crawford, 1993; Zeichner, 1993), which presents a problem for the large numbers of ELL students in mainstream classes.

Further, the educational reform movement has had a direct impact on English-language learners, as states have moved to implement high-stakes testing and standards-based instruction for all students. In most states, classroom instruction is guided by standards for core subjects such as social studies, mathematics, science, and language arts. In many mainstream classes, little or no accommodation is made for the specific language needs of English-language learners, placing them at a deficit when they are expected to achieve high academic standards in English. Imagine the difficulty of being expected to perform at grade level in a language the student is still in the process of learning. Many times, the difficulties students experience in school are caused by inappropriate modes of instruction that do not take into account students' linguistic needs (Wiley, 1996). Moreover, under new state-level accountability measures, all students are expected to pass end-of-grade tests in order to be promoted and graduate, although most states offer an exemption for ELL students for one to three years.

In order to address the instructional needs of English-language learners, sheltered content teaching (described in detail in Chapter 3) has been identified as an effective way for students learning English to gain access to content material while acquiring English skills. The teacher using this approach takes into consideration students' English-language skills and modifies the delivery of instruction through slower speech, giving information verbally as well as visually, and using controlled vocabulary while also striving for academically rigorous instruction that includes grade-level content, age-appropriate interactive activities, and higher-level questioning. Sheltered instruction gives students an opportunity to learn English as they master important content and skills. If ELL students are to be successful academically, graduate from high school, and reach cognitive levels similar to their U.S.-born peers, they must have access to content material and opportunities to practice academic skills and tasks common to mainstream classes (Short, 1999; Henze & Lucas, 1993).

## *Learning Theories*

Since one of the goals of sheltered instruction is to teach content—including new concepts, information, and skills—to English-language learners, it is worthwhile to examine the learning theories underpinning methods and practices. Although many teachers consider theory irrelevant to practice, it is important to keep in mind the theoretical perspective driving a given instructional method or approach. Most teachers have a "folk theory," or implicit theory, that influences their teaching but may be unaware of the established theory underlying it. Teachers benefit from having a decision-making model rooted in theory to assist them in making instructional modifications that meet the learning needs of their students.

Individuals differ in their preferences and learning styles, and one single approach rarely meets the needs of all students. If students are not responding to instruction, teachers need to ask these questions:

1. What are the assumptions underlying the approach I'm using?
2. Do these assumptions apply to my students?
3. Do I obtain my desired outcome using this approach?

The process of reflecting on the instructional approach being used, examining the theoretical base for the approach, and appraising student learning needs may yield valuable information for maximizing student learning and performance.

The best teachers we have observed are able to use various approaches, depending on the context and the goals of the lesson, enhancing learning opportunities for students. Examining the components of various modes of instruction helps teachers develop a concept of and put into operation new or alternate teaching approaches. Teachers should draw from a continuum of teaching models (Saunders & Goldenberg, 1996).

In looking at the following overview of learning theories, it is important to keep in mind that classroom practices rarely are pure examples of single theories. Rather, effective teachers typically use a balanced approach that includes choices rooted in different learning theories. Many instructional methods and practices make use of aspects of several theoretical approaches. Similarly, sheltered instruction is not driven by a single theory but rather exhibits influences of several theoretical perspectives.

## Humanistic Learning Theory     *Aristotle & Plato, Maslow*

The *humanistic teacher* is one who desires students to learn to interact well with others and to feel as good as possible about themselves. The affective well-being of students is a central focus of this approach (see Chapter 6) and is always a consideration when planning the schoolday. Personality development, including cooperation and consideration, is a primary value and is the focus of education.

> Mrs. Leung believes that student learning is enhanced when students feel good about themselves and the class operates as a community of

learners. She frequently uses cooperative learning because it provides opportunities for students to contribute equally and to cooperate with one another (Slavin, 1995). She also schedules a daily sharing time for students to discuss personal interests, share a favorite book, show pictures of family and friends, or tell about a favorite school project or successful school effort. Through this process, Mrs. Leung learns a great deal about each student, which enhances her ability to teach in a way that focuses on the strengths of each individual learner.

Mrs. Leung's classroom reflects humanistic learning theory. *Humanistic learning theory* is a general term for those theories that contend that the central focus of human learning is to develop high self-esteem and a healthy personality. Sternberg and Williams (2002) describe it as "a meaningful educational environment in which students are encouraged to see themselves as capable; development of self-esteem; teachers acting warm and supportive; explaining why things must be done a certain way—no rules for the sake of rules." (See Woolfolk [2001] for more information on the affective domain, Maslow's hierarchy of needs, Ericson's stages of psychosocial development, Kohlberg's stages of moral reasoning, and Marsh and Shavelson's structure of self-concept.)

## Developmental Learning Theory    *Piaget*

Woolfolk (2001) defines *development* as naturally occurring stages that occur in an orderly fashion. These stages usually appear gradually and develop at different rates in different people. (See Woolfolk [2001] for more information on Piaget's theory for the development of thinking and Vygotsky's theories for development of language, general linguistic development, and reading development. Also see Sternberg and Williams [2002] for implications for teaching.)

> Mr. Fleming believes in allowing each student to progress at his or her own pace. He structures class activities so that students can all participate at their own level. He evaluates students' journals according to their ability level. Some students write a few words with an illustration, while others compose whole stories. Mr. Fleming often uses a *language experience approach,* in which students tell their own stories and he functions as a scribe. Students are taught Writer's Workshop (see Chapter 5), where they compose at their level of functioning.

Teachers whose practices are influenced by *developmental learning theory* subscribe to stagelike views of development and do not push students into development or force them to skip a stage. These teachers believe that in-born factors largely account for the unfolding of a child's ability over time and allow this unfolding to take place in its own time, when the child is ready.

## Social Interactionist Learning Theory

*Vygotsky Dewey*
*Constructive  Progressive*

Influenced by the work of Vygotsky (1978), the sociocultural view of learn-ing recognizes the unique role adults and older children play in learning, emphasizing the importance of modeling and the use of language to facili-tate learning. These "more capable others" provide the child with the in-formation and support necessary for intellectual growth by listening to the child and providing just the right help to advance his or her understand-ing. Assisted learning in the classroom involves giving prompts, remind-ers, and encouragement at the right time and in the right amounts to foster understanding.

According to this view, the social side of learning is important be-cause interaction with teachers and peers has both cognitive and affective consequences. Through social interaction, students confront other people's points of view and discover how other people respond in various situations. This process of understanding others' points of view and learn-ing to explain and defend one's own view not only gives students new information, but the social interaction adds a verbal level to their under-standing. Social interaction, according to Vygotsky, contributes to the de-velopment of language.

Vygotsky viewed language as a child's first tool for social interaction. As children mature, they internalize speech and use it in their own private interactions with the environment. Children can often be seen talking aloud during play and directing their own actions, which eventually leads to language directing thought. One example of an instructional approach that facilitates this type of learning is the *instructional conversations* ap-proach (see Chapter 6).

In Ms. Nelson's class, a lot of student-to-student and teacher-to-student interaction can be heard and observed. As a teacher, Ms. Nelson sees her role as providing the right amount of information and support to students necessary for intellectual growth. During a lesson, Ms. Nelson listens to the children and provides just the right help to advance the children's understanding. She does this by giving prompts, reminders, and encouragement at the right time and in the right amount to foster understanding. Rather than dominating the lesson and seeking specific correct answers, she is careful to ask ques-tions that will draw out the children's ideas and assists them in con-structing meaning from the text based on their own experiences and backgrounds. You will hear questions such as "Why do you think he will do that?" "Tell me more about that," and "Would you react that way under the same circumstances? Why?"

## Cognitive Learning Theory  *Chompsky*

Although there is no one *cognitive learning theory,* cognitivists tend to focus on such factors as kinds of knowledge; the information-processing model of learning, including perception, attention, memory, and metacognition; discovery learning; learning strategies; and problem solving (Woolfolk, 2001). They also tend to explore internal mental processes such as memory, reasoning, and strategies for acquiring facts and concepts. Most cognitive theorists do not try to explain all learning through a single theory but instead share a generally agreed upon philosophical orientation. Generally, cognitive psychologists believe that people are active learners who initiate experiences, seek out information to solve problems, and reorganize what they already know to achieve new insights.

Perhaps the major contribution of cognitivists has been in the area of memory as it relates to learning theory. For example, confirmation of mnemonic strategies (procedures that facilitate memory) has been gained through research into such subjects as verbal rehearsal, chaining, and the keywords strategy (see Chapter 5). Instructional choices focused on cognitive theory are those that encourage students to think about their own learning and those that focus students on their own learning. For example, when the teacher says, "Let's repeat this a few times so we can remember it," he or she is using verbal rehearsal to enhance knowledge gained and relying on cognitive theory. Or a teacher may insist that each time students solve a problem in class, they use the following steps: (1) define and clarify the problem, (2) experiment, reflect, and apply examples, and (3) solve the problem or draw conclusions.

*Discovery learning* is an instructional approach that Mr. Gimplin uses often in his class. This is an intuitive approach in which students are provided with pieces of the knowledge "puzzle" and encouraged to induce the principle or rule. For example, in one lesson, Mr. Gimplin gave students 20 Popsicle sticks and told them to make groups of 2. He asked how they would find out how many sticks they had. Some students said they would count them ("1, 2, 3 . . ."). But one or two of the students said they would count by 2s to make it easier. These students had essentially discovered multiplication. The teacher pointed out to the students that some of them had found an easier way to find out "how many": Counting by 2s or 3s is multiplying, which is an easier way to add. Mr. Gimplin also uses mnemonic strategies to help students learn and retain information.

## Behavioral Learning Theory    *Pavlov & Skinner*

While cognitivists are concerned with knowledge and how it is gained, saved, used, and lost, behaviorists believe learning is manifested through behavioral changes that can be observed and measured. (See Woolfolk [2001] for elaboration.) For behaviorists, language is a skill like any other behavior that we learn. Language is learned by presenting language with attractive experiences in the environment and by rewarding the learner once language occurs.

The best-known approach to behavioral learning is *operant conditioning*. The goal of the operant learning approach is to change behavior by manipulating antecedents and consequences. Modern behaviorists tend to focus on antecedents of behavior more than on its consequences, realizing that setting up the environment for success can do more to change behavior than waiting to enforce consequences. According to behaviorists, teachers can modify antecedents and assist learning by (1) demonstrating skills and asking students to imitate them, (2) walking students through an organized series of steps in a process, (3) clarifying concepts by providing examples and nonexamples, (4) providing clear, simple wording that is easy to imitate and that can be reinforced easily when reproduced, (5) and involving students actively throughout the learning process to provide ample practice.

> Mrs. Bobkowski begins most lessons by writing objectives on the board that indicate the precise behaviors students are to adopt to be judged successful. Usually, the behaviors, or tasks, are sequenced from simple to more difficult and instructional activities are carefully planned to increase learning. She also focuses on consequences in the form of positive reinforcers for increases in appropriate behavior, such as positive teacher affect, verbal praise, privileges such as computer time or free time, and any other reinforcers that are effective with the students. Students are dealt with individually, with target behaviors reflecting the needs of the student. New behaviors are taught through continuous reinforcement. Mrs. Bobkowski reduces inappropriate behavior by ignoring it and attending to appropriate behavior.

Behaviors are discussed in observable terms, and learning is measured by the acquisition of new behaviors. For example, Ms. Smith asked students to write reports about their trip to Seaworld. She specified that each student was to write a paragraph with a main idea and three detail sentences about the field trip. She also specified that students should indent, punctuate, and use capital letters correctly. She required a handwritten first draft; a self-corrected second draft, to be signed by a peer editor and the teacher; and a final version printed from the computer. After each phase, students were to take notes home to parents explaining their accomplishments. The teacher walked around class during each phase, giving support for participation and hard work. She assessed the results of each student's efforts and set goals for each accordingly. Over time, students were required to become more and more independent, with a focus on generalizing or using the newly learned skills in many different situations with increasingly reduced teacher supervision.

*Modern Behavior Learning Theory*
*teachers can modify to fit*

### Overview

An understanding of learning theory can become a decision-making model when a teacher realizes that certain educational goals are more likely to be accomplished using specific approaches. If a teacher finds that some students are struggling in a given learning environment, it may be wise to think about which approaches are currently in use, which are missing, and what changes might be implemented to yield a balanced approach to support student learning.

As previously stated, sheltered instruction involves learning new content *and* learning English. Since English-language development is an important component of sheltered instruction, the next section will discuss theories of second-language development.

## Theories of Second-Language Acquisition

While there are a number of important theories of second-language acquisition (see Baker, 1993; McLaughlin, 1987), the work most often cited and discussed is that of Stephen Krashen. We will begin with a presentation of Krashen's monitor model and then address some of James Cummins's contributions to understanding the relationship between the development of one's native language and of a second language.

The *monitor model* is the theory of second-language acquisition most familiar to practitioners but also the most widely debated. There are five hypotheses comprising this theory, each presented briefly here. (For a complete presentation of these hypotheses, see Krashen [1994]. For a critique, see McLaughlin [1987] and Barasch and James [1994].)

1. *The acquisition-learning hypothesis* makes a distinction between second language acquired through natural communication and second language learned formally, where the focus is on correct grammar, vocabulary, and other linguistic features. In *language learning*, students consciously think about language rules and what they know about the language. Classrooms in which students drill the target language, memorize dialogues, and spend time conjugating verbs reflect a language-learning environment. In

*language acquisition,* language use is driven by what feels like the correct and appropriate usage, without the learner being consciously aware of the rules. Students are given opportunities to hear and use the new language by a teacher who makes the language intelligible through simplified speech, gestures, and context. Students learn correct usage through modeling and practice, not overt correction by the teacher.

**2.** *The natural order hypothesis* suggests that there is a universal order to acquiring language; certain rules tend to be acquired before others, similar to the order used in learning the first language. This hypothesis assumes that both adults and children learn a second language in a predictable order, although variations among individuals can be expected.

**3.** *The monitor hypothesis* explains the relationship between second-language acquisition and second-language learning. An individual learns and internalizes rules of the second language. As he or she uses acquired language, the internal *monitor* edits errors based on the rules the individual has learned. The monitor may be used in two ways: editing before an utterance is spoken or as a correcting device after the utterance is spoken. Speakers invoke the monitor in situations where, time allowing, correct grammar is necessary and they know the correct rules to be followed.

**4.** *The input hypothesis* explains how language learners progress from one developmental stage to the next. Krashen assumes that language is acquired in a developmental sequence by receiving abundant *comprehensible input,* making messages understood to the learner. When those messages contain new structures and are comprehensible, learners move a little beyond their current level of competence. As Krashen (1985) puts it, "We move from $i$, our current level, to $i + 1$, the next level along the natural order, by understanding input containing $i + 1$" (p. 2).

In applying this hypothesis to the classroom, the teacher strives to be cognizant of the students' level of functioning and introduce new vocabulary and grammatical structures in context, using simplified speech and visual clues to make them understandable, thus moving students to a higher level of competence. Simply hearing higher levels of language—in a mainstream classroom with no modifications, for instance—does not allow students to acquire English, since they do not understand the message.

**5.** *The affective filter hypothesis* is related to the emotional side of language use. It relates to such aspects as attitude, anxiety, motivation, and self-confidence. The assumption of this hypothesis is that a filter exists that affects how much a person will learn. If a learner is anxious or lacks self-confidence, these affective variables can block or impede learning of a second language. This hypothesis suggests that a positive affective environment will enhance language learning. Teachers adhering to this theory make sure that their classroom environments are as stress free as possible.

During language-learning lessons, students are not put on the spot to give correct answers but encouraged to participate at their own level of comfort. When errors are made, the teacher models correct usage or elaborates. For example, a social studies teacher might ask, "What was one of the causes of the Civil War?" A student might answer, "One cause was the differences between farming peoples and city peoples." The teacher would reply, "Good answer, Farook. There were differences in the way people thought, which were influenced by their lifestyle. The South was a farming or agrarian society *(teacher writes terms on the overhead projector),* and the North was largely an industrialized society. Good answer. So Farook said there were differences between the thinking of farming people *(teacher points to "farming/agrarian" on the overhead)* and city people *(teacher points to "city/industrialized" on the overhead).* Good. What else?" Notice how the teacher makes it easy for the student to participate by accepting his answer in the form given. The teacher then models and elaborates on the student's answer. Without insisting on correct speech, students are more relaxed and willing to participate, lowering the affective filter.

Krashen points out that sheltered content lessons can serve as excellent language lessons, as long as the content is comprehensible. Many of the components of sheltered instruction originate in Krashen's work.

## *The Contributions of Cummins*

As Crawford (1991) suggests, James Cummins's contributions to understanding the relationship between first- and second-language development "shattered a number of misconceptions about bilingualism" (p. 105). In Chapter 1, we discussed one of Cummins's most influential contributions: the concept of two types of language proficiency. The conversational/academic (or BICS/CALP) distinction recognizes that students acquire basic interpersonal communication skills relatively quickly, but the language necessary for school tasks (such as reading, writing, mathematics, and other content subjects) is cognitive-academic language proficiency, a more complex type of language proficiency that takes longer to acquire. Two of Cummins's other notions relate to the BICS/ CALP distinction: the linguistic interdependence model and the range of communicative demands.

The *linguistic interdependence hypothesis* (Cummins, 1994, 1981a, 1981b) holds that cognitive-academic skills learned in the native language will transfer to the new language (English) and that such skills are interdependent across languages. For example, once the code of reading has been cracked, an individual can learn to read in other languages without relearning the concept of sound-symbol relationship with each new language. The concepts acquired in the language the student understands most completely (the native language) are called the *common underlying proficiency*. These concepts will transfer into the second language. The process of transfer, however, is neither automatic nor inevitable (Gersten, Brengelman, Jiménez, 1994). It is a process that requires guidance by the teacher, with explicit links made to past learning. For students to draw on previously learned skills or information, they frequently need prompting, reminders, and explicit teaching behaviors. This is especially true for students with language or learning difficulties.

Communicative tasks (listening, speaking, reading, and writing) may be easier or more difficult for second-language learners, depending on the task itself and the amount of contextual support available. The range of communicative demands is conceptualized as two continuums (see Figure 2.1):

• The *horizontal continuum* represents contextual support, ranging from contextually embedded communication, wherein meaning can be derived from a variety of clues such as gestures, visual clues, and feedback, to context-reduced communication, which relies primarily on linguistic messages or written texts, which give few, if any, contextual clues. (A straightforward, spoken message without any visual clues could mean anything.)

• The *vertical continuum* relates to the cognitive demands of the task. For example, a cognitively undemanding task can be performed with little or no conscious thought, such as reciting one's own name and phone

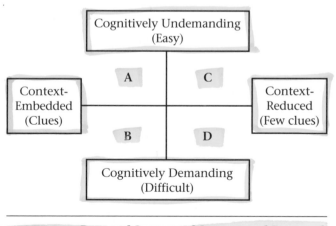

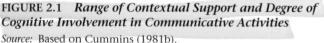

FIGURE 2.1   *Range of Contextual Support and Degree of Cognitive Involvement in Communicative Activities*
*Source:* Based on Cummins (1981b).

number, while listening to a lecture on an unfamiliar topic is a cognitively demanding task.

Students with limited English proficiency often achieve communicative competence more rapidly than academic competence. Therefore, tasks in the A quadrant (Figure 2.1) should be relatively easy for English-language learners, since they rely on contextual clues and are less dependent on academic language. However, the most common types of instructional tasks are found in quadrant D. They are also the most difficult. These tasks offer few contextual clues. They include reading a text (without visual clues), understanding math concepts, doing math word problems, writing compositions, listening to lectures, and taking tests.

Cummins hypothesizes that children must attain grade-level cognitive-academic language proficiency if they are to experience success in academic tasks that are typically context reduced and cognitively demanding. Time spent developing academic skills in the language the student understands is not time lost, since these skills are transferable to English.

## *Factors That Affect Second-Language Acquisition*

Snow (1992) concludes that "second language acquisition is a very complex process; its success or failure will not be explained by a single factor or theory." Many factors can influence acquisition of English. These include, but are not limited to, the following:

- Motivation
- Age
- Access to the language
- Personality
- First-language development
- Quality of instruction
- Cognitive ability

### Motivation

While there is great variation in motivational levels from learner to learner, the importance of high motivation for second-language acquisition is clear. In this regard, Fillmore (1985) asserts that recognizing the need to learn the second language and being motivated to do so are key ingredients for second-language learning. (This factor will be discussed in more depth in Chapter 7.)

What are motives for learning a second language? Baker (1992) discusses two types of motivation: integrative and instrumental. When students are motivated to identify with or join another language group—that is, integrate into the group—the process is termed *integrative motivation.* This type of motivation increases the likelihood of becoming proficient in the second language because it involves developing personal relationships that are potentially long lasting. *Instrumental motivation* describes a situation in which individuals learn another language for a practical reason, such as getting a job, enhancing their career possibilities, or passing an exam. This type of motivation may not be as effective in leading to mastery of the second language, since it tends to involve short-term goals. Once a goal is achieved—the exam is passed, the job is obtained—this type of motivation may diminish.

## Age

Debate continues regarding the optimal age for beginning second-language acquisition. Recent research seems to indicate that younger learners are more efficient at certain aspects of language acquisition related to natural settings, such as the home, playground, and other environments where they interact naturally with native speakers. They tend to pick up the communicative aspects of language more readily, prompting them to learn more. Young learners are also relatively free from personality issues that can have a negative impact on language learning, such as self-consciousness, mental rigidity, the desire for perfect pronunciation, and so forth. Older learners may respond better to formal instruction in a second language because of their advanced cognitive abilities and larger repertoire of learning strategies (Snow, 1992; Collier, 1987; Fillmore, 1985; Krashen, 1982; Scarcella & Higa, 1982; Cummins, 1980; Elkind, 1970).

## Access to the Language

Opportunities for learning about the target language are promoted by successful communicative exchanges with native speakers of the target language (Snow, 1992). Such heterogeneous groupings and a learning environment that encourages student-to-student interaction both foster second-language acquisition.

## Personality

Extroverts may enjoy initial success with the language because they tend to prefer the social aspects of relationships—such as talking, playing, and working with others—and thus have increased opportunities for interaction and access to native-language models. However, there are not likely to be long-term language-learning differences based on introversion and extroversion.

Risk taking is a personality characteristic that can greatly affect language learning. A willingness to experiment with vocabulary and forms of the language, as well as drawing generalizations from what has been learned, will improve proficiency (Fillmore, 1985).

## First-Language Development

As was shown in Chapter 1, learning a first language is a complex task, requiring a minimum of 12 years (McLaughlin, 1984) and with certain aspects of development, such as vocabulary expansion, continuing for a lifetime. Although a tremendous amount of language is acquired from birth to age 5, children from ages 6 to 12 continue to develop more complex forms of semantics, phonology, morphology, and syntax, as well as more elaborate speech acts (McLaughlin, 1984).

Researchers suggest that the level of first-language development significantly influences second-language development. Students who have had solid schooling in their native language are more efficient acquiring a new language. Those who achieve full cognitive development in both languages will gain cognitive benefits, whereas when development of the first language is discontinued, there may actually be negative consequences (Collier, 1989). Native-language instruction enhances the cognitive development of students learning English and raises the status of second-language learning. Particularly for students who have low literacy levels, it is difficult to catch up in the second language, a language they do not yet fully comprehend, so continued native-language instruction is ideal. The deeper the conceptual foundation, the higher the ability to build. Saville-Troike (1984) found that opportunities for continuing cognitive development in the native language through contact with peers and adults correlated significantly with English academic achievement. Moreover, the practical benefits of continued instruction in the native language are bilingualism and biliteracy. The cases of two immigrant students illustrate the importance of a solid foundation in the primary language.

> *Wasyl* was six months old when his family arrived in the United States from Ukraine. The family was driven to start a life in a strange land by the promise of a better future for their children. The father decided that in order for his children to learn English and have an edge when they entered school, the family would speak English at home. The father learned basic English on the job, and the mother picked up phrases here and there. Although hindered by lack of proficient English, they both were committed to their decision and struggled to use the new language as often as possible with their children.

*Natalia's* family also made many sacrifices in order to come to the United States to seek a better future. For the first five years of her life, Natalia's father worked long and hard in this new land while her mother, who spoke no English, stayed home. To keep them from forgetting their homeland, Natalia's mother spent many hours telling Natalia and her baby sister stories of their village in Ukraine. She taught the children traditional songs and rhymes, and Natalia helped her mother prepare the father's favorite meals.

Which child has the advantage when entering school? Although Wasyl's family had the best of intentions, his language will not be as fully developed as that of Natalia. Because native language use was restricted in the home, Wasyl does not have a solid linguistic foundation in either language. He has not had the kinds of preliteracy experiences that Natalia has had. Through her experiences, Natalia has a foundation in preliteracy—she is familiar with word order and patterns, rhyming, vocabulary and concept development—as well as background knowledge upon which to build. She will not have to relearn acquired concepts when she begins to speak English; the concepts will transfer to the new language.

## Quality of Instruction

What happens in the classroom is vitally important. The teacher's daily routines, level of lesson preparation, expectations of the students, use of essential teaching behaviors, instructional strategies, knowledge of the subject matter, and techniques for modifying instruction for English-language learners all impact learner outcomes, including language acquisition. The challenge for teachers of students with diverse abilities is to create classroom conditions in which learners can and will learn by adjusting texts, tasks, and instructional settings to match the learners' needs (Lipson & Wixson, 1999). It has been suggested that many learning problems experienced by students learning English are pedagogically induced, or the result of instructional practices that are not suited to the learner, often resulting in inappropriate placement in special education (Cummins, 1984). The prereferral interventions discussed in Chapter 1 are one way of eliminating inappropriate placement. These interventions are used along with instructional practices that reflect effective teaching for second-language learners. If instruction is not made comprehensible and accessible for students, the opportunity to learn both English and content material decreases. Good instruction requires good input.

Effective language learning takes place in well-organized classrooms where there are opportunities for interaction with the teacher and peers and adequate practice in the target language. Interactive instruction allows students to use elaborated language around relevant topics, building English skills while at the same time developing content knowledge.

## Cognitive Ability

Many of the cognitive processes that are important for second-language acquisition are related to general cognitive abilities, such as verbal memory, auditory perception, and categorization. These abilities affect the language-learning process (Fillmore, 1985), although wide variation among learners is expected in this area. Individuals with lower cognitive ability have the ability to acquire a second language, but proficiency levels will be equal to or lower than those in the first language. Further, Canadian studies found that students in bilingual programs who had learning disabilities and low academic ability performed as well as equivalent students in English-only programs (Cummins, 1980b).

## *Summary*

A variety of language backgrounds and proficiency levels are represented in U.S. classrooms today. Teachers can use their knowledge of theories that underlie practice to adjust instruction in order to better meet the individual needs of students. An understanding of second-language acquisition assists teachers in designing lessons that facilitate learning for English-language learners. For example, a firm foundation in the native language facilitates English-language acquisition, as we saw with the students profiled in Chapter 1. When English instruction is introduced, the cognitive and linguistic demands of academic tasks should be addressed and instruction modified to meet the needs of the students.

## *Activities*

1. Discuss which "folk theories," or implicit theories, underlie your ideas about teaching.

2. Select three instructional approaches with which you are familiar (for instance, cooperative learning, the language experience approach, direct instruction, or thematic teaching). Identify the theories that influence each approach.

3. Using Cummins's grid (Figure 2.1), discuss what level of cognitive demand and context (quadrant A, B, C, or D) is represented by a student who performs each of the following activities:

   a. Reads for comprehension  *D*
   b. Acts out a historical event  *C*
   c. Points to items in the classroom  *A*
   d. Writes short paragraphs  *D*
   e. Watches a movie with academic content  *B*

    **f.** Participates in a baseball game
    **g.** Listens to a lecture on the atom

**4.** Take the activities in quadrant D, and discuss how they can be changed to fit quadrant B.

## *References*

Arias, M. B. (1986). The context of education for Hispanic students: An overview. *American Journal of Education, 95,* 26–57.

Baker, C. (1992). *Attitudes and language.* Clevedon, England: Multilingual Matters.

Baker, C. (1993). *Foundations of bilingual education and bilingualism.* Philadelphia: Multilingual Matters.

Baker, C. (1996). *Foundations of bilingual education and bilingualism* (2nd ed.). Philadelphia: Multilingual Matters.

Barasch, R., & James, C. (1994). *Beyond the monitor model.* Boston: Heinle & Heinle.

Bunch, G., Abram, P., Lotan, R., & Valdes, G. (2001). Beyond sheltered instruction: Rethinking conditions for academic language development. *TESOL Journal, 10*(2/3), 28–33.

Collier, V. (1987). Age and rate of acquisition of second language for academic purposes. *TESOL Quarterly, 21,* 617–641.

Collier, V. (1989). How long? A synthesis of research on academic achievement in a second language. *TESOL Quarterly, 23,* 509–531.

Collier, V. (1995). Acquiring a second language for school. *Directions in Language and Education, 1*(4), 1–12.

Crawford, J. (1991). *Bilingual education: History, politics, theory and practice* (2nd ed.). Los Angeles: Bilingual Educational Services.

Crawford, L. (1993). *Language and literacy learning in multicultural classrooms.* Boston: Allyn and Bacon.

Cummins, J. (1980a). The cross-lingual dimensions of language proficiency: Implications for bilingual education and the optimal age issue. *TESOL Quarterly, 14*(2), 175–187.

Cummins, J. (1980b). Psychological assessment of immigrant children: Logic or intuition? *Journal of Multilingualism and Multicultural Development, 1,* 97–111.

Cummins, J. (1981a). Age on arrival and immigrant second language learning in Canada: A reassessment. *Applied Linguistics, 2,* 131–149.

Cummins, J. (1981b). The role of primary language development in promoting educational success for language minority students. In *Schooling and language minority students: A theoretical framework.* Los Angeles: California State University, National Evaluation, Dissemination and Assessment Center.

Cummins, J. (1984). *Bilingualism and special education: Issues in assessment and pedagogy.* Clevedon, England: Multilingual Matters.

Cummins, J. (1994). Primary language instruction and the education of language minority students. In *Schooling and language minority students: A theoretical framework* (2nd ed.). Los Angeles: California State University, National Evaluation, Dissemination and Assessment Center.

Elkind, D. (1970). *Children and adolescents: Interpretive essays on Jean Piaget.* New York: Oxford University Press.

Faltis, C., & Arias, M. (1993). Speakers of languages other than English in the secondary school: Accomplishments and struggles. *Peabody Journal of Education, 69*(1), 6–27.

Fillmore, L. W. (1985). *Second language learning in children: A proposed model.* Proceedings of a conference on Issues in English Language Development for Minority Language Education, Arlington VA. (ERIC

Document Reproduction Service No. ED 273 149)

Genesee, F. (1994). Introduction. In F. Genesee (Ed.), *Educating second language children: The whole child, the whole curriculum, the whole community.* New York: Cambridge University Press.

Gersten, R., Brengelman, S., & Jiménez, R. (1994). Effective instruction for culturally and linguistically diverse students: A reconceptualization. *Focus on Exceptional Children, 27,* 1–16.

Gold, N. (1993). Solving the shortage of bilingual teachers: Policy implications of California's staffing initiative for LEP students. *Proceedings of the third national research symposium of limited English proficient student issues.* Washington, DC: U.S. Department of Education, Office of Bilingual Education and Minority Language Affairs.

Henze, R., & Lucas, T. (1993). Shaping instruction to promote success of language minority students: An analysis of four high school classes. *Peabody Journal of Education, 69*(1) 6–29.

Krashen, S. (1982). Accounting for child-adult differences in second language rate and attainment. In S. Krashen, R. Scarcella, & M. Long (Eds.), *Child-adult differences in second language acquisition.* Rowley, MA: Newbury House.

Krashen, S. (1985). *The input hypothesis: Issues and implications.* New York: Longman.

Krashen, S. (1994). Bilingual education and second language acquisition theory. In *Schooling and language minority students: A theoretical framework* (2nd ed.). Los Angeles: California State University, National Evaluation, Dissemination and Assessment Center.

McLaughlin, B. (1987). *Theories of second-language learning.* London: Arnold.

Molesky, J. (1988). Understanding the American linguistic mosaic: A historical overview of language maintenance and language shift. In S.

McKay & S. Wong (Eds.), *Language diversity: Problem or resource.* Boston: Heinle & Heinle.

National Coalition of Advocates for Children. (1988). *New voices: Immigrant students in U.S. public schools.* Boston: National Coalition of Advocates for Children.

National Commission on Teaching and America's Future (NCTAF). (1996). *What matters most: Teaching for America's future.* New York: Columbia University, Teachers College.

Lipson, M., & Wixson, K. (1999). *Asessment and instruction of reading and writing disability* (2nd ed.). New York: Longman.

Ogbu, J., & Matute-Bianchi, M. (1986). *Beyond language: Social and cultural factors in schooling language minority students.* Los Angeles: California State University, National Evaluation, Dissemination and Assessment Center.

Olebe, M. (2001). A decade of policy support for California's new teachers: The beginning teacher support and assessment program. *Teacher Education Quarterly, Winter,* 71–84.

Olsen, R. (1997). Enrollment, identification and placement of LEP students increase (again). *TESOL Matters, 7*(4), 6–7.

Orfield, G. (1986). Hispanic education: Challenges, research and policies. *American Journal of Education, 95,* 1–25.

Saunders, W., & Goldenberg, C. (1996). Four primary teachers work to define constructivism and teacher-directed learning: Implications for teacher assessment. *The Elementary School Journal, 97*(2), 139–161.

Saville-Troike, M. (1984). What really matters in second language learning for academic achievement? *TESOL Quarterly, 18*(2), 199–219.

Scarcella, R., & Higa, C. (1982). Input and age differences in second language acquisition. In S. Krashen, R. Scarcella, & M. Long (Eds.), *Child-*

*adult differences in second language acquisition.* Rowley, MA: Newbury House.

Short, D. (1999). Integrating language and content for effective sheltered instruction programs. In C. Faltis & P. Wolfe (Eds.), *SO much to say: Adolescents, bilingualism and ESL in the secondary school* (pp. 105–137). New York: Teachers College Press.

Slavin, R. E. (1995). *Cooperative learning* (2nd ed.). Boston: Allyn and Bacon.

Snow, C. (1992). Perspectives on second-language development: Implications for bilingual education. *Educational Researcher, 21*(2), 16–24.

Sternberg, R., & Williams, W. (2002). *Educational psychology.* Boston: Allyn and Bacon.

U.S. Census Bureau. (1990). *Language spoken at home and ability to speak English for United States, regions and states: 1990* (Report Number CPH-L-133). Washington, DC: Population Division, Statistical Information Office, Census Bureau.

U.S. Census Bureau. (1980). *1980 census of population,* vol. 1, chap. D, pt. 1 (PC80-1-D1-A).

U.S. Census Bureau. (2000). Data available online: <censtats.census.gov/data/us/01000.pdf>.

Vygotsky, L. S. (1978). *Mind in society: The development of higher psychological processes* (M. Cole, V. John-Steiner, & E. Souberman, eds. & trans.). Cambridge, MA: Harvard University Press.

Wiley, T. G. (1996). *Literacy and language diversity in the U.S.* Washington, DC: Center for Applied Linguistics and Delta Systems.

Wong-Fillmore, L., & Valadez, C. (1986). Teaching bilingual learners. In M. C. Wittrock (Ed.), *Handbook of research on teaching* (3rd ed.). New York: Macmillan.

Woolfolk, A. (2001). *Educational psychology* (8th ed.). Boston: Allyn and Bacon.

Zeichner, K. (1993). *Educating teachers for cultural diversity* (NCRTL Special Report). East Lansing, MI: Michigan State University, National Center for Research on Teacher Learning.

# Sheltered Instruction in the Content Areas

- *Mrs. Nash* presents a student-centered lesson, using grade-level curriculum with a lot of visuals and hands-on activities to make the lesson understandable for English-language learners. What would such a lesson be called?
- *Mr. Hightower,* a tenth-grade science teacher, completed each step of his lesson plan. Should he be confident that students learned the material?
- *Ms. Alvarez* has three students in her sheltered math class who have been identified as learning disabled. What special adaptations should she make for those students?

"Sheltered instruction is nothing more than good teaching—and I already do that." This statement is commonly heard from teachers who have English-language learners in their classrooms. True, sheltered instruction shares many of the characteristics of effective instruction (also known as *direct instruction*), but it is more than simply good teaching—much more. This chapter begins by discussing what sheltered instruction is and then examines a social studies unit that illustrates the distinction between effective and sheltered instruction. The chapter ends with a discussion of the needs of students with learning difficulties.

## Components of Sheltered Instruction

*Sheltered instruction* is a means for making grade-level content, such as science, social studies, and math, more accessible for English language learners (ELLs) while also promoting English development. Sheltered instruction is said to be the most influential instructional innovation since the 1970s, particularly because it addresses the needs of secondary students (Faltis, 1993). The approach was first introduced in the early 1980s by Stephen Krashen as a way to use second-language acquisition strategies while teaching content area instruction. The approach teaches academic subject matter and its associated vocabulary, concepts, and skills by using language and context to make the information comprehensible.

Faltis (1993) discusses the origins of sheltered instruction and the differences among its variations, such as content-based English language teaching (CELT). The term *sheltered* indicates that such instruction provides refuge from the linguistic demands of mainstream instruction, which is beyond the comprehension of ELLs. Sheltered instruction provides assistance to learners in the form of visuals, modified texts and assignments, and attention to their linguistic needs. The term *sheltered* is used widely in schools across the United States to speak of content area classes for English-language learners, such as sheltered math, sheltered science, and sheltered social studies.

While sheltered instruction utilizes and compliments sound instructional methods and strategies recommended for both second-language and mainstream classes, a number of features make sheltered instruction more than good teaching. Some of those unique features, illustrated in Figure 3.1, include adapting academic content to the language proficiency level of the students; using supplementary materials to a high degree;

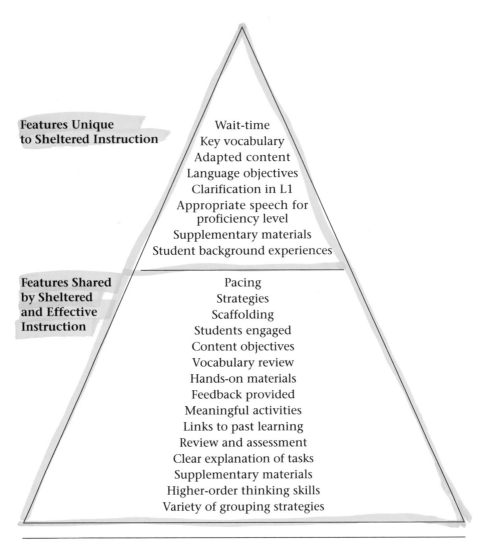

**Features Unique to Sheltered Instruction**

Wait-time
Key vocabulary
Adapted content
Language objectives
Clarification in L1
Appropriate speech for proficiency level
Supplementary materials
Student background experiences

**Features Shared by Sheltered and Effective Instruction**

Pacing
Strategies
Scaffolding
Students engaged
Content objectives
Vocabulary review
Hands-on materials
Feedback provided
Meaningful activities
Links to past learning
Review and assessment
Clear explanation of tasks
Supplementary materials
Higher-order thinking skills
Variety of grouping strategies

FIGURE 3.1 *A Comparison of Sheltered Instruction and Effective Instruction: Unique and Shared Features*

emphasizing key vocabulary; using speech that makes information comprehensible to students, including sufficient wait time; and emphasizing language development.

A model of sheltered instruction, *sheltered instruction observation protocol, or SIOP* (Echevarria, Vogt, & Short, 2000), was developed to provide a way for teachers to systematically implement instructional features for improving the academic achievement of ELLs. The SIOP is comprised of 30 items organized around the categories of preparation, instruction, and review/assessment (see Figure 3.2, page 56). In SIOP classes, language and content objectives are woven into the lessons in a particular subject area so that the teacher develops both subject matter competence and students' English-language abilities. Teachers use the SIOP as both a lesson-planning guide and a way to reflect and improve upon the effectiveness of their teaching (Short & Echevarria, 1999). Research has shown that students whose teachers implemented the SIOP made significant improvement in their writing (Echevarria, Short, & Powers, in preparation).

In addition to language and content objectives, sheltered lessons are characterized by an abundance of supplementary materials, clear and meaningful lessons, and concrete examples. Information that is embedded in context allows ELLs to understand and complete more cognitively demanding tasks. Since lectures and pencil-and-paper tasks centered around a text are difficult for these students, use of supplementary materials and student-centered activities are necessary to bring meaning to the text, making lessons relevant and purposeful for the students. For example, the idea that products costing the same may vary in quality (last longer or work better) can take on more meaning when students have the products to examine and compare. A textbook discussion of the idea is more easily understood when students are actually looking at the items. Figure 3.2 shows the components of effective sheltered instruction. Certain features require thought and preparation ahead of time, whereas others are part of the lesson's delivery. Interaction should take place throughout the lesson, with the teacher making the information comprehensible throughout.

Numerous techniques for contextualization exist. The following examples are drawn from a variety of subject areas:

**1.** *Modeling.* The teacher models what is expected of the students. Before students begin solving word problems in math, the teacher takes the students through a word problem step by step, modeling useful strategies for solving such problems. Students with diverse levels of ability benefit from concrete, step-by-step procedures presented in a clear, explicit manner.

**2.** *Hands-on manipulatives.* This approach can include learning aids from Cuisenaire rods in math to microscopes in science to globes in social studies.

FIGURE 3.2   *The Sheltered Instruction Observation Protocol (SIOP)*

Observer:_____

Date:_____

Grade:_____

Class:_____

Teacher:_____

School:_____

ESL level:_____

Lesson:  Multi-day   Single-day

*I. Preparation*

1. Clearly defined *content objectives* for students
2. Clearly defined *language objectives* for students
3. *Content concepts* appropriate for age and educational background level of students
4. *Supplementary materials* used to a high degree, making the lesson clear and meaningful (graphs, models, visuals)
5. *Adaptation of content* (e.g., text, assignment) to all levels of student proficiency
6. *Meaningful activities* that integrate lesson concepts (e.g., surveys, letter writing, simulations, constructing models) with language practice opportunities for reading, writing, listening, and/or speaking

*II. Instruction*

**(1) Building Background**

7. *Concepts explicitly linked* to students' background experiences
8. *Links explicitly made* between past learning and new concepts
9. *Key vocabulary emphasized* (e.g., introduced, written, repeated, and highlighted for students to see)

**(2) Comprehensible**

10. *Speech* appropriate for students' proficiency level (e.g., slower rate, enunciation, and simple sentence structure for beginners)
11. *Explanation* of academic tasks clear
12. Uses a variety of *techniques* to make content concepts clear (e.g., modeling, visuals, hands-on activities demonstrations, gestures, body language)

**(3) Strategies**

13. Provides ample opportunities for student to use *strategies*
14. Consistent use of *scaffolding* techniques throughout lesson, assisting and supporting student understanding such as think
15. Teacher uses a variety of *question types throughout the lesson including those that promote higher-order thinking skills*

throughout the lesson (e.g., literal, analytical, and interpretive questions)

**(4) Interaction**

16. Frequent opportunities for *interactions* and discussion between teacher/student and among students, which encourage elaborated responses about lesson concepts
17. *Grouping configurations* support language and content objectives of the lesson
18. Consistently provides sufficient *wait time for student response*
19. Ample opportunities for students to *clarify key concepts in L1*

**(5) Practice/Application**

20. Provides *hands-on* materials and/or manipulatives for students to practice using new content knowledge
21. Provides activities for students to *apply content and language knowledge* in the classroom
22. Uses activities that integrate all *language skills* (i.e., reading, writing, listening, and speaking)

**(6) Lesson Delivery**

23. *Content objectives* clearly supported by lesson delivery
24. *Language objectives* clearly supported by lesson delivery
25. *Students engaged* approximately 90–100% of the period
26. *Pacing* of the lesson appropriate to the students' ability level

*III. Review/Assessment*

27. Comprehensive *review* of key vocabulary
28. Comprehensive *review* of key content concepts
29. Regularly provides *feedback* to students on their output (e.g., language, content, work)
30. Conducts *assessment* of student comprehension and learning of all lesson objectives (e.g., spot checking, group response) throughout the lesson

*Source:* From Jana Echevarria, Maryellen Vogt, & Deborah Short, *Making content comprehensible for English language learners: The SIOP model.* Published by Allyn and Bacon, Boston, MA. Copyright © 2000 by Pearson Education Inc. Reprinted with permission of the publisher.

**3.** *Realia.* For a unit on banking skills, students might practice filling out actual bank deposit slips and check registers. When learning about geology, students might be given samples of rocks and minerals. For consumerism, students might read actual labels on products.

**4.** *Commercially made pictures.* There are a variety of photographs and drawings on the market that depict nearly any object, process, or topic covered in the school curriculum.

**5.** *Teacher-made pictures.* As an alternative to buying pictures to enhance lessons, the teacher can draw pictures or cut them out of magazines.

**6.** *Overhead projector.* As material and information are introduced, the overhead projector can be used to give constant clues to students. Teachers jot down words or sketch out what they are presenting. The written representation of words gives students learning English a chance to copy the words correctly, since certain sounds may be difficult to understand when presented orally. Students with learning problems often have difficulty processing auditory information and are helped with the visual clues offered through an overhead projector. For example, rather than relying solely on verbal presentation of the water cycle in a biology class, the teacher uses the overhead projector to write the basic terms as they are being discussed (see Figure 3.3, page 58). These additional visual clues help students understand the spoken words and the meaning of *cycle*. In the consumerism lessons, the sheltered teacher frequently used the overhead projector as a visual reinforcement of words and ideas presented orally.

**7.** *Demonstration.* In a middle school class studying archeology, a student asked how artifacts get buried deep underground. Rather than relying on a verbal explanation, which would have been meaningless to many of the students learning English, the teacher demonstrated the process. First, he placed a quarter in a pie pan and proceeded to blow dirt on the quarter, covering it slightly. He then put dried leaves on top, followed by a sprinkling of "rain." Finally, he put some sand on top, and the quarter was then underneath an inch or so of natural products. Although the process was described in the text, most students did not have the reading skills or English proficiency to understand it. The demonstration made a much greater impression on the students and was referred to later when discussing the earth's layers and other related topics.

**8.** *Multimedia.* Technology offers a multitude of options in this area, from something as simple as listening to a tape recording of Truman's announcement of the dropping of the atomic bomb to an interactive laser computer display. Videos, CD-ROM programs, tape recordings, and online websites are examples of multimedia that can enhance comprehension for English-language learners.

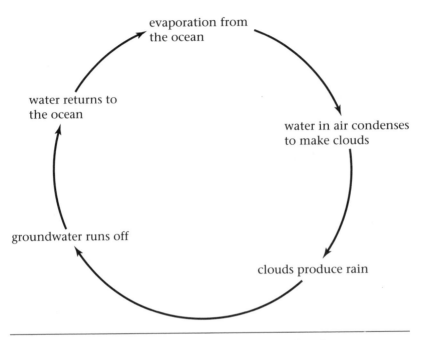

FIGURE 3.3 *Water Cycle as Displayed by Overhead Projector*

**9.** *Timelines.* These are particularly useful in the social sciences. As one lesson progressed through Western civilization, a timeline was mounted along the length of a wall that visually represented each historical event as it related to other events and periods in history. As an event was studied, the teacher made some visual representation on the timeline and continued adding to it throughout the course of the year.

**10.** *Graphs.* Information represented visually often makes greater impact and is easier to remember. Graphing the students' weekly consumption of junk food, fruits and vegetables, and milk products is more interesting and meaningful than simply reading about the various food groups and recommended servings. The text becomes more understandable when the graphing activity is completed before reading the text. Many of the terms and concepts will then already be familiar to the students.

**11.** *Bulletin boards.* Visual representations of lesson information can be put on bulletin boards for reference, such as an example of a business letter, some friendly letter formats, or a three-dimensional paper model of stalactites and stalagmites with labels.

**12.** *Maps.* A map can be one of the most effective means of easily creating context, since many subjects relate to geography. When talking about the rainforest in science, its location can be shown on a map. History class lessons about wars can become more meaningful if the territories are shown on maps.

Another component of sheltered instruction that sets it apart from effective instruction is the extent to which the text is adapted to meet students' language and learning needs, while still reflecting high expectations. Most content area teachers are required to use texts that tend to be difficult for English-language learners to read with comprehension. (Chapter 6 details ways teachers can make subject area curriculum, including textbooks, understandable for English-language learners.)

Since sheltered instruction is student centered, students are assigned real-life activities (for example, surveys, letter writing, simulations, or constructing models) with lots of opportunities for listening, speaking, reading, and writing. In a lesson on values, for instance, students could get into small groups and be given scenarios to discuss and write about. One might be "You come across the answer key to the upcoming science test. Do you put it on the teacher's desk, keep it and study from it, or give it to friends so you'll all do well on the test?" Another might be "Your grandmother is ill and you agree to stay with her for the weekend while your parents work. Later you get an invitation to a party where the most popular kids will be. What do you do?" The students spend time discussing the dilemma and then write down their solution to the situation.

New key words are introduced, highlighted, and written for students to see. Vocabulary knowledge in English is one of the most important aspects of oral English proficiency for academic achievement. To be most effective, vocabulary development needs to be closely related to subject matter (Saville-Troike, 1984). Krashen and Terrell (1983) suggest that comprehension of new vocabulary is acquired through context and calls for students to infer meaning from the text. On the other hand, there is a body of experimental research supporting the explicit teaching of vocabulary and the use of memory strategies to enhance recall of words and their meanings (Scruggs & Mastropieri, 1990).

Consider, for example, a class of tenth-grade students at the intermediate level of proficiency. One approach to vocabulary building would be to structure an interesting lesson around an issue that has meaning for the students, such as the influence of gangs in the inner city. The teacher would provide abundant comprehensible input and introduce vocabulary within the context of the lesson. Those on the side of direct teaching would agree that such a lesson would be effective but that vocabulary could be taught explicitly, outside the context of the lesson, as well. McLaughlin (1992) proposes an eclectic approach to vocabulary teaching, including both direct teaching and use of context, thus providing a more balanced approach. Vocabulary words can be brainstormed, mapped, and clustered, or visual associations can be generated for new words.

In a sheltered lesson, the teacher selects several key terms that are critical to understanding the lesson, writes them on an overhead projector or a wall chart, and discusses each one at the outset of the lesson. Perhaps a mnemonic strategy could be employed. Then, as students encounter these words throughout the lesson, they can recall the definition or can infer meaning from the context. In both cases, students are exposed to new vocabulary and see its application within the text.

The vocabulary words or terms can then be added to a word bank written on butcher paper and posted around the room. These word banks become reference points for students to remember definitions and relationships between terms and to model correct spelling.

Another unique component of sheltered instruction is reducing the linguistic load of teachers' speech. Natural but slower speech, clearly enunciated, can increase comprehensibility, particularly when effort is made to use shorter sentences with simpler syntax. Take, for example, the sentence "To add or subtract numbers with exponents, whether the base numbers are the same or different, you must simplify each number with an exponent first and then perform the indicated operation." A preferable delivery might be (pointing to examples on the board), "To add or subtract numbers with exponents, you must complete two steps: (1) simplify each number with exponents and (2) perform the operation. This is true whether the base numbers are the same or different."

The use of more pauses between phrases allows students time to process what has been said before the next utterance begins. Although many teachers of ELLs believe they are consciously making an effort to pause between phrases, audiotaping of lessons usually yields surprising results. One method for ensuring pauses are long enough for students to process the information is to count two seconds between utterances—for example, "An equation is a mathematical sentence, a relationship between numbers or symbols. *(The teacher counts silently: 1001, 1002)*. Remember that an equation is like a balance scale, with the equal sign being the fulcrum, or center *(1001, 1002)*." Naturally, this technique will be more effective when the teacher employs other techniques simultaneously, such as showing a visual of a balance scale, pointing to the fulcrum when reference is made to it, and writing an equation and equals sign on the board or overhead projector.

Another way to increase the comprehensibility of the message is to use consistent vocabulary and appropriate repetition. Repetition, or natural redundancy, reinforces language. Songs, chants, raps, and patterned stories give students opportunities to practice using the language and can provide reinforcement of vocabulary, language structures, and intonation (Richard-Amato, 1996). During instruction, use consistent vocabulary as much as possible. To expand vocabulary, communicate the same idea repeatedly using different words. In the example above, the term *mathematical sentence* was elaborated and the synonym *center* was given for the term *fulcrum*. It may be useful to emphasize the original expression by repeating it, giving students the opportunity to hear the same idea expressed in more than one way.

The next component of sheltered instruction lessons is one of the most important: *interaction between students*. While an opportunity for student interaction is also a characteristic of effective instruction, it is especially important for ELLs to practice using the new language in meaningful ways. Elaborated utterances around substantial questions are greatly encouraged in sheltered lessons.

Typically, teachers dominate linguistic interactions in the classroom. Studies have revealed the extraordinary paucity of opportunities for students to participate in meaningful discussions and question-answer sessions. (For more discussion of interaction, see Chapter 6.) Sheltered lessons give ample opportunity for discussing and questioning between teacher and students and among students in a variety of group configurations. Grouping becomes more critical when working with students with a variety of language and learning abilities. Heterogeneous grouping is encouraged, both with respect to language proficiency and academic skill level. Group activities offer students with diverse abilities an advantage by utilizing one student's strengths to compensate for a classmate's weakness. Grouping gives students the opportunity to clarify key concepts in their primary language as needed, by consulting an aide, peer, or primary-language text. One of the benefits of sheltered instruction is that students are exposed to good models of English language as well as the opportunity to practice using English in academic settings. However, English-language learners are in the process of acquiring a new language and will benefit from clarifying concepts in their native language when needed.

## Sheltered Instruction and Effective Instruction

There is a well-established body of literature on *effective teaching*, the instruction to which many people are referring when they speak of good teaching. The effective teaching literature offers findings associated with gains in student achievement in basic skills. These findings emerged from studies conducted from the 1970s through the early 1980s. They dispell the notion of teaching as an art rather than an applied science. The characteristics of effective teaching fall into two broad categories: (1) teaching behaviors and (2) organization of instruction (Bickel & Bickel, 1986). Teaching behaviors include emphases on direct instruction, demonstration, recitation, drill, and practice. Teachers conduct their classrooms in a task-oriented, businesslike manner, with a brisk instructional pace and material presented in small, sequential steps. Students are given many examples and the teacher uses frequent recall-level questions. Feedback and correction are provided, particularly in the initial stages of learning new material, and students are given ample opportunity to practice the skills they are learning.

Effective classroom management has been shown to promote positive achievement in students (Englert, 1984; Brophy & Everson, 1976). Characteristics of effective teachers include "with-it-ness" (the ability to monitor the entire class continuously); the ability to do two or more things simultaneously without having to break the flow of classroom events; a talent for moving along at a good pace without confusion or loss of focus; the ability to offer a variety of seatwork at the proper difficulty level and that maintains the students' interest and attention; and the ability to look around the classroom, select randomly, lead students in choral response, and call on everyone frequently when questioning students. In terms of organization of instruction, effective instruction is characterized by well-planned lessons and high levels of academic engaged time. Sheltered instruction shares these characteristics (Gersten, Taylor, & Graves, 1999).

## A Well-Planned Lesson

The amount of time a teacher spends preparing is often reflected in the effectiveness of the lesson. A well-planned lesson includes a brief review of previous learning to orient the students, including reteaching if necessary. It also includes presenting new content and skills in a way that is understandable, as well as offering an opportunity to students to practice using the new skills or material.

For example, in a sheltered science class where middle school students were studying the function of arteries and veins, the lesson began with a display of the following review questions by the overhead projector:

1. Why do you think we need both arteries and veins in order to live?
2. Why do you think arteries need to be thicker and heavier than veins?

Students were given 5 minutes to answer the questions. After the students gave their answers aloud, the teacher told the class to form work groups so they could do an activity that involved creating a model of arteries and veins in the body. Although the students complied, they did so slowly, taking 5 minutes to form groups. The teacher then gave each of the five groups a large sheet of butcher paper and told them to trace one group member's body on the paper. A couple of the groups began the assignment, but 9 minutes passed before one group began tracing, according to observational notes. The students' next step was to go to the front of the class, where there were drawings of the heart and spools of red and blue yarn. Students were told to cut out the paper drawings of the heart and cut several lengths of yarn to represent veins and arteries. However, there were no instructions as to which group member was to do which job. The result was that one person from the group went up and waited in line to get the items while the other group members sat around talking. It took 15 minutes to get the items needed to complete the project. Students then worked together to glue yarn from the heart to various places in the body. When students had questions, such as which color should be used for which veins, they asked the teacher. After approximately 50 minutes, students cleaned up. Finally, the teacher concluded the period by asking the students what they had done. They replied that they had traced the body and glued yarn. At the end of the period, only one group was near completion of the project. The teacher told them that they would complete their work the following day.

This was a creative, interesting lesson, but it lacked sufficient planning. How could it have been improved with more preparation? The teacher should have planned specific tasks for each member of the groups by having two students trace, one get the heart paper, and another get the yarn. What took 15 minutes could have taken 2 to 3 minutes. Also, the teacher should have precut the yarn so that students would not have to stand in line for 5 to 10 minutes waiting for the spools. The teacher could have instructed students to bring their notebooks with them to the group and use their notes to answer questions that arose before asking the teacher questions. Finally, the lesson wrap-up should have been planned to reinforce the concepts and vocabulary of the lesson. The goal of every lesson needs to be student *learning*, not simply the completion of activities. Unfortunately, lack of focus and poor planning resulted in a lesson that included little more than having middle school students tracing and gluing, as the students mentioned at the conclusion of the lesson.

## Academic Engaged Time

There is a high correlation between student achievement and the amount of time students are actively engaged in learning tasks. Too often, important academic time is wasted on noninstructional events, such as taking attendance and passing out papers. In some sheltered classes, there are practices that maximize instructional time with positive results. These practices include beginning the lesson immediately after the bell rings. The lesson usually begins with a review of past learning and then moves into the objectives for the current lesson, making a connection between the two. Presentation of lesson content begins, maximizing student interest and involvement through either a direct instruction approach or interactive format. The key issue is keeping students actively engaged in learning, regardless of the format. The lesson ends by refocusing students on the lesson's objectives and reviewing what was learned.

Academic engaged time and lesson preparation are interrelated because it takes planning to keep students engaged throughout the period. Students, particularly English-language learners, cannot afford lost academic time. In some classes, like the science class described above, the last 10 minutes of the period are used for clean up, which means 30 seconds of gathering books and papers, followed by $9\frac{1}{2}$ minutes of sitting around. In classes that use every minute of class time wisely, the same students can be seen on task and performing to a high degree. The science lesson could easily have been completed in one class period, yet the teacher devoted two full class sessions to it, wasting valuable academic time.

Regardless of the type of student—mainstream, English-language learner, or special education—meaningful, effective lessons must be well planned and engage students to a high degree.

## A Comparative Case Study

Effective instruction and sheltered lessons share many characteristics. A series of middle school social studies lessons can demonstrate the similarities and differences. These lessons were part of a pilot study (Echevarria, Greene, & Goldenberg, 1996) in which three teachers taught the same content to English-language learners, two using a sheltered approach and one using effective instruction.

The lessons were part of a four-day unit on consumerism. The first day's lesson introduced key vocabulary: *brand name, ingredient, consumer, false advertising, effective,* and *myths.* The content objectives of the unit were as follow:

1. What health values to look for in products and services consumers buy or use
2. How product labels can help consumers
3. How advertising can help consumers

The language objective was to use key vocabulary in context.

Students read the textbook definition of *consumers:* "those who buy and use products." In the effective instruction group, each student individually looked up vocabulary words in the glossary and wrote his or her definitions. In the sheltered group, each word was assigned to a group of five students to look up in the glossary, and each group then reported its definition to the class and paraphrased the definition of the word.

The objective of the second day was to learn how consumers can make informed decisions. The lesson began with all groups reviewing the definition of *consumer* and other vocabulary words. Students then began reading a section in the text titled "You Can Make Good Decisions." The effective instruction students read the section silently to themselves; the sheltered students read as a group, with the teachers providing paraphrasing and clarification as needed. After reading, both groups discussed the need for consumers to examine the quality of the item as well as the price. Teachers in both groups mentioned that cheap prices sometimes indicate poor quality, but some brand name prices are based on the name, not the quality. In the sheltered group, teachers showed a sample of cheap shoes and well-made shoes, writing the cost of each pair on the board. Then the shoes were passed around for students to compare. They discussed cost and quality.

The effective instruction group was given a worksheet containing these four questions:

1. You want a new jacket. The Laker jacket is almost twice the price of a similar jacket sold by Sears. Do you buy the expensive Laker jacket or the Sears brand? Why?
2. Two cameras are the same price, but one comes with a zoom lens. Which would you buy? Why?
3. An 8-ounce tube of toothpaste costs $3.00, and a 4-ounce tube of the same type costs $2.00. Which would you buy? Why?
4. Shasta Cola costs $2.50 for a six-pack, and Coke costs $3.25 for a six-pack. Which do you buy? Why?

The sheltered instruction group participated in a hands-on activity in which items were arranged in stations around the room. At each station, students compared two items and decided if the quality was the same and if the difference in price was worth it. Students completed worksheets at each station (see Figure 3.4, page 66), rotating from one station to the other. All groups had the same closure at the end of the lesson: "Today you learned that consumers should make informed decisions. What are some things you should consider before buying something? Tomorrow we'll find out how we can be more informed to make better decisions."

The third day of the unit followed a similar format: The sheltered instruction lessons were more student centered, proving more context and hands-on activities, while the effective instruction lessons were paper-and-pencil oriented, relying on the teacher and textbook as sources for learning. Again, both groups reviewed what a consumer is and why consumers should make informed decisions. Review of vocabulary was oral for the effective instruction group; the sheltered group benefited from having the words on an overhead projector. All teachers opened the lesson by saying, "Today we're going to learn about how product labels help consumers."

Both groups began by reading a section in the textbook about reading labels and the important information they give consumers. In both

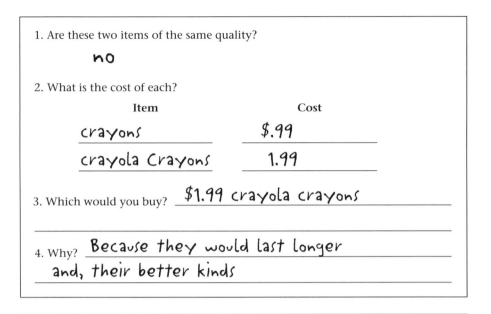

1. Are these two items of the same quality?

   no

2. What is the cost of each?

   | Item | Cost |
   | --- | --- |
   | crayons | $.99 |
   | crayola Crayons | 1.99 |

3. Which would you buy?  $1.99 crayola crayons

4. Why?  Because they would last longer and, their better kinds

FIGURE 3.4  *Activity Worksheet*

groups, students were asked, "Can consumers believe the information they read on health product labels?" Students were assigned either to a group that argued yes or a group that argued no. Each group was required to defend its answer using information from the textbook.

After the brief debate, the effective instruction group answered questions posed in the textbook about labels, while the sheltered instruction group participated in a hands-on activity to further their understanding of the concepts presented in the textbook. The teacher brought in a variety of food containers, medicine containers, and clothing with labels, and the students formed groups. Each group was given one food container, one medicine container, and one clothing item. As a group, they completed a worksheet about reading labels (see Figure 3.5).

All the teachers closed the lesson by saying, "Today you learned how a consumer can learn about products and make good decisions. Why would you not buy a sweater that has to be dry cleaned, even if the price is good? Why would you not buy vitamins where the first ingredient labeled is sugar? Tomorrow we're going to see how advertising affects our choices."

On the final day of the unit, both groups reviewed the definition of *consumer* and the things they had learned about being more informed consumers, such as considering cost and quality and reading labels. The objective of the final day was to show how advertising can help consumers and how it can trick consumers.

**Medicine**

1. What are the **directions** for using this product?

The directions are that you only have to use a small amount, spreading and rubbing in well.

2. What can you learn from the **warning**?

that we have to keep out of reach of children.

**Food**

1. What is the major ingredient of this product?    Sugar is a major ingredient

2. What other health information is on the label?

Nutrition information. Calories & vitamins

**Clothing**

1. What material is the clothing made from?

It is 55% Ramie   45% cotton

2. According to the label, how should it be cleaned?

Hand wash cold water

**FIGURE 3.5**   *Label-Reading Activity*

Students in both groups were directed to look at a shampoo ad in the textbook depicting an attractive couple riding bikes. The teachers asked if the ad had useful health information about the shampoo. The effective instruction teacher led students in a question-and-answer session about the ad and what it communicated. The sheltered students formed pairs and were given 2 minutes to write down words that described the people in the ad (*happy, healthy, fun, pretty, handsome*). Students were asked to share some of their words. The sheltered teachers wrote the words on the overhead projector as students said them. Teachers in both groups pointed out that ads give consumers the impression that using the product will make them resemble the people in the ad. Teachers further asked students, "If the people in the ad were smoking, would you think that the brand being smoked was healthful?"

Both groups then turned to the textbook to read and discuss. The sheltered teachers used a variety of reading options, such as having students read with a partner, read aloud, or read in groups, with the teacher paraphrasing, clarifying, discussing, and checking for understanding frequently. The effective instruction group relied more on independent silent reading. Checks for understanding consisted of brief teacher-student interactions with fewer opportunities for elaboration and discussion than the sheltered format. In the textbook passage, students were directed to the term *brand name* and asked to give examples based on their experience. The sheltered teachers wrote students' responses on overhead transparencies. Students were asked questions such as whether consumers have any protection from false health information in advertising.

Next, a variety of laminated magazine and newspaper advertisements were distributed to students. Effective instruction students individually completed the worksheets and then compared their scores with those of their partners. Teachers modeled how students were to score each ad. Sheltered instruction students, preassigned by the teacher in groups of three, rated each ad (see Figure 3.6). A timer was then set for 4 minutes. When the timer went off, the group had to have the ad scored and go on to the next ad. When the timer went off again, groups exchanged ads with another group for scoring. After 8 minutes (4 minutes per ad), the groups compared their scores. Sheltered teachers directed this portion of the lesson by asking questions such as "How did group 1 score this ad? and group 2? Group 1, why did you give it a score of 9? Group 3, how did you score this ad? Compare your score with group 4." The class discussed how some people like certain things while others like others. The teacher pointed out that this distinction is what advertising is about: targeting certain groups (young mothers, teenagers, senior citizens) and trying to put together an ad to which a certain group will respond.

All teachers ended the lesson with this statement: "Today we have seen how advertising can help consumers and how consumers can use ads to get important information. We've also seen how advertising is used to influence consumers. How does advertising differ from the information you get on labels?"

On the final day, students in both groups were also given a test that included multiple-choice items, definitions of vocabulary items, and short-answer questions.

This social studies unit gives an idea of what might occur during a sheltered lesson. Sheltered lessons unfold as the result of thoughtful planning done at the beginning of the year. Teachers who work with ELLs must first develop a vision for the students of where they want to take them and

Score each ad in this way:

0 = No useful information
5 = A lot of useful information

Circle the score you give to each ad.

**Ad #1**  1  2  3  4  ⑤

Why? <u>**Becous It has how your hear will loke and**</u>
    <u>**the vitamins will make your hear beter and**</u>
    <u>**its beter for your hear**</u>

**Ad #2**  1  2  3  4  5

Why? _____

Circle the score you give to the other group's ads.

**Ad #1**  ①  2  3  4  5

Why? <u>**I think that is not good becous it**</u>
    <u>**doesnt say If your lips will be dry.**</u>

**Ad #2**  1  2  3  4  5

Why? _____

Your group members:

1. <u>**Francisco**</u>
2. <u>**Eric**</u>
3. <u>**Joel**</u>

---

**FIGURE 3.6  *Advertisement Activity***

develop lessons around that vision (see Chapter 1). Gonzales (1994) suggests developing an annual plan, whereby teachers review the textbooks, content standards, state framework guides, curriculum guides, and teachers' manuals for purposes of determining the essential content for a specific grade level or course. Planning involves weaving critical concepts and ideas related to each topic into meaningful, connected units that build upon each other. Once the most important concepts have been determined, the nonessential details can be eliminated and the broad range of students' academic needs can be addressed by using a planning pyramid (Schumm, Vaughn, & Leavell, 1994). Such a process is guided by these questions: What do I want *all* students to learn? What do I want *most* students to learn? and What do I want *some* students to learn? This final question acknowledges that while all students can learn, not all students can be realistically expected to learn everything in content area textbooks, given the variety of levels of literacy and English proficiency.

This type of big-picture planning assists teachers in formulating a vision for the students that translates into cohesive lessons that build on one another, providing English-language learners with continuity and reinforcement of major concepts and vocabulary. It also lends itself to thematic teaching.

In the social studies class just described, the theme was an individual's power to make choices. With thematic teaching, the teacher selects a concept or theme and weaves it across the curriculum. The teacher analyzes the content for the entire course and determines the relevant information to be covered throughout the year, formulating ways to weave the theme into the information. When presenting the key concepts from the unit, the teacher emphasizes an individual's ability to choose between products and make wise decisions. Students could be asked about products available in their home countries and whether they were able to choose from among several brands. In the discussion on advertising, students learned that they can choose to buy or not. Using recurrent themes when introducing new learning provides linkages that render the material more understandable.

The extent to which teachers use sheltered elements is difficult to capture in a written description. In a description of sheltered lessons, the high level of student interaction, the student-centered focus of the instruction, and the many ways the teacher uses visuals and other means to create a context for information and discussions are not evident. Further, many features are unique to sheltered instruction, not so much in their essence but in the degree to which they are used. For example, tapping into students' background knowledge is useful in most instructional situations, but when working with culturally diverse students learning English, it is essential to make the connection between students' knowledge and experience and the lesson at hand. In sheltered lessons, the connection needs to be made much more explicitly than in other situations. This is one of the characteristics that makes sheltered instruction unique.

Finally, not every component of sheltered instruction is present in each lesson, but most should be implemented throughout a series of lessons. In other words, one day's lesson may be a hands-on cooperative activity designed as a follow-up to the previous day's lesson that involved reading from the text. In this case, modifying the text wouldn't be applicable, but many of the other components would be evident.

## *Discussion of the Case Study*

In the unit on consumerism, the content level of the sheltered instruction and effective instruction lessons were the same, both based on the core curriculum. Since lesson objectives must always reflect grade-level content (although it is permissible to cover background information that the student needs for understanding), it would be inappropriate to teach ELLs a curriculum intended for younger students simply because they are in the process of acquiring English. In both the sheltered and effective instruction lessons, the objectives were clearly supported by lesson delivery. Each lesson had a focus that was easily identified as the lesson unfolded. In addition, major concepts were explicitly identified. In the sheltered and effective lessons, the teacher wrote the major concepts on the board or overhead projector, discussed each one, and referred back to each as it was covered during the lesson. Both teachers in the consumerism lessons told students they were going to learn about how product labels help consumers and tied information back to this concept throughout the reading and discussion.

Concepts are also reinforced by linking them to students' background. This process is twofold: It taps the students' previous knowledge on the topic being studied and ties it to the lesson, and it validates students' cultural background and experiences by providing opportunities for students to talk about their lives and relating them to the topic. The first step can be accomplished in a number of ways, such as a through pretest or discussion. Secondary students in particular may have a wealth of knowledge acquired through exposure to a variety of experiences typical of most immigrant students. The known information is used to link previous learning to new learning.

The second step, bringing in students' cultural background, is especially effective with English-language learners. The teacher explicitly draws parallels between the topic and the students' experiences. The teacher might ask, "How many of you have bought something and had it break right away? How many of you have wanted something because you saw a commercial, but when you got it, it wasn't as good as you thought?" Using their own experiences to introduce new learning is a good way to engage students in a topic. Also, when discussing myths associated with products, such as the myths that mouthwash prevents colds or that protein shampoo feeds hair, students are encouraged to share cultural beliefs about certain products. In preparation for the lesson on advertising, immigrant students may be asked to bring in newspapers or magazines in their native languages to compare their ads to American advertising styles.

Content material is organized so it relates to previous lessons. English-language learners need relationships between new learning and past lessons explicitly stated to clarify the connection between lessons. Timelines and word banks facilitate this process, since events, previous vocabulary, and terms are posted for students to see and remember. For example, prior to the unit on consumerism, students had studied about pollution and about household items that contain dangerous chemicals. That information could be revisited when students study the value of reading labels. The presence of chemicals in products may affect consumer decisions. The unit following consumerism should be a topic that logically follows. Using state curriculum frameworks and curriculum guides facilitates connected lessons that build on one another.

Another feature that is common to both sheltered and effective instruction is that the teacher consistently varies delivery modes. A recitation or lecture mode is possibly the least effective way of teaching students learning English (Tharp & Gallimore, 1988). It relies heavily on comprehending verbal input and provides limited contextual clues for the learner. Effective instruction offers a variety of learning opportunities for students, including explanation, modeling, demonstration, and visual representation. Sheltered instruction does the same, perhaps to a higher degree. When students are acquiring a new language, varying delivery modes assists in comprehension and helps keep students engaged in learning throughout the lesson. What they may not understand presented one way may become clearer when presented in a different fashion. The importance of academic engaged time was discussed previously and cannot be overstated. Teaching is not going on unless students are learning. In order to learn, the student must attend to and be cognitively engaged in the task.

Frequent checks for understanding characterize both effective instruction and sheltered instruction. These checks can be done individually or by asking group questions, such as "Everyone who thinks a consumer is only a person who buys goods and services, raise one finger; everyone who thinks a consumer is someone who buys and uses goods and services, raise two fingers."

Ample variation in reading options is a feature of both approaches, with sheltered lessons using variation more frequently. Options include teacher read-aloud, buddy reading, and silent reading. Listening to reading on tape is effective for English-language learners and is used more commonly in a sheltered class. Reading for meaning is one of the more challenging activities for students learning English. Students' reading fluency is limited, since many do not have the vocabulary necessary to read with ease, while others lack the advantage of a strong academic background on which to draw. Students with learning problems often have comprehension difficulties, as well. Varying the reading format allows students to have reading experiences that are assisted or scaffolded by others. *Scaffolding* is the process of providing support as needed, with less support required as students move toward independent functioning. As the teacher reads aloud, he or she can pause at natural breaks. During sheltered lessons, paraphrasing and clarification are a routine part of the reading process.

With both approaches, lessons are designed to provide opportunities for students to use higher-level skills, including problem solving, hypothesizing, organizing, synthesizing, categorizing, evaluating, and self-monitoring. In a lesson on economics, a teacher showed the covers of several weekly news magazines with headlines about massive layoffs. She then asked, "How do you think workers feel when they see these headlines? Why does it make them nervous?" Students were asked to work with partners and come up with three ways that massive layoffs affect everyone. Opportunities such as this for higher-level thinking should be presented throughout a lesson.

Scaffolding is used with both sheltered and effective instruction. However, the implementation differs in that effective instruction teachers typically use questioning techniques to guide students, prompting and prodding verbally to get students to the correct answer. In sheltered instruction, scaffolding is used frequently throughout the lesson, since the varying levels of English proficiency and academic background of students necessitates doing so. The teacher accepts the students' ideas without correcting their form but instead adds clarification and elaboration as needed. The teacher does not rely on verbal scaffolding alone but may use context clues to clarify meaning and promote understanding. When conducting whole-group lessons in sheltered or effective instruction classes, students participate by giving signals such as thumbs-up or thumbs-down to indicate their opinion or answer.

## Specific Considerations for Students with Learning Disabilities

Students with language and learning disabilities need extra support in acquiring English. They most likely will not learn at the same rate as other students and often need more repetition and clarification of terms. Many of the features of the SIOP model of sheltered instruction are considered as the best practice for students with learning difficulties, as well. In one study, ELLs identified as learning disabled were included in sheltered classes whose teachers implemented the SIOP model. Using pre- and posttest data, these students made significant overall improvement in writing and specifically in the areas of language production, support/ elaboration, and mechanics (Echevarria, 2001).

A focus on specific objectives, written for students to see, along with selected vocabulary provides the kind of structure that many of these students need. Using supplementary materials to make lesson concepts clear and meaningful and adapting the content to the students' academic and linguistic levels are also important features of instruction for ELLs with learning difficulties.

Further, the use of extralinguistic clues, such as gestures and body language, helps students understand the message and focuses their attention. For example, in the consumerism lesson, the teacher pointed to the words *cheap* and *expensive* on the board as she said, "Would you rather buy the cheap pair of shoes *(holding them up)* or the expensive pair *(holding them up)?*"

An abundance of positive reinforcement encourages students' participation. Students who have experienced learning problems may be particularly reticent in using a new language. A positive affective environment can facilitate language use (Krashen, 1981).

The type of instructional tasks that tend to engage English language learners with learning difficulties are those that draw on students' prior experiences and interests and that relate those experiences to new learning. In addition, these students benefit from tasks that foster intrinsic motivation and a sense of success and pride in accomplishment (Yates & Ortiz, 1991). Figure 3.7 provides some suggestions for adapting instruction to meet these students' needs.

## *Summary*

Sheltered instruction is designed to teach English language learners content area material in a way that both makes it understandable to them and also develops their English language proficiency. There is no step-by-step sheltered plan, but certain features should be present in all sheltered lessons, such as having language and content objectives, emphasizing key vocabulary, scaffolding instruction, using comprehensible input, reviewing material, and assessing students' learning (see Figure 3.2).

Not all students learn in precisely the same way. Thus, instruction should be tailored to the needs of individual students. Some may respond well to direct, explicit instruction, whereas others may perform better when given an opportunity to develop ideas in a cooperative group. The academic task itself often dictates the type of instructional approach to be used. Better-defined subjects, such as math computation and grammar, may call for a direct instruction approach, while exploring ideas presented

FIGURE 3.7   *Considerations for ELLs with Language and Learning Difficulties*

- Provide abundant guided practice for acquisition of concepts.
- Adjust the pace of instruction according to students' needs.
- Allow extra time to complete assignments.
- Praise students' efforts and use positive reinforcement.
- Partner students with others sensitive to their learning needs.
- Provide alternative activities when a task may draw undue attention to students' disabilities (e.g., reading aloud, a task that requires fine motor skills or substained periods of attention).
- Plan and use apropriate behavior management techniques.
- Employ learning strategies known to be effective with students with disabilities (see Chapter 5).

*Source:* Based on J. Echevarria (May 1995), Sheltered instruction for students with learning disabilities who have limited English proficiency, *Intervention in School and Clinic, 30*(5), 302–305.

in a social studies book lends itself to a more conversational approach (Goldenberg, 1992–93).

Sheltered content area instruction may be seen as a framework for instruction in which lessons are designed and adapted to meet the needs of the students. Sheltered lessons may include explicit teaching, group work, curricular adaptations, infusion of learning strategies (see Chapter 5), or an interactive approach. While sheltered lessons clearly share some of the characteristics of effective instruction, they expand on others to meet the needs of ELLs and include some characteristics that are unique to these individuals. Many of the characteristics of a sheltered lesson will enhance the ability of students with learning difficulties to make sense of the content, such as the use of visuals, repetition, and active involvement. Therefore, sheltered instruction is good instruction, but it involves more. Teachers adapt effective lessons to make them understandable and more appropriate for students learning English.

## *Activities*

1. Using a textbook from a given subject area, develop a lesson using the features of sheltered instruction outlined in Figure 3.2.

2. In small groups, brainstorm ways to make a sheltered lesson more comprehensible.

3. List at least five different ways a teacher can check for students' understanding.

## *References*

Bickel, W. E., & Bickel, D. D. (1986). Effective schools, classrooms, and instruction. *Exceptional Children, 52*(6), 489–500.

Brophy, J., & Everston, C. (1976). *Learning from teaching: A developmental perspective.* Boston: Allyn and Bacon.

Cummins, J. (1989). *Empowering minority students.* Sacramento: California Association for Bilingual Education.

Echevarria, J. (2001). *Improving content literacy for English language learners.* Paper presented at the California Reading Association Conference, Ontario, CA.

Echevarria, J., Greene, G., & Goldenberg, C. (1996). *A comparison of sheltered content instruction and effective instruction.* Unpublished pilot study.

Echevarria, J., Short, D., & Powers, K. (in preparation). *Using sheltered instruction to improve the achievement of English language learners.* Manuscript submitted for publication.

Echevarria, J., & Vogt, M. (1996). *Measuring the effects of sheltered instruction on English language learners.* Paper presented at the annual meeting of the American Educational Research Association, New York.

Faltis, C. (1993). Critical issues in the use of sheltered content instruction in high school bilingual programs. *Peabody Journal of Education, 69*(1), 136–151.

Gersten, R. M., Taylor, R., & Graves, A. W. (1999). Direct instruction and diversity. In R. Stevens (Ed.), *Teaching in American schools: A tribute to Barak Rosenshine.* Upper Saddle River, NJ: Merrill/Prentice Hall.

Goldenberg, C. (1992–93). Instructional conversations: Promoting comprehension through discussion, *The Reading Teacher, 46*(4), 316–326.

Gonzales, L. (1994). *Sheltered instruction handbook.* Carlsbad, CA: Gonzales & Gonzales.

Krashen, S. (1981). *Second language acquisition and second language learning.* London: Pergamon Press.

Krashen, S., & Terrell, T. (1983). *The natural approach: Language acquisition in the classroom.* Englewood Cliffs, NJ: Alemany/Prentice-Hall.

McLaughlin, B. (1992). *Babes and bathwaters: How to teach vocabulary.* Working papers of the Bilingual Research Group, University of California, Santa Cruz.

Richard-Amato, P. (1996). *Making it happen* (2nd ed.). White Plains, NY: Longman.

Saville-Troike, M. (1984). What really matters in second language learning for academic achievement? *TESOL Quarterly, 18*(2).

Schumm, J., Vaughn, S., & Leavell, A. (1994). Planning pyramid: A framework of planning for diverse student needs during content area instruction. *The Reading Teacher, 47*(8), 608–615.

Scruggs, T., & Mastropieri, M. (1990). Mnemonic instruction for students with learning disabilities: What it is and what is does. *Learning Disability Quarterly, 13*(3), 271–283.

Short, D., & Echevarria, J. (1999). *The sheltered instruction observation protocol (SIOP): A tool for teacher-researcher collaboration and professional development* (Educational Practice Report 3). Washington, DC: Center for Research on Education, Diversity and Excellence.

Tharp, R., & Gallimore, R. (1988). *Rousing minds to life.* New York: Cambridge University Press.

Yates, J., & Ortiz, A. (1991). Professional development needs of teachers who serve exceptional language minorities in today's schools. *Teacher Education and Special Education, 14*(1), 11–18.

# 4

## *Affective Issues*

- *Pon,* the fourth-grader from Chapter 1, has behavior problems and learning problems in school. Teachers wonder if the problems he is experiencing can be attributed in part to cultural and linguistic differences that set him apart from most of his peers. How can Pon's teachers help him feel a greater sense of belonging?
- *Araceli,* a Mexican immigrant, spoke only Spanish when she began school. By the eighth grade, she has learned to read in Spanish, but reads in English at a second-grade level. How can Araceli's teachers provide emotional support and enhance her self-esteem?

When students experience challenges in school, their *affective,* or social-emotional, reactions are often counterproductive. Challenges in learning English or in performing well in school, when coupled with the general diversity of society, can often produce intensification of racial and ethnic tensions (Pang, 2001; Obi, Obiakor, & Algozzine, 1999; Lessow-Hurley, 1996; Gay, 1993). The purpose of this chapter is to give readers information about creating a learning environment that promotes emotional and intellectual fairness and security. A good learning environment can enhance self-esteem in all learners (Lynch & Hanson, 1998; Ruiz, 1995a, 1995b; Bandura, 1986).

Emotions and feelings of inadequacy tend to be stronger when students are trying simultaneously to learn English and to meet other school responsibilities (Altwerger & Ivener, 1994). Beginning English-language learners (ELLs) are in a new cultural setting and do not have their usual support systems (Faltis & Hudelson, 1994; Faltis & Arias, 1993). The students are in a survival mode; they are unable simultaneously to consider others' feelings, plan for their own future, and function outside an egocentric concern for their own survival (Baca & Almanza, 1996; Walker de Felix, Waxman, Paige, & Huang, 1993). The new culture is practically inaccessible to these students, because they draw extensively on first-language strategies and resources (Harry, 1992). The students typically encounter new information or processes in school that are unfamiliar and therefore difficult to learn (Cazden, 1992; Figueroa, 1989).

Many theories about affective issues indicate that a student who is trying to learn English may experience extraordinary school challenges (M. N. Torres, 2001; C. C. Torres, 2000; Fitzgerald, 1995; Moll, 1988). The English-language learner may experience ridicule or rejection by peers and teachers when trying to use English (Ramirez, 1989). The English-language learner may also experience challenges and perceive failure in communicating effectively with peers and school personnel. Encountering these challenges, the student is likely to resist learning English and may experience emotional blocks or trauma when trying to speak English (Cummins, 1992).

Students like Pon and Araceli are likely to feel a greater sense of belonging, feel more supported emotionally, and have higher self-esteem when teachers take the following steps (Graves, 1995):

1. Provide constructivist activities in reading and writing.
2. Provide ample practice and careful corrections.
3. Focus on relevant background knowledge.
4. Actively involve learners.
5. Use alternate grouping strategies.
6. Provide native-language support.
7. Focus on content and activities that are meaningful to students.
8. Create roles in the classroom for family and community members.
9. Hold high expectations for *all* learners.
10. Be responsive to cultural and personal diversity.

## Providing Constructivist Reading and Writing Activities

Students have a more positive feeling toward school and are more successful when they construct their own meaning during writing and reading assignments (Allen, 1989; Cheng, 1995; Bos, 1988; Lim & Watson, 1993; Moll, 1988). Students tend to be successful when they are actively and personally involved. Activities such as language experience approaches and writing-as-a-process are among the most valuable for youngsters who are learning English. Literature-based instruction in reading and writing typically provides rich and exciting activities for students. Abundant information is now available regarding this type of instruction (Waldschmidt et al., 1999; Cloud, 1993).

Ruiz and her colleagues have investigated the effects of the *optimal learning environment (OLE)* program on literacy development in several studies of ELLs with learning disabilities (Ruiz, 1995a, 1995b). The OLE program includes an integration of oral language, listening, speaking, reading, and writing along with a combination of writing-as-a-process and strategy instruction. The learning environment is designed in a way that facilitates this development by including the following elements:

1. Interactive journals, in which the teacher responds to students' daily entries in writing each day to provide modeling of written dialog
2. Writer's Workshop based on writing-as-a-process, in which students go through planning, drafting, editing, revising, final drafting, and publishing each time they produce a written product

3. Patterned writing and reading, in which students read and copy key phrases from children's literature, such as the works of Eric Carle
4. Creating text for wordless books
5. Shared reading with predictable text
6. Literature conversation with read-alouds
7. Literature study with response journals
8. Student-made alphabet wall charts
9. Drop everything and read time (DEAR)

Ruiz found that the use of OLE improved the writing performance of these individuals and provided a mechanism for nonwriters and readers in English and Spanish to develop improved performances in English and Spanish.

Several additional studies of Spanish-speaking youngsters with learning disabilities have provided information about the OLE project and its effects on writing outcomes (Graves, Valles, Prodor, & Rueda, in press; Ortiz & Graves, 2001; Graves, Valles, & Rueda, 2000a, 2000b). The first was a descriptive case study comparison of writing instruction in four bilingual special education settings (Graves et al., 2000a, 2000b). The second study was a quasi-experiment study of two groups of Spanish-speaking students in special education settings comparing the effects of OLE with those of traditional writing instruction (Graves et al., in press). Both studies indicate significant progress for students who were part of the OLE project. Progress on meaningful tasks tends to promote positive affect in the learner (Baca & Cervantes, 1998).

In one eighth-grade class, 97 percent of the students were Latino, the majority of whom were not born in the United States. The students were at varying levels of English and Spanish proficiency. The teacher used English reading materials not consistent with the lives of the students and far below the students' grade level, and some of these phonics-based materials had mundane story lines. One young man in the class sat with a scowl on his face and constantly sought attention from his peers through inappropriate behavior. The teacher reported that this student and many others were frustrated and that their parents were concerned about their lack of progress. It was recommended that this teacher start to use a more meaningful approach by providing constructivist activities relevant to the students' lives.

The teacher devised practice exercises to develop vocabulary, spelling, sequencing, and identification of main ideas and developed other activities based directly on student-generated work. When the teacher used this approach, the behavior problems virtually vanished and the troubled students became happier and more cooperative. Providing constructivist activities to students can change their attitudes and their performances. For students like Pon and Araceli, they can enhance feelings of belonging at school because they are able to bring their own ideas to the task. These types of activities are also likely to enhance students' self-esteem, as they begin to take pride in their work and to experience success.

Journal writing at the beginning of each class day or at the beginning of each unit appears critical for the development of secondary students' writing skills. It can also reinforce positive feelings toward school (Peyton, Jones, Vincent, & Greenblatt, 1994). For example, one middle school math teacher had students use a binder as a journal. The teacher assigned various types of writing throughout the year. For 3 minutes at the start of each math period, the students made journal entries about their thoughts and feelings concerning the math homework. At other times, the students wrote for 3 minutes about how the concepts they were learning applied to their lives. The students were asked to share their writing in small groups or to read journal entries to the class without disclosing the student writer. Each week, the teacher collected the journals, read the entries, and provided written comments in the journals. The comments created a written interaction, or dialogue, with each student and established an opportunity for language development, even in a math class.

Written expression is a common method used to assess subject matter knowledge. However, written expression is often problematic for students who are ELL. Alternate ways of allowing students to demonstrate knowledge are to let them speak into a tape recorder, to a peer, or to the teacher. Students can work in pairs to complete written assignments or can express their ideas in graphic or pictorial form rather than in words alone.

## *Providing Ample Practice and Careful Corrections*

Students remember and reuse information better with ample practice. Successful students generally feel better about school and have higher self-concepts. Teachers can provide successful experiences by giving abundant practice and applying new knowledge in ongoing, authentic experiences. Consider an example of a unit on Coastal Native Americans, in which students practiced report writing, finding main ideas, and sharing writing in the context of the unit. Students continued to practice these skills within the context of future units.

In order to minimize anxiety, teachers must approach correction during practice cautiously (Flores, Rueda, & Porter, 1986). In particular, students who have experienced school failure or who are learning to speak English as a second language often need encouragement and they need to be told when they have responded correctly. For example, teachers are advised to approach error correction indirectly as follows:

*Enrico:*   When animals move from place to place, they midrate.

*Teacher:*   Did you say *migrate,* Enrico *(with emphasis on the gr)?* That's right, Enrico. When animals move from place to place, they *migrate.* Good. *(The teacher writes the word on the board once again.)*

The teacher responds positively to the correct content and models the correct pronunciation by repeating the word.

## *Focusing on Relevant Background Knowledge*

Educational theories and research from many different perspectives indicate that students learn better when teachers refer to relevant student experiences during instruction (Woolfolk, 1996; Lim & Watson, 1993; Allen, 1989; Bos, 1988; Moll, 1988; Vygotsky, 1978). Establishing relevance near the beginning of a lesson and continuing to connect and associate the lives of students to the lesson throughout improves student learning. Using connections and associations from the lives of students serves the dual purpose of bringing the learners consciously and actively to the task at hand and validating their own life experiences. This addition to a lesson maximizes the amount students learn by linking new knowledge to already existing knowledge. This focus on relevant background knowledge lowers anxiety and heightens motivation. Students are more interested in school and likely to experience positive feelings toward school and themselves as learners.

Teachers can ask the students for relevant background knowledge about a topic. A brainstorming session can produce student examples in association with the topic. These student-generated examples can then be used to help establish relevance to the topic. For example, when asked for a direct application of a geometry lesson in math class, students might say that it could be used to build a bridge, to cut pizza, to build houses, or to install a carpet. The teacher needs to plan daily activities that center around these student-generated applications of knowledge (García, 1993b).

In a study of mathematics and middle-school students of Mexican descent, Henderson and Landesman (1992) found that students had better success in mathematics when involved in student-formed construction companies. Each student group named its own construction company and assigned roles within. Each company was allotted $1.5 million to purchase supplies and pay the workers for the construction of a bridge. Purchases from the "school warehouse" required bookkeeping and double-checking of math skills. All math skills on the scope and sequence for middle school were encountered during the project. Students learned adult responsibilities such as budgeting, check writing, and accounting. Each company was required to file tax returns each year and budget for state and federal tax assessments.

In another example, a fifth-grade teacher presenting a math unit on fractions began by showing pieces of pie that when put together made one whole pie. On another occasion, she used a cut-up egg crate and then put it together to make a whole crate. Students talked about whether they ate eggs or pie. Students were then asked how many pieces of pie would need to be cut in their house to serve their family. The teacher further provided opportunities for students to develop knowledge of and experience with fractions by giving each student a square of material and telling them to cut their square into five equal pieces. They were also asked to survey family members about their use of fractions. They were provided with different classroom experiences, such as folding a piece of paper into four equal parts to make a card for family members or determining how many parts or chapters were in a whole book. This allowed students to develop some background knowledge by way of their own recent experiences (Gay, 1993; Krashen, 1985).

## *Actively Involving Learners*

Learning theorists and researchers from many perspectives concur that active learning produces the greatest success (Woolfolk, 1996). Successful learning enhances positive emotional feelings and self-esteem. When a student is highly active, greater student involvement is even more crucial for maximizing learning opportunities (Henze & Lucas, 1993). A student like Pon benefits when teachers give students a number of choices to involve them actively in the learning process. A teacher can use routine questioning, small-group and cooperative-group activities, partner and individualized sharing opportunities, and role-playing to keep students physically active and involved in their learning.

Teachers who actively engage students meaningfully often are more successful than teachers who do not (Gersten & Jiménez, 1994; King, 1990; Palincsar, 1986). Successful teachers ask many questions, including many high-level questions of all students (Gersten & Jiménez, 1994). Approaches that have teachers ask many questions that do not have specific answers, such as instructional conversations (see Chapter 7), improve the language skills of learners and the comfort levels of students in school (Echevarria & McDonough, 1995; Goldenberg, 1992–93; Rosebery, Warren, & Conant, 1992; Palincsar, 1986).

When a teacher decides to use concise wording to define a concept such as that in the lesson on animals that migrate, a short segment in which the students repeat "Animals that migrate move from place to place" is recommended (Short, 1994; Allen, 1989; Pierce, 1988). Such segments are likely to facilitate memory and long-term use of the information. When teaching students who are learning English, the opportunity to repeat and at times rehearse terminology and sentence structure has been shown to produce improved English-language skills (Peyton, Jones, Vincent, & Greenblatt, 1994; Good & Brophy, 1991; Krashen, 1985; Saville-Troike, 1984).

Individualized sharing opportunities, such as talking, reading, and role-playing, contribute to language development in students (Englert & Mariage, 1992). Teachers can use segments of time for individualized sharing. For example, in a high school class of 30, 3 students a day are asked to present 5-minute oral reports. In two weeks, each student in the class will have presented a report and the teacher will have used only 15 minutes of the 50-minute period each day.

A teacher is more successful in promoting learning when students are physically involved in the learning process. Some excellent tools for promoting physical learning are manipulatives for teaching math (for instance, Popsicle sticks or dice). An example not as obvious is the use of a timeline for teaching history. Students can learn to understand a timeline by charting out their own lives. After timelines are introduced, each history lesson can begin with a student writing the historical time period for the lesson on the timeline. Personal timelines can be displayed in the classroom, and the historical timeline can be displayed on a large scale and updated regularly. Other examples of techniques that can keep students actively involved in a history lesson are role-playing, displaying actual objects from a historical time period, and videotaped reenactments.

## Using Alternate Grouping Strategies

Partner sharing, peer tutoring, and cooperative grouping are also important activities in which students can participate and feel valued (Greenwood, Arreaga-Mayer, Gavin, & Terry, 2001; Slavin & Madden, 1999; Schunk & Hanson, 1985). However, several researchers advise that alternative grouping should be approached with caution (Greenwood et al., 2001; Beaumont, 1999). One strength of partner sharing and cooperative grouping is the random nature of the activities. Students of different cultural and academic backgrounds work together. Another strength is that teachers can pair individuals together who have different academic strengths so that students can learn from each other. Partner sharing and cooperative grouping can guarantee an equal opportunity for all to participate actively.

Peer tutoring works best when structured and thus requires careful planning by the teacher. Specific and pointed instruction can be provided by peer tutors, and both the tutors and tutees often show academic benefits from their interaction. (See Greenwood et al. [2001] for a full review.)

Cooperative groups promote problem solving by allowing students to share among themselves (Slavin, 1990; Arreaga-Meyer, 1998). Teachers typically structure cooperative group activities so students know exactly what is expected, how much time they have to complete a task, and the exact role for each member of the group. For a history lesson called "Looking at the Revolution from Different Points of View" (Short, 1993), the teacher divided students into cooperative groups. Each group represented a different cultural element in America. The cooperative groups (Native American, African American, Spanish, French, English, and Loyalists) considered how their assigned culture felt about the Revolutionary War. The Short study (1993) indicated that the group designated as Native Americans reported pro-independence attitudes. The group thought independence would allow the Native Americans to make their own laws and to be free again. The students were able to think like eighteenth-century Native Americans without letting the actual historical events affect their answers.

Regarding grouping, teachers can choose many different grouping structures during instruction to maximize active involvement and success (Reyes, 1992). Rigid, consistent ability grouping is not recommended. Research, however, indicates that forming small groups of students with similar needs can be very beneficial (Reyes, 1992). When all the students in a group need the same information but the instruction requires more teacher attention than can be offered in a large group, the teacher can choose small-group instruction (Brice & Rosemary-McKibbin, 1999; Good & Brophy, 1991; Slavin, 1987). Teachers can often save time by grouping three to nine students together. Each small student group recites the same information at once, and the teacher can efficiently monitor performance. The teacher can usually provide more active student involvement in small groups by asking individualized questions and requiring group responses. When compared to large-group instruction, the teacher can move at a faster pace and provide more individual attention within a small group. Continually changing student groups should prevent any stigmas associated with fixed-group structure.

## Providing Native-Language Support

When a student's native language is included in the classroom, students learn that their language is respected and valued. The students, in turn, tend to feel respected and valued because their native language and culture are recognized (Scarcella & Chin, 1993). Respect for and the utilization of a student's native language and culture are integral to responsive teaching and can improve the transfer and comprehension skills necessary for learning a new language (Grant & Gomez, 2001; García, 1993a; Perez, 1993; Cazden, 1992; Chang, 1992). When beginning writers are encouraged to write journal entries in their native language, the writers are more comfortable in school and gain English skills faster than those who do not have native-language opportunities for writing (Peyton, Jones, Vincent, & Greenblatt, 1994).

A case study shows how a limited-Spanish-speaking science teacher became a role model for English-language learners. The teacher spoke Spanish with his pupils to demonstrate the value he placed on the learners' native language and became a role model regarding the learning of a new language (Pease-Alvarez & Winsler, 1994). Though his knowledge of Spanish was quite limited, he sought help from students in using Spanish properly. He taught all the scientific terms in the lesson in both Spanish and English. Each class started with a Spanish translation of the key vocabulary for the topic. Students responded well to this teacher, and their English skills improved. In another situation, a history teacher provided key words about the Pilgrims and Thanksgiving in both Spanish and English (Hornberger & Michaeu, 1993). She conducted a discussion in which she wrote the key words in both languages (for example, *Thanksgiving = Día de Gracias*) to facilitate understanding and interest.

In terms of both communication skills and academic progress in English, native-language instruction seems to improve the performance of students. Sioux children receiving weekly instruction in their tribal language outperformed students who did not (Franklin & Thompson, 1994). In this school, tribal members came to assist teachers with the delivery of instruction. The students who received the native-language instruction participated for only several hours a week. When compared to other Sioux students who did not receive native-language instruction, those who did receive native-language instruction learned more English and did better in school.

Teachers not fluent in various languages have numerous sources for assistance and support. Other school personnel and community members can help even when multiple languages are represented in a class (Cheng, 1995; Walker de Felix, Waxman, Paige, & Huang, 1993; Gollnick & Chinn, 1990; Lucas, Henze, & Donato, 1990). There are a number of ways to incorporate native languages in the classroom when the teacher does not speak a language other than English. The teacher can use bilingual dictionaries, library books in native languages, or ask students, other teachers, or the school staff for help. Students can assist or tutor other students, ask questions or write in the native-language, and interact socially with students to learn more language (Lucas & Katz, 1994). An excellent source of native-language help is parents. Parents can communicate with other parents in the native language, encourage other parents to read to the students in the native language, and volunteer in the classroom to provide additional native-language interaction.

One monolingual teacher found a useful way to show value and re-spect for native languages as well as to empower students. The teacher or-ganized a Translation and Bridging Committee of students in grades 2 through 6. The committee was responsible for preparing notes for parents and programs for school assemblies in Tagalog and Spanish. The teacher found a useful way to empower parents and to give students a sense of pride about the role of their native language in the school environment.

## Focusing on Content and Activities That Are Meaningful to Students

Theories about language acquisition generally support native-language instruction to facilitate underlying academic proficiency. The instruction can later be "transferred in" and applied to English-language learning (Baca & Cervantes, 1998; Cummins, 1989; Krashen, 1985). However, native-language instruction is not always available in schools. To help native-language speakers, teachers can create a nonthreatening atmo-sphere where students can share information about their own cultural and ethnic backgrounds (Franklin & Thompson, 1994; Banks, 1991). For ex-ample, the teacher can arrange partner sharing and cooperative group ac-tivities to facilitate feelings of safety and comfort. The students in each group can learn how problems are solved or how stories are told within each unique cultural and linguistic perspective.

Moll (1988) writes extensively about the value of the "funds" of knowledge that students bring to the classroom. These funds of knowledge can be tapped through daily journal entries. The knowledge gained by the teacher about the students should be incorporated into lessons and coursework. For example, in an American history lesson on the design of the first American flag, students can be instructed to draw a picture of any flag with which they are familiar. They can be assigned to study and draw flags representing their countries of origin for either themselves or for fam-ily members. This might also be a good parent-involvement activity; par-ents might be asked to bring in real flags or to draw pictures of the flags of their countries of origin.

## Creating Roles in the Classroom for Family and Community Members

The celebration of cultural and linguistic diversity in the schools is not likely to feel real to parents and community members until a comfortable place is created for the families of all students (Goldenberg, Gallimore, Reese, & Garnier, 2001; Baca & Cervantes, 1998; Lynch & Hansen, 1998;

Gay, 1993; Gonzalez, Moll, Floyd-Tenery, Rivera, Rendon, Gonzales, & Amonti, 1993; Chang, 1992; Chan, 1990). Teachers must establish relationships with family members and should invite families to serve in the classroom. Family members in the classroom might help students learn about other cultures and can serve as role models for all students (Torres-Burgo, Reyes-Wasson, & Brusca-Vega, 1999; Ogbu, 1992; Lynch & Stein, 1987). In one class, a parent who claimed to have made over one hundred piñatas was asked to guide a piñata art project. On the other hand, classroom service does not have to be culturally specific. It is designed to bring parents and community members into the class on a regular basis to provide a multiplicity of cultural leadership. For example, any parent could be asked to share life experiences or job-related experiences (Hildebrand, Phenice, Gray, & Hines, 2000).

Parents and family members can be encouraged to volunteer for many different roles in the classroom. Volunteers can read stories to students or work with small groups. They can help students with science projects with learning math facts or participate in field trips. Parents or community members with special skills can occasionally teach classes. For example, one teacher invited a father who works on a fishing boat to speak to the class about ocean animals. The student assisted his father with English and they worked together to present fish stories and pictures to the class. In another example, a fifth-grade teacher planned a unit entitled "Viva San Diego." The teacher invited parents to participate. Each student was to pick an area of the city he or she wanted to learn more about, such as Balboa Park or San Diego State University. Students and parents were to do research and to visit their chosen areas to learn as much as they could about them. In the end, each student wrote a report and made a model of the area selected. All of these models and reports were displayed in the school showcase.

## Holding High Expectations for All Learners

Treuba, Jacobs, and Kirton's research (1990) showed that high school English teachers had low expectations of Latino students. The teachers interviewed felt that Latino students were incapable of completing higher-level projects. As part of an experiment, the teachers assigned students higher-level projects with topics relevant to their own lives. The students conducted authentic research from their own experiences and from the community. The results of the experiment indicated that they could complete high-quality projects. Trueba and colleagues (1990) concluded that Latino students could produce relatively high-level work when they understood the connection between schoolwork and out-of-school experiences.

A fourth-grade teacher wanted to ask each student a higher-order question at least once a week. The teacher composed at least six higher-order questions for each 50-minute period. He kept a box containing each student's name on a piece of paper, and drew five names from the box each day. He wrote those names on the board and checked off the names as he asked one of the higher-order questions of each student. The names drawn one day were taken from the box so that the remaining names for the next days of the week were those students who had not yet received questions. The questions were not necessarily asked in succession but were spread throughout the period, coupled with different parts of the plan for the day.

Students are more likely to perform well when asked and expected to answer higher-order questions (Henze & Lucas, 1993). For example, one middle school science teacher designated a weekly problem-solver for the classroom. Any class problem during the week was assigned to the problem solver. The problem-solver could work independently or use a self-selected committee. Students responded well to the responsibility and to their new roles in the classroom. One week, the student problem-solver was faced with a situation in which the teacher had scheduled a field trip to the beach as part of a marine biology unit, but the school could not supply enough adult supervision. The field trip was not approved. The principal told the teacher that if adult supervision was obtained by the class members, the class could still make the trip. The student of the week proposed sending notes home to all the parents and to community members asking for support supervising the field trip. The effort was entirely student initiated, and the notes were handwritten by the problem-solver and her committee. The students were successful in obtaining enough adult supervision, and the field trip was approved. The students were pleased with their efforts and their new responsibilities in the classroom.

Teachers can create challenging environments for students by arranging activities in which the students form collaborative or cooperative problem-solving groups. For example, during the unit on marine biology, the science teacher asked a student group to list how they thought an oil spill had affected sea life. The teacher then had the students pair off and write reports on how an oil spill would affect the grey whales.

## Being Responsive to Cultural and Personal Diversity

Teachers have a responsibility to promote cross-cultural understanding throughout the school (Pang, 2001; Harry, 1996; Cloud & Landurand, 1987). Students from ethnolinguistically diverse backgrounds may have experienced ignorance, prejudice, or disrespect or may even have been targets of abuse. A teacher plays an important role in promoting a positive social climate at school. Schoolwide implementation of rules for appropriate ways of interacting in a democratic, pluralistic community are essential. Rules created with student input and facilitated by student mediators can enhance students' understanding of democratic processes. School personnel and teachers must conscientiously provide classrooms and school grounds where learning and respect are primary values.

Successful teachers know each of their students and take an active interest in their students. A sixth-grade teacher of students who were designated as ELL was also the faculty advisor for the Homework Club. The teacher encouraged students from all cultural and linguistic groups to join the Homework Club. During the daily lunchtime meeting, the students were allowed to eat lunch, play music, and receive help with their homework. The teacher created a safe atmosphere for fun and learning. Parents could attend the meetings, as well.

In another example, a high school teacher of students who were in sheltered English classes spent time in class explaining campus activities and assisting the students in filling out applications for campus programs and activities. The teacher became an advocate for the students by ensuring decisions about campus clubs, programs, and after-school activities were fairly made. This seemed to help students feel as much a part of school as everyone else. When the students learned that the teacher was their ally and that she was always facilitating their participation in school activities, students were more motivated to learn from this teacher. From time to time in class, this teacher would raise questions about school issues that may have involved prejudice or stereotyping. She encouraged open discussions in which students were challenged to think about interpersonal conflicts from a variety of perspectives. The teacher wanted the students to understand that actions have consequences. They were encouraged to see the benefits of nonviolent, logical, problem solving when interpersonal conflicts arise.

## *Summary*

Affective issues enhance the learning capabilities of English-language learners. Students like Pon and Araceli are among the many who teachers must learn to consider when arranging the classroom environment. Psychological and emotional support from the teacher are likely to affect the student's sense of belonging at school. Teachers can alienate learners and block their progress without careful planning and consideration of the 10 factors mentioned in this chapter. Teachers can work to facilitate positive emotional responses and high self-esteem in students by adding important dimensions to the classroom and the school environment.

## Activities

1. Outline ways in which a teacher might help Pon (see Chapter 1) feel like a vital and respected member of his class.

2. Interview someone for whom English is not a first language. Probe deeply into the types of school experiences he or she has had. In particular, inquire about any desirable school experiences. Ask the person about the 10 recommendations for teachers in this chapter.

3. Ponder the following statement made by a teacher: "I tried to learn Spanish in college, but it's just too difficult. I don't know how anyone learns to speak a second language." With a classmate or in a small group, discuss the ramifications for students and teachers if this type of statement is acceptable. Discuss the ramifications for students and teachers if this type of statement is unacceptable.

4. Suppose Cambodian American and Vietnamese American students were engaging in physical fights at school. What are some possible strategies for resolving problems between the groups and fostering nonviolent interactions?

## References

Allen, V. G. (1989). Literature as a support to language acquisition. In P. Rigg & V. G. Allen (Eds.), *When they don't all speak English* (pp. 55–64). Urbana, IL: National Council of Teachers of English.

Altwerger, B., & Ivener, B. L. (1994). Self-esteem: Access to literacy in multicultural and multilingual classrooms. In K. Spangengerg-Urbschat & R. Pritchard (Eds.), *Kids come in all languages: Reading instruction for ESL students*. Washington, DC: International Reading Association.

Arreaga-Mayer, C. (1998). Language sensitive peer mediated instruction for language minority studies in the intermediate elementary grades. In R. Gersten & R. Jiménez (Eds.), *Promoting learning for culturally and linguistically diverse students: Classroom applications from contemporary research*. Belmont, CA: Wadsworth.

Baca, L., & Almanza, E. (1996). *Language minority students with disabilities*. Reston, VA: Council for Exceptional Children.

Baca, L., & Cervantes, H. (1998). *The bilingual special education interface* (2nd ed.). Columbus, OH: Merrill.

Bandura, A. (1986). *Social foundations of thought and action*. Englewood Cliffs, NJ: Prentice-Hall.

Banks, J. A. (1991). A curriculum for empowerment, action, and change. In C. E. Sleeter (Ed.), *Empowerment through multicultural education* (pp. 125–141). Albany, NY: State University of New York.

Beaumont, C. J. (1999). Dilemmas of peer assistance in a bilingual full inclusion classroom. *Elementary School Journal, 99*, 233–254.

Bos, C. (1988). Process-oriented writing: Instructional implications for mildly handicapped students. *Exceptional Children, 54*, 521–527.

Brice, A., & Roseberry-McKibbin, C. (1999). Turning frustration into success for English language learners. *Educational Leadership, 24*, 53–55.

Cazden, C. B. (1992). *Language minority education in the United States: Implications of the Ramirez report* (Educational

Practice Report: 3). Santa Cruz, CA: National Center for Research on Cultural Diversity and Second Language Learning.

Chamot, A. U., & O'Malley, J. M. (1994). *The CALLA handbook: Implementing the cognitive academic language learning approach*. Reading, MA: Addison-Wesley.

Chan, S. (1990). Early intervention with culturally diverse families of infants and toddlers with disabilities. *Infants and Young Children, 3*, 78–87.

Chang, J. M. (1992). Current programs serving Chinese-American students in learning disabilities resource issues. In *Proceedings of the Third National Research Symposium on Limited English Proficient Issues: Focus on Middle and High School Issues* (pp. 713–736). Washington, DC: U.S. Department of Education, Office of Bilingual Education and Minority Language Affairs.

Cheng, L. L. (1995). *Intergrating language and learning for inclusion: An Asian-Pacific focus*. San Diego, CA: Singular.

Cloud, N. (1993). Language, culture and disability: Implications for instruction and teacher preparation. *Teacher Education and Special Education, 16*, 60–72.

Cloud, N., & Landurand, P. M. (1987). *Multisystem: Training program for special educators*. New York: Teachers College.

Cummins, J. (1989). A theoretical framework for bilingual special education. *Exceptional Children, 56*, 111–128.

Cummins, J. (1992). Bilingual education and English immersion: The Ramirez report in theoretical perspective. *Bilingual Research Journal, 16*, 91–104.

Echevarria, J., & McDonough, R. (1995). An alternative reading approach: Instructional conversations in a bilingual special education setting. *Learning Disabilities Research and Practice, 10*, 108–119.

Englert, C. S., & Mariage, T. V. (1992). Shared understandings: Structuring the writing experience through dialogue. In D. Carnine & E. Kameenui (Eds.), *Higher order thinking* (pp. 107–136). Austin, TX: Pro-Ed.

Faltis, C. J., & Arias, M. B. (1993). Speakers of languages other than English in the secondary school: Accomplishments and struggles. *Peabody Journal of Education: Trends in Bilingual Education at the Secondary School Level, 69*(1), 6–29.

Faltis, C. J., & Hudelson, S. (1994). Learning English as an additional language in K–12 schools. *TESOL Quarterly, 28*(3), 457–468.

Figueroa, R. A. (1989). Psychological testing of linguistic-minority students: Knowledge gaps and regulations. *Exceptional Children, 56*(2), 111–119.

Fitzgerald, J. (1995). English as a second language learners' cognitive reading processes: A review of research in the United States. *Review of Educational Research, 65*(2), 145–190.

Flores, B., Rueda, R., & Porter, B. (1986). Examining assumptions and instructional practices related to the acquisition of literacy with bilingual special education students. In A. Willig & H. Greenberg (Eds.), *Bilingualism and learning disabilities* (pp. 149–165). New York: American Library.

Franklin, E., & Thompson, J. (1994). Describing students' collected works: Understanding American Indian children. *TESOL Quarterly, 28*(3), 489–506.

García, E. (1993a). *Education of linguistically and culturally diverse students: Effective instructional practices* (Educational Practice Report: 1). Santa Cruz, CA: National Center for Research on Cultural Diversity and Second Language Learning.

García, E. (1993b). Project THEME: Collaboration for school improvement at the middle school for language minority students. In *Proceedings of the Third National Research Symposium on Limited English Proficient Issues: Focus on Middle and High*

*School Issues* (pp 323–350). Washington, DC: U.S. Department of Education, Office of Bilingual Education and Minority Language Affairs.

Gay, G. (1993). Building cultural bridges: A bold proposal for teacher education. *Education and Urban Society, 25,* 285–299.

Gersten, R., & Jiménez, R. (1994). A delicate balance: Enhancing literature instruction for students of English as a second language. *The Reading Teacher, 47,* 438–449.

Goldenberg, C. (1992–93). Instructional conversations: Promoting comprehension throuh discussion. *The Reading Teacher, 46,* 316–326.

Goldenberg, C., Gallimore, R., Reese, L., & Garnier, H. (2001). Cause or effect? A longitudinal study of immigrant Latino parents' aspirations and expectation, and their children's school performance. *American Educational Research Journal, 38,* 547–582.

Gollnick, D. M., & Chinn, P. C. (1990). *Multicultural education in a pluralistic society.* Columbus, OH: Merrill.

Gonzalez, N., Moll, L. C., Floyd-Tenery, M., Rivera, A., Rendon, P., Gonzales, R., & Amonti, C. (1993). *Teacher research on funds of knowledge: Learning from households* (Educational Practice Report: 6). Santa Cruz, CA: National Center for Research on Cultural Diversity and Second Language Learning.

Good, T. L., & Brophy, J. E. (1991). *Looking in classrooms* (5th ed.). New York: HarperCollins.

Grant, C. A., & Gomez, M. L. (2001). *Campus and classroom: Making schooling multicultural* (2nd ed.). Columbus, OH: Merrill.

Graves, A. (1995). Teaching students who are culturally and linguistically diverse. *Teacher Educator's Journal, 15*(3), 32–40.

Graves, A., Valles, E., & Rueda, R. (2000a). Variations in interactive writing instruction: A study of four bilingual special education settings. *Learning*

*Disabilities Research and Practice, 15,* 1–10.

Graves, A., Valles, E., & Rueda, R. (Fall, 2000b). Variations in interactive writing instruction: A study of four bilingual special education settings. Available online: <www.ciera.org/ciera/publications/online-at-ciera/>.

Graves, A., Valles, E., Prodor, C., & Rueda, R. (in press). A study of the effects of optimal learning environment compared to eclectic writing instruction in bilingual special education settings. *Reading and Writing Quarterly.*

Greenwood, C. R., Arreaga-Mayer, C., Utley, C. A., Gavin, K. M., & Terry, B. J. (2001). Class-wide peer tutoring management system: Applications with elementary-level English language learners. *Remedial and Special Education, 22,* 34–47.

Harry, B. (1992). *Culturally diverse families and the special education system.* New York: Teachers College Press.

Harry, B. (1996). These families, those families: The impact of research identities on the research act. *Exceptional Children, 62,* 292–300.

Henderson, R. W., & Landesman, E. M. (1992). *Mathematics and middle school students of Mexican descent: The effects of thematically integrated instruction* (Research Report: 5). Santa Cruz, CA: National Center for Research on Cultural Diversity and Second Language Learning.

Henze, R. C., & Lucas, T. (1993). Shaping instruction to promote the success of language minority students: An analysis of four high school classes. *Peabody Journal of Education: Trends in Bilingual Education at the Secondary Level, 69*(1), 54–81.

Hildebrand, V., Phenice, L. A., Gray, M. M., & Hines, R. P. (2000). *Knowing and serving diverse families* (2nd ed.). Columbus, OH: Merrill.

Hornberger, N., & Michaeu, C. (1993). Getting far enough to like it: Biliteracy in the middle school. *Peabody Journal of Education: Trends in Bilingual Education at the Secondary School Level, 69*, 54–81.

King, A. (1990). Enhancing peer interaction and learning in the classroom through reciprocal questioning. *American Educational Research Journal, 27*, 664–687.

Krashen, S. D. (1985). *The input hypothesis: Issues and implications.* New York: Longman.

Lessow-Hurley, J. (1996). *The foundations of dual language instruction.* White Plains, NY: Longman.

Lim, H.-J. L., & Watson, D. (1993). Whole language content classes for second-language learners. *The Reading Teacher, 46*, 384–395.

Lucas, T., Henze, R., & Donato, R. (1990). Promoting the success of Latino language minority students: An exploratory study of six high schools. *Harvard Educational Review, 60*, 315–340.

Lucas, T., & Katz, A. (1994). Reframing the debate: The roles of native languages in English-only programs for language minority students. *TESOL Quarterly, 28*, 537–562.

Lynch, E. W., & Hanson, M. J. (1998). *Developing cross-cultural competence: A guide for working with young children and their families* (2nd ed.). Baltimore, MD: Paul H. Brookes.

Lynch, E. W., & Stein, R. C. (1987). Parent participation by ethnicity: A comparison of Hispanic, Black, and anglo families. *Exceptional Children, 54*, 105–111.

Moll, L. C. (1988). Some key issues in teaching Latino students. *Language Arts, 65*, 465–472.

Obi, S. O., Obiakor, F. E., & Algozzine, B. (1999). *Empowering culturally diverse exceptional learners in the 21st century: Imperatives for U.S. educators* (Report No. EC307730). Washington, DC: National Institute of Education. (ERIC Document Reproduction Service No. ED439551)

Ogbu, J. U. (1992). Understanding cultural diversity and learning. *Educational Researcher, 21*(8), 5–14.

Ortiz, A., & Graves, A. W. (2001). English language learners with literacy related learning disabilities. *International Dyslexia Association Commemorative Booklet Series, 52*, 34–39.

Palincsar, A. S. (1986). The role of dialogue in providing scaffolded instruction. In J. Levin & M. Pressley (Eds.), *Educational Psychologist, 21* (Special issue on learning strategies), 73–98.

Pang, V. O. (2001). *Multicultural education: A caring-centered, reflective approach.* Boston: McGraw-Hill.

Pease-Alvarez, L., & Winsler, A. (1994). Cuando el maestro no habla Espanol: Children's bilingual language practices in the classroom. *TESOL Quarterly, 28*(3), 507–536.

Perez, B. (1993). Biliteracy practices and issues in secondary schools. *Peabody Journal of Education: Trends in Bilingual Education at the Secondary School Level, 69*(1), 117–135.

Peyton, J. K., Jones, C., Vincent, A., & Greenblatt, L. (1994). Implementing writing workshop with ESOL students: Visions and realities. *TESOL Quarterly, 28*(3), 469–488.

Pierce, L. V. (August, 1988). *Facilitating transition to the mainstream: Sheltered English vocabulary development.* Washington, DC: National Clearinghouse for Bilingual Education.

Ramirez, O. (1989). Mexican American children and adolescents. In J. Taylor Gibbs & L. Nahme Huang (Eds.), *Children of color: Psychological interventions with minority youth* (pp. 224–250). San Francisco: Jossey-Bass.

Reyes, M. de la Luz (1992). Challenging venerable assumptions: Literacy instruction for linguistically different students. *Harvard Educational Review, 62*(4), 427–446.

Rosebery, A. S., Warren, B., & Conant, F. R. (1992). *Appropriating scientific discourse: Findings from language minority classrooms* (Research Report: 3). Santa Cruz, CA: National Center for Research on Cultural Diversity and Second Language Learning.

Ruiz, N. T. (1995a). The social construction of ability and disabilitiy I: Profile types of Latino children identified as language learning disabled. *Journal of Learning Disabilities, 28*, 476–490.

Ruiz, N. T. (1995b). The social construction of ability and disability II: Optimal and at-risk lessons in a bilingual special education classroom. *Journal of Learning Disabilities, 28,* 491–502.

Saville-Troike, M. (1984). What really matters in second language learning for academic achievement? *TESOL Quarterly, 18,* 117–131.

Scarcella, R., & Chin, K. (1993). *Literacy practices in two Korean-American communities* (Research Report: 8). Santa Cruz, CA: National Center for Research on Cultural Diversity and Second Language Learning.

Schunk, D. H., & Hanson, A. R. (1985). Peer models: Influence on children's self- efficacy and achievement. *Journal of Educational Psychology, 77,* 313–322.

Short, D. (1993). *Integrating language and culture in middle school American history classes* (Educational Practice Report: 8). Santa Cruz, CA: National Center for Research on Cultural Diversity and Second Language Learning.

Short, D. (1994). Expanding middle school horizons: Integrating language, culture, and social studies. *TESOL Quarterly, 28*(3), 581–608.

Slavin, R. E. (1987). Ability grouping and student achievement in elementary schools: A best-evidence synthesis. *Review of Educational Research, 60,* 471–500.

Slavin, R. E. (1990). *Cooperative learning.* Englewood Cliffs, NJ: Prentice-Hall.

Slavin, R. E., & Madden, N. A. (1999). *Success for all/roots and wings. Summary of research on achievement outcomes* (Report No. CRESPAR-TR-41). Washington, DC: Office of Educational Research and Improvement. (ERIC Document Reproduction Service No. ED438363)

Torres, C. C. (2000). *Emerging Latino communities: A new challenge for the rural south* (Report No. RC 022 605). Chicago, IL: ERIC Clearinghouse on Rural Education and Small Schools. (ERIC Document Reproduction Service No. ED444806)

Torres, M. N. (2001). Teacher-researchers entering into the world of limited-English-proficiency (LEP) students: Three case studies. *Urban Education, 36,* 256–289.

Torres-Burgo, N., Reyes-Wasson, P., & Brusca-Vega, R. (1999). Perceptions and needs of Hispanic and non-Hispanic parents of children receiving learning disabilities services. *Bilingual Research Journal, 23,* 319–333.

Treuba, H., Jacobs, L., & Kirton, E. (1990). *Cultural conflict and adaptation.* New York: Falmer.

Vygotsky, L. S. (1978). *Mind in society: The development of higher psychological processes.* Cambridge, MA: Harvard University Press.

Waldschmidt, E. D., Kim, Y. M., Kim, J., Martinez, C., & Hale, A. (1999). *Teacher stories: Bilingual playwriting and puppetry with English language learners and students with special needs* (Report No. FL026293). Montreal, Quebec, Canada: ERIC Clearinghouse on Languages and Linguistics. (ERIC Document Reproduction Service No. ED442288)

Walker de Felix, J., Waxman, H., Paige, S., & Huang, S. Y. (1993). A comparison of classroom instruction in bilingual and monolingual secondary school classrooms. *Peabody Journal of Education: Trends in Bilingual Education at the Secondary School Level, 69*(1), 102–116.

Woolfolk, A. (1996). *Educational psychology* (6th ed.). Boston: Allyn and Bacon.

# *Learning*
# *Strategies*

- *José* was unable to use his native language to supply cues to English vocabulary. What type of learning strategy would help him?
- *Marisol* constantly confused the steps for solving math word problems. What kind of instruction could the teacher choose?
- *Thongsy* seemed lost when reading and writing tasks were assigned in history. What learning strategies might improve his performance?

Sheltered instruction is a process by which subject matter instruction is made more meaningful and accessible to English-language learners (ELLs). As Chapter 3 indicates, there are many components to an effective sheltered content lesson and not all will be present in every lesson. However, teachers should strive to incorporate the features regularly in their sheltered lessons. For example, use of higher-order thinking skills is an important feature of sheltered instruction that should be a regular part of lessons.

Teachers must be sensitive to the fact that ELLs have extraordinary cognitive burdens when learning new information in English. Students with learning and behavioral challenges also experience cognitive overload when learning new information. Hence, English-language learners with learning and behavioral difficulties can have exceedingly taxing cognitive burdens when learning in English. Students can be so overwhelmed by deriving meaning from a second language that they do not spontaneously generate the strategies needed for efficient and effective learning (Ortiz & Graves, 2001; Yang, 1999). Teachers can facilitate learning by directly teaching strategies. Explicit instruction of learning strategies increases the comfort and learning potential of students needing support (Vaughn, Gersten, & Chard, 2000; Carnine, Silbert, & Kameenui, 1997; Chamot & O'Malley, 1994; Deschler & Schumaker, 1994; Gaffney & Anderson, 1991; Archer, 1990).

Those students needing learning-strategies instruction often have content area, academic, and English-language development issues. They present learning challenges and require language sensitive instruction (Gersten & Baker, 2000; Baca & Cervantes, 1998; García, 1993). Language-sensitive instruction focuses simultaneously on developing (1) content area knowledge, (2) academic proficiency, and (3) English-language proficiency (Graves, 1998; Baca & Almanza, 1996; Chamot & O'Malley, 1994).

The purpose of this chapter is to (1) define *learning strategy* and delineate types of learning strategies, (2) provide guidelines for selecting learning strategies, (3) describe lesson formats for teaching learning strategies, (4) identify presentation methods to use in teaching learning strategies, and (5) present examples of specific strategies for reading, writing, and content areas. Each section contains specific lesson and classroom descriptions.

## *Types of Learning Strategies*

A *learning strategy* is a series of steps that can be repeated over and over again to solve a problem or to complete a task. Some students develop learning strategies on their own. Obviously, the teacher would not teach these students strategies explicitly. Instead, the teacher should simply encourage them to use effective strategies.

A teacher can formulate and explicitly teach strategies when students do not develop them on their own. To use learning strategies in thinking, reading, and writing in content area work, teachers can provide a minilesson (about 15 minutes daily) on the strategy (Ellis & Graves, 1990). Using a minilesson allows students to learn the strategy in a controlled practice situation during a designated period of time. Teachers can provide opportunities to memorize and use the strategy during a practice session before requiring strategy use in a content area application. Learning strategies can be developed not only for academics but for language acquisition and many other areas, such as social skills and vocational skills.

Learning strategies are not a curriculum. Instead, strategies are used as a part of the curriculum to enhance access to content, academic, or life-skills proficiency. Strategies enhancing access to content are used in literature, science, social studies, and math classes and facilitate gaining knowledge. For example, the steps for writing about an experiment is a science strategy taught at the beginning of the schoolyear. It should increase the knowledge a student gains from science lessons (see Figure 5.1). The science strategy can be reused for future science work and can be used as a general problem-solving method by studying information systematically.

Strategies can enhance language acquisition and second-language listening and thinking skills. Such learning strategies provide a series of steps to integrate language knowledge and content knowledge (Herrell, 2000; Gersten, Taylor, & Graves, 1999; Jiménez, García, & Pearson, 1996; Chamot & O'Malley, 1994). For example, the use-of-cognates strategy has

---

**FIGURE 5.1    *Science Strategy: Steps for an Experiment***

Step 1:  Write or state the purpose of the experiment and the expected outcome.

Step 2:  Gather materials.

Step 3:  Write or review procedures.

Step 4:  Carry out the experiment (observe and take notes).

Step 5:  Write exact results.

Step 6:  Discuss expectations versus actual results and what the results mean.

---

---

**FIGURE 5.2** *Use of Cognates Strategy*

---

Step 1: Read the unfamiliar word in English.

Step 2: Note the spelling of the word.

Step 3: Think of a word that looks or sounds like the English word, a *cognate,* in your primary language.

Step 4: Think of what that *cognate* means in your primary language.

Step 5: Guess at the meaning of the unfamiliar word in English.

---

*Source:* Adapted from R. T. Jiménez, G. E. García, & P. D. Pearson, Three children, two languages, and strategic reading: Case studies in bilingual/monolingual reading, *American Educational Research Journal, 32* (1995), 67–97.

five steps (see Figure 5.2). Other language-acquisition strategies can be used to think back and forth between languages and to help focus thinking while listening (Jiménez et al., 1996; Chamot & O'Malley, 1994).

Strategies enhancing academic proficiency can improve the reading, writing, language, or math work of students (Pritchard, 1990). For example, finding main ideas is a reading strategy important to academic proficiency and useful in many different learning situations (see Figure 5.3). This learning strategy can benefit a student in all pursuits involving reading.

Life-skills strategies enhance proficiency in social, vocational, and transition skills. Enhanced proficiency in these areas improves the interpersonal skills and job-related abilities of students and prepares them for the future. To help students learn to get along with peers and teachers, social skills strategies and interpersonal strategies can be taught as early as preschool. For example, in social situations, students may need to learn how to solve a problem (see Figure 5.4, page 100). Students can be taught the series of steps necessary to solve a social problem. As they mature, the life-skills strategies could relate more to community or work-related situations. Teaching social skills is very important as students progress through school and pursue adult activities.

---

**FIGURE 5.3** *Finding Main Ideas*

---

Step 1: Read the paragraph.

Step 2: Decide what the whole paragraph is about.

Step 3: Test to make sure you have the best answer (the answer that tells what the whole paragraph is about).

Step 4: Reread and start over if you are not sure.

Step 5: If you are sure, write the main idea down.

---

---

**FIGURE 5.4** *Social Skills Strategy: Solving a Problem*

Step 1: Say the problem.

Step 2: Keep a calm body (count to 10).

Step 3: Think of three possible solutions.

Step 4: Decide which is the best solution and do it.

Step 5: Use positive self-talk afterward, telling yourself you did the best you could.

---

# Guidelines for Selecting a Learning Strategy

Students can learn strategies that provide maximum benefits and that can be used in a multiplicity of settings. The following guidelines can assist teachers in determining the strategies most beneficial to students. First, determine the exact knowledge or proficiency level of the student. Second, determine the strategies the student would use the most. Consider teaching the simplest and most useful strategies first, and introduce them in an order that reflects the content curriculum and proficiency goals for the year. Finally, use simply wording and the fewest number of steps when teaching each strategy.

## Determine Levels of Knowledge

Teachers are concerned about students' levels of content knowledge and academic and language proficiency (Espin, Scierka, Skare, & Halverson, 1999). A teacher must determine the level of knowledge students possess in literature, math, science, or social studies and then mold his or her instruction to fit what the students do or do not know. The teacher can use information assessment to determine the current reading, studying, and computational skills of students and teach accordingly.

Based on the informal assessment phase, the teacher can construct new materials or use existing materials to test students. The tests may be traditional or nontraditional. For example, the nontraditional test might ask students to choose a book and read a few pages out loud. From the test, the teacher can gather baseline information on reading skills, reading level, and reading comprehension. Examples of tests that provide value performance information on basic skills include the Diagnostic Indicators of Basic Early Literacy Skills (Kaminski & Good, 1996) and Curriculum-Based Measurement (Espin et al., 1999; Deno, 1985).

The tests allow the teacher to determine what students know and what to teach. Strategies may be part of the curriculum. For example, if at the beginning of the year the teacher finds that history students do not know the steps needed for making an outline, the teacher might teach everyone a strategy for outlining. If the teacher determines that students have difficulty writing an expository paragraph, the teacher might teach the steps for writing a paragraph and provide a useful strategy for improved academic proficiency. For example, the teacher might teach students to use an introductory sentence describing the intended content, three detail sentences elaborating on the content, and a conclusion sentence summarizing the content.

## Determine Which Strategies Will Be Most Useful

A teacher teaching the paragraph-writing strategy fulfills the second guideline for choosing a strategy, because the learning strategy is useful in other subjects and other life tasks. Grade and performance level and life goals are important considerations when determining the strategies most useful to students. For example, in middle-school math, for students struggling with English and who have very weak math skills, a teacher would be more likely to teach a check-writing strategy than a scientific notation strategy.

Teachers should teach strategies that students can use over and over again. For example, strategies for finding the main idea in reading or regrouping in math obviously have significant applications. On the other hand, teachers may need to teach scientific notation as part of math instruction, but they would be wise *not* to create a formal strategy for this because it may not have broad enough application. If teachers create strategies for everything students are learning, students will be less likely to remember the key strategies and their long-term applications.

## Decide Order of Instruction

Once the most beneficial strategies are determined, the teacher must decide the teaching order. He or she should analyze the strategies and decide if they are embedded in one another or if one strategy is a prerequisite of another. For example, when students need to learn notetaking from chapters in a book, finding main ideas is a prerequisite. The teacher can focus on the steps for finding main ideas until the skill is mastered by the students. The notetaking strategy will be easier to teach once students can successfully find the main ideas in a section or chapter and then writes notes about them.

## Use Simple Wording and the Fewest Number of Steps

For students to understand a strategy, each step must be as simple as possible. Students are more likely to remember a strategy if it is stated in clear, concise words. Teachers should highlight or underline keywords within

---

**FIGURE 5.5**    *The COPS Strategy*

---

- Capitalization
- Overall appearance of paper
- Punctuation
- Spelling

---

steps and encourage the students to memorize the keywords. Unnecessary words and steps should be eliminated to simplify the strategy. The teacher must think: Is the strategy as simple as possible? Are all the words clear and necessary?

Many times, students will start to memorize strategy steps and re-word what teachers have specified. The teacher can facilitate learning by changing the strategy to conform to the student-created version if it improves the efficiency of the strategy or the economy of words.

Some teachers use acronyms when teaching strategies by taking the first letter of each of the steps to form a new word. This mnemonic device often facilitates the memorization of a strategy. For example, the capitalization, overall appearance, punctuation, spelling (COPS) editing strategy is a great acronym (see Figure 5.5). The teacher can reinforce the strategy with the visual image of a "cop" looking over the paper to make sure everything is correct.

An acronym should not be used as a mnemonic device if it must be forced in place. Teachers should not try to create an acronym by using sophisticated wording or stretching the strategy to accommodate it. Students focus on memorizing the keywords of a simple strategy quickly and often do not need an acronym to remember the strategy. If a strategy becomes more complex in order to create an acronym that works, the teacher can defeat the purpose of the learning strategy (that is, to enhance the academic and language proficiency of the learner).

## *Lesson Phases When Teaching Learning Strategies*

Research indicates explicit instruction in learning strategies facilitates and improves proficiency for students with learning and behavioral challenges and for language (Chamot & O'Malley, 1994; Graham & Harris, 1993; Graves & Montague, 1991; Lenze, Schumaker, & Deshler, 1991). Explicit instruction requires sound lesson structure, lesson preparation, and extensive teacher-student interaction to enhance learning.

Optimal learning strategy instruction requires a teacher to (1) determine the necessary preskills students need to learn the strategy and to teach them, (2) arrange lessons with an opening, a body, and a closing, and (3) plan a series of lessons over time to allow the mastery and generalized use of the strategy.

## Determine Preskills and Teach Them

The teacher can analyze the strategy and list all of the preskills a student must know before the strategy will be easy for the student to learn. A strategy involves a multiplicity of actions. Students will learn the strategy more easily if the difficult steps are taught before the complete strategy is introduced. If students are unable to perform the difficult steps, the entire strategy will be more difficult to accomplish.

Embedded in the steps of a strategy are preskills, concepts, and rules. For example, if a teacher decides to teach an editing strategy to students, such as the COPS strategy (see Figure 5.5), necessary preskills are the ability to write a paragraph, the ability to use correct sentence structure, and handwriting proficiency. Some concepts for the successful use of this strategy are capitalization, neatness, punctuation, and spelling. Some rules for the successful use of this strategy are (1) capitalize the first word in each sentence, (2) capitalize proper nouns, (3) write on the line, (4) use the one-finger rule between words, (5) use the two-finger rule between sentences, (6) indent paragraphs, (7) use an end mark, and (8) try to spell words correctly but check to determine correctness. Students may need significant instruction in these underlying concepts and rules before they can successfully learn the editing strategy.

Rules are taught by focusing on *critical attributes,* which are the defining elements of each rule. Defining elements are used to create examples to illustrate a rule. Defining elements are also used to create nonexamples to sharpen understanding of the application of the rule. The nonexamples serve as distractors in an example set and hone the discrimination skills necessary for correct rule applications. For example, in teaching students to indent paragraphs, the teacher will show what a proper indentation is and what it is not in order to clarify exactly how to follow the rule. Lessons that focus on the rules are important precursors to strategy instruction. Once the identified concepts and rules are mastered, students are better prepared to learn a strategy. Learning a strategy requires automatic knowledge of all preskills. This allows the student to focus on the application of the strategy and helps the student avoid a struggle with the semantic or procedural knowledge that is inevitably embedded in the strategy.

## Include an Opening, a Body, and a Closing

*Opening.*   At the beginning of each strategy instruction minilesson, the teacher should review relevant preskills. For example, in the COPS strategy lesson, the teacher might review rules for capitalization, neatness, and punctuation before introducing the strategy. The teacher should also describe the strategy and explain how the strategy can be used. For example, to introduce a strategy on good listening, the teacher tells the students about the importance of listening and talks to them about when not listening could affect them adversely (for example, if the teacher tells them to raise their hands if they like ice cream, because Juan's mother is bringing ice cream for everyone who raises a hand). The teacher might also ask students to think of times when good listening is important.

After the students understand why the strategy is important, the teacher should state the goal of the lesson. The teacher might tell them that for the next few weeks, they are going to work very hard on becoming good listeners and that today they are to learn some steps to follow to become good listeners. Teachers must use language the students understand to emphasize what is being taught and why the students will benefit from learning the strategy.

*Body.*    The body of the strategy instruction minilesson contains three basic steps: (1) the teacher demonstrates or models, (2) the teacher and students practice together, and (3) students practice on their own.

The demonstration and modeling by the teacher is the most critical part of the lesson. A strategy should be taught using a two-stage model. The first stage is verbal rehearsal. The steps of the strategy are explicitly stated, and the students practice the words of the steps over and over again. If the students are readers, the students should be given a list of the steps and the steps should be written on a wall chart or shown on the overhead projector.

The teachers can underline or highlight the key words for each step and illustrate any action involved in the step. For example, if students are learning a good-listening strategy, the teacher might draw a set of eyes beside the step "Look at the person" (see Figure 5.6). In a more elaborate

Step 1:   Look at the person

Step 2:   Keep your hands and body still

Step 3:   Keep a pleasant face

---

FIGURE 5.6   *Good Listener Strategy (including use of visuals)*

strategy, such as COPS, for the step "Capitalization," the teacher might write capital letters beside the step and write the two rules for capitalization in smaller print underneath or beside it (see Figure 5.7).

The second stage of modeling is the physical model. During this stage, the teacher actually demonstrates the strategy step by step for the students. As part of the demonstration, the teacher might think-aloud through each step. In teaching the COPS strategy, the teacher might say,"Step 1: Check for capitalization. Hmmm, I'd better think about each rule for capitalization. The first one is: Each sentence must begin with a capital letter. Hmmm, does each sentence begin with a capital letter? Yes, but here's one that doesn't; I'd better fix it." The teacher can continue to demonstrate each step by correcting a writing sample shown on an overhead.

After the teacher has demonstrated the steps of the strategy sufficiently, students can be asked to practice the process with the teacher. The teacher uses new examples of sentences that need to be corrected and continues to apply the steps of the strategy, working together with the students. For the COPS strategy, the teacher and the students go through each step talking about it and answering together. Students are encouraged to ask questions and to continue practicing the steps of the strategy until no errors occur. If errors do occur, the teacher can repeat the demonstration, modeling in a similar manner to the original. Hearing the same words from the teacher and seeing the same behaviors reinforces the steps for the students and helps clear up any misunderstandings.

In the final part of the body of the lesson, teachers give feedback while the students practice the strategy on their own. The students may work in small groups, in pairs, or on their own when practicing the steps and completing the strategy. The first practice examples should be short and simple. The following samples should progress to grade-appropriate and perhaps to more difficult examples. After enough varied practice, students should be able to apply the strategy to different situations. The examples show how the strategy is applied to other subjects and to real-life situations such as letter writing.

**FIGURE 5.7**   *Capitalization in the COPS Strategy\**

Step 1:  Check for Capitalization
          (Capitalization Rules)

   • Each sentence must begin with a capital letter.
   • Each proper noun must begin with a capital letter.

\*See Figure 5.5 for the complete COPS strategy.

*Closing.*    At the end of each lesson, the teacher may focus the students on homework or on the lessons to follow. During the closing, the teacher typically assigns independent practice for a later time during class or as homework. The teacher can also preview the next lesson or review the strategy by repeating the steps or by asking the students to reflect on uses for the strategy.

## Plan a Series of Lessons

A lesson plan for most days should include work on the strategy preskills, concepts, or rules. Over time, given enough instruction and practice, students can master the strategy. A 10- to 15-minute minilesson on the strategy works best as part of the instructional period (see Figure 5.8). For example, in elementary school, a teacher may designate an hour and a half for language arts. During that time, the students may be engage in various 15- to 20-minute activities. Focusing on an important learning strategy could be just one of the segments of the language arts period.

Strategy instruction is not intended to be a one-time lesson; instead, the instruction becomes a strand stretching across several weeks. A series of

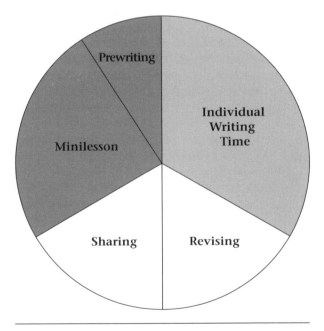

FIGURE 5.8    *Writing Instruction Time Management*

lessons provide the students ample time to practice, apply, and master the strategy.

# Presentation Methods Used to Teach Learning Strategies

The type of interaction a teacher chooses to maximize student learning is based on many of the aspects of sheltered instruction. For strategy instruction, teachers can focus on (1) active student involvement with maximum student participation, (2) the appropriate pace that helps students to move neither too rapidly nor too slowly through the material, (3) careful monitoring so error correction occurs immediately, or (4) independent practice, controlled practice, and grade-appropriate practice.

## Active Student Involvement with Maximum Student Participation

Active student involvement is a recurrent theme throughout this book, as it is in the literature on instruction for English-language learners. In the context of learning-strategy instruction, teachers may ask students to tell them about why a strategy will be useful. Teachers can ask students to talk more about when a strategy could be used and what has happened when they have used the strategy. They can ask what made the strategy work and what could be done to make it work better the next time.

The teacher can also ask students to engage in verbal rehearsal of the steps of the strategy. During practice the teacher can ask, "Did we use the strategy properly? How do you know?" When the teacher poses questions like this often throughout demonstration and practice sessions, accuracy can be monitored to ensure maximum learner involvement. The teacher can require the students to think about the strategy and can determine whether each student is absolutely sure of the correct application of a strategy or lacks confidence or knowledge. The more active involvement the teacher can elicit from the students, the more likely the students are to learn (Jiménez & Gersten, 1999; Gersten, Brengelman, & Jiménez, 1994).

## Appropriate Pacing

Effective teacher interaction is characterized by precise, slow speech, gestures, and controlled vocabulary. Controlled vocabulary involves the use of cognates and the limited use of idiomatic expressions. Consistent wording without the use of synonyms is critical for efficient language development. Teachers are most successful when they avoid references to reading materials and cultural information that are not familiar to the learners (Gersten & Jiménez, 1994).

Pacing is also important. Teachers need to know when to move through lessons quickly and when to move through them slowly. A teacher should quicken the pace when the confidence and accuracy level of the students increases. The opposite is true when students make errors or struggle with the strategy application. When students are learning information for the first time, a teacher must pace the lesson carefully so the students capture the content. It is better for a teacher to proceed slowly during the modeling and prompting than to go back and correct errors or to repeat lessons. Of course, at times the latter is necessary and can be the appropriate choice.

## Monitor and Correct Errors

The teacher can monitor each phase of a lesson to decide how to pace the lesson, which lesson parts to repeat, and which examples will maximize learning. This monitoring provides teachers with information on when to mediate learning and when to provide student feedback. During strategy instruction, error correction is determined by the type of response the student gives. If the error is careless, the teacher may ask the student to repeat the answer. If the error is due to a lack of knowledge, the teacher should return to the model, repeat the steps, and involve the student in additional practice. The teacher should work with the student to practice the strategy.

One point of contention between researchers and practitioners is when to provide corrective feedback. Whole language and writing-as-a-process approaches often prohibit error correction, particularly at the beginning of reading and writing development. It is commonly believed that as students progress, they will begin to notice correct forms and begin to use them spontaneously. Reyes (1992) claims that this practice is not always best for learners. Her research indicated that students who were not corrected did not progress and were often left further and further behind. These conclusions lend support to the "perfect final copy" requirement of the Writer's Workshop approach. Many teachers insist that students continually rewrite their work until everything is perfect, hence insisting on self-correction.

To minimize anxiety, teachers can approach error correction cautiously when students are learning content material (Flores, Rueda, & Porter, 1986). Students who have experienced school failure or who are learning to speak English as a second language often need to be praised when they have responded correctly. Teachers can approach error correction indirectly (Graves, 1998). For example, in a sixth-grade sheltered class, a student described a close-up picture by saying, "It looks more big." The teacher responded indirectly and said, "Yes, it looks bigger." The student understood the correction and repeated, "Yes, it looks bigger." The student seemed to appreciate the information.

Reyes (1992) and Short (1994) report positive results from direct teaching of vocabulary, academic strategies, and English language, followed by teacher monitoring and nonthreatening error correction. The direct feedback approach requires the teacher to model the correct response and asks the student to repeat or copy it. The teacher then asks a related question that requires the student to use the correct information. If an ELL writes *bruder* in his journal instead of *brother,* the teacher can write the correct word above the misspelling and ask the student to spell the word correctly the next time. At the same time, the teacher should compliment the student's work, respond in writing to its content, and point out correctly spelled words.

## Controlled, Grade-Appropriate Practice and Independent Practice

Practice is necessary when students are learning strategies. Once they have memorized the steps of a strategy, they must practice on clear examples. The first practice phase is *controlled practice.* For example, a student has learned to sound out a word by looking at the word, saying all the letter sounds without stopping between sounds, and saying the word the "fast way." The controlled practice examples are words that are absolutely decodable, such as *on, cat,* or *mast.* The examples provide practice of the sounds the student knows.

After students master controlled practice, *grade-appropriate practice* should follow (Ellis & Graves, 1990). This will include grade-level reading words that might be found in content area reading assignments. Grade-appropriate practice shows students the range of a strategy's application and how to generalize and transfer the knowledge they have gained. In this process, students learn that the strategy works better with some words than with others. They learn the limitations and the value of the strategy as it applies to their own life experiences.

*Independent practice* is appropriate only after students have mastered a strategy. A student can practice a strategy without supervision when it can be performed without frustration and error. If students practice applying the strategy to grade-appropriate words for homework too soon, errors may go uncorrected and cause confusion. The strategy is likely to be more valuable to students when the teacher avoids assigning homework or independent practice before students are quite familiar and comfortable with a strategy. An alternate homework assignment when students are learning a strategy is practicing one of the early example sets that have already been mastered. The assignment would then be relevant but would not require the student to perform the strategy prematurely in a frustrating situation.

## *Examples of Specific Strategies in Teaching Reading and Writing in Content Areas*

In a recent study in the San Diego schools, nine multiple-language, first-grade classroom teachers were observed and rated. Their students were assessed on oral reading fluency as part of a small battery of assessments (Graves, Plasencia-Peinado, & Deno, 2002; Haager, Gersten, Baker, & Graves, 2002). The classrooms were very diverse; for example, in one room, there were five Spanish speakers, seven Somali speakers, three Cambodian speakers, three Vietnamese speakers, and two native-English speakers. Teachers in these classrooms were compelled to teach in English because it provided common ground for all of the students. Native-language instruction was a logistical impossibility.

Results of this study indicated extremely positive ratings for two teachers, and predictably, those teachers' students earned the highest outcome scores on oral reading fluency. Both teachers demonstrated a skill for maximizing time ontask, amount of work produced, time spent reading, appropriate length for teaching segments, specialized small-group instruction, structured daily routines, consistent homework assignments, daily writing tasks, assessment of reading and writing progress, and English-as-a-second language development. Written work was corrected on a daily basis, and students were often required to self-correct errors. Both teachers had amassed multiple sets of decodable texts and used them regularly to enhance student reading. Students had their own boxes of books at their desks, including books of different genres and reading levels, but at least 50 percent of the books in each student's box were at his or her own level of decoding.

Mara, the teacher who received the highest score (3.75), used a structured reading instruction program that included a comprehensive curriculum with special emphasis on phonological awareness and phonics. She appeared to enjoy the challenge of following the linear scope and sequence that the reading series provided along with structured lesson plans. She tended to be quite systematic in her approach to teaching language arts, including consistent assessment and remediation for low performers.

Dana, who also received a very high score (3.5), tended to teach reading by pulling materials from many sources of many eclectic origins. She used leveled readers and assigned students to homogeneous small groups that met on a regular basis, and she was diligent about assessment of reading and writing progress. The scope and sequence she used was part of an oral tradition that she can talk about when interviewed but for which she does not have an exact written source. Because she does not use a specific reading series, her activities and segments of instruction are often unique and draw from a range of sources. She was observed delivering instruction in critical domains for reading instruction, such as phonological awareness, phonics, concepts about print, spelling, writing, comprehension, and critical thinking. She is particularly skilled at comprehension questions related to reading material and critical thinking.

A videotaped interview of the two teachers is currently being created, with footage of their instruction. Both teachers use sheltered techniques and consider affective issues, as outlined in Chapters 3 and 4 of this book. The video, as well as the paper that will follow, both provide numerous examples.

## Teaching Reading Strategies in Content Area Classes

This section contains a series of classroom observations of teachers teaching English as a second language (Graves, 1998). To illustrate good reading strategy instruction, three classroom observations are presented. First, in the context of teaching a unit on coastal Native American tribes, a sixth-grade ELL teacher taught the concept of finding main ideas. Similarly, a seventh-grade science teacher taught the compare-and-contrast technique as part of a unit on ecosystems. Finally, an eighth-grade history teacher taught about using a timeline for notetaking while beginning a unit on the colonial period.

The sixth-grade teacher started the Native American tribes unit by showing pictures of coastal tribes and recovered artifacts. The teacher also read some information about various tribes. As part of the effort to teach reading explicitly while covering content, the teacher established a lesson plan based on informal student assessment. The teacher used about 15 minutes a day to develop reading skills specifically during the history unit.

Typically, at the beginning of the period, the teacher put a simple paragraph about a Native American tribe with a definite main idea on the overhead projector and gave each student a copy of the paragraph (see Figure 5.9). The overhead projector and handouts provided visual reinforcement for the students. On the first day, the teacher taught main ideas explicitly. He said, "A main idea tells what the whole paragraph is about. It does not tell what *part* of the paragraph is about, but it tells what the *whole* paragraph is about. Watch me as I read this paragraph and decide what the

FIGURE 5.9   *Finding the Main Idea*

---

The Chumash once flourished on the southern coast of California. They traveled back and forth between the mainland and the Channel Islands, which are just off the coast. They fished and grew crops for food. The artifacts that they left behind let us know that the most important animal to the Chumash was the dolphin. They made many picture stories in caves and on rocks that include dolphins. War with the Spanish conquestadors and others caused the decline of this great people.

---

whole paragraph is about." He continued, "Ask yourself if you know the main idea. If you do, make a check at the bottom. If not, go back and re-read." The series of steps used by the teacher was based on research demonstrating the effectiveness of the steps (Graves, 1986).

On subsequent days, the teacher and the students found main ideas together. The students then worked alone and started to develop confidence and competence. Each day, the students looked pleased with their success. The teacher learned that students taught explicitly and then given a range of practice opportunities learned faster and were able to use the skills mastered longer. Later in the year, the students used their strategy for finding the main idea to write reports about what they were reading.

A seventh-grade science teacher had students construct freshwater and saltwater aquariums for a unit on ecosystems. The students wrote reports about the aquariums before constructing them and were integrally involved in the planning and building of each aquarium. After the aquariums were completed, the students wrote about their observations and formulated hypotheses about observed changes in the aquariums.

The teacher combined the activities with daily minilessons in reading to provide strategies for increasing reading comprehension. For example, she developed a series of 15- to 20-minute segments of instruction on appropriate strategies to use when students were asked to compare. On the first day of the series of lessons, the teacher said, "Watch while I show you a way to compare two items." She drew a Venn diagram (two overlapping circles) on the board. The students were then asked to compare a seahorse to an octopus. The teacher held up a picture of each animal and taped one picture in the outside portion of each circle. She asked the students to describe each animal and made notes under the pictures in each circle. One student said a seahorse is a fish and has a head like a horse. The teacher then asked, "How are they alike?" and wrote the students' comments in the overlapping part of the circles. Students said that both animals live in the ocean, and the teacher added that females in both animals lay eggs. After this initial example the teacher said, "Now, in your groups, compare the freshwater ecosystem to the saltwater ecosystem." Each student group was given a large Venn diagram drawn on posterboard. Each diagram had a picture of the saltwater ecosystem taped above the left circle and a picture of the freshwater ecosystem taped above the right circle. The students appeared to transfer the knowledge rapidly and learned a strategy for comparing.

An eighth-grade history teacher used many demonstrations and visual images, such as maps, globes, graphs, charts, and timelines. To teach the students how to maximize comprehensible input while reading, the teacher demonstrated making a timeline. To provide students explicit instruction, the teacher started the unit by making a timeline of his own life from birth to that day. A personal timeline was drawn on the board with major life events entered in order. The teacher then assisted the students in constructing their own personal timelines and posted the timelines on the bulletin board. In the last 20 minutes of class, the teacher had the students read through the assigned chapter. The teacher made a historical timeline beginning with the settlement in Jamestown, Virginia, and ending with the settlement at Plymouth, Massachusetts. Students filled in a blank timeline along with the teacher. With each new chapter, the students were asked to fill in a blank timeline with the information from the chapter.

## Teaching Writing Strategies in Content Area Classes

Research in the last 10 years has yielded valuable information about teaching writing to students who are struggling in school (Ruiz, 1995a, 1995b; Peyton, Jones, Vincent, & Greenblatt, 1994; Englert & Mariage, 1992; Graves & Montague, 1991; Box, 1988). Because good writers seem to use a recursive or circular process during composing (Graves, Semmel, & Gerber, 1994), students should learn five basic writing steps: prewriting or planning, composing, revising, editing, and final draft or publishing. The circle in Figure 5.10 represents writing-as-a-process, and the arrows pointing each way indicate that a writer can take any number of courses in composing. The writer could start with planning and composing, go back to planning for revising, start composing again, and then go back to revising and editing before completing the final draft.

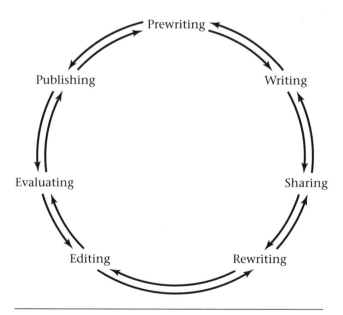

FIGURE 5.10   *Writing-as-a-Process*

Writer's Workshop, developed largely by Donald Graves (1983), consists of journal writing, prewriting activities for narrative or expository compositions, the five stages described as writing-as-a-process, and sharing and publishing final drafts. Writer's Workshop is a viable approach up through sixth grade for students learning English (Graves, Valles, & Rueda, 2000; Ruiz, 1995a, 1995b; Peyton, Jones, Vincent, & Greenblatt, 1994; DuCharme, Earl, & Poplin, 1989), although it can also be effective with older students who have had uneven school expereince and are poor writers. Writer's Workshop has been used extensively for students who are having problems in school (Englert et al., 1995; Ruiz, 1995a, 1995b; Peyton, Jones, Vincent, & Greenblatt, 1994; Zaragoza & Vaughn, 1993; Bos, 1988).

To illustrate good writing strategy instruction, three classroom observations will be presented. A fourth-, a sixth-, and a ninth-grade classroom are described in each of which teachers used Writer's Workshop while teaching writing to students learning English. In each of these classrooms, teachers often taught strategies and skills explicitly as a supplement to Writer's Workshop, and researchers support that choice (Chamot & O'Malley, 1994; Gersten & Jiménez, 1994; Englert & Mariage, 1992; Graves & Montague, 1991; Graves, Montague, & Wong, 1990).

In a fourth-grade class, the teacher used explicit strategy instruction in writing. After teaching the students each step of the writing process overtly, the teacher used different colors of paper to represent the stages of writing (Englert & Mariage, 1992). Planning was completed on yellow paper, the first draft on orange paper, and the final draft was completed on the computer or on white paper. Revising was accomplished on the orange paper by marking through and correcting spelling and punctuation. Students engaged in the process at least once a week. The students learned to start the writing process by expressing ideas. The writing process occurred in predictable stages.

A sixth-grade social studies teacher devoted 20 of her 50 minutes per class to Writer's Workshop. The teacher consistently used about one-third of the time for writing; one-third for sharing, presenting, revising, or editing; and one-third for minilessons or teacher direct learning (see Figure 5.7). The teacher did not accomplish all three aspects each day but spent at least 1 hour each week on writing.

The teacher asked the students to pretend they lived at the time of the California gold rush and to write stories about their adventures (Klinger & Vaughn, 1996; Stokes, 1989). The students had 20 minutes each day during the week to complete the assignment. The teacher chose the narrative genre because students are usually comfortable with story structure. When writing in a new language, students must be comfortable with the genre. Story writing often makes history come alive for students. The teacher led a student brainstorming activity to help them get started. The students created their own story webs or outlines, created illustrations, and wrote first drafts.

For students floundering on the narrative story structure, the teacher used the *story grammar cueing system* (Graves, Montague, & Wong, 1990). The cueing system is a list of the story grammar parts (setting, characters, problem, resolution, ending). The students were instructed to think about the parts as they wrote and revised their stories (Graves & Hague, 1993; Graves & Montague, 1991). The cueing system required the students to reflect on the steps.

During the next lesson, the students formed peer pairs and made corrections and changes in their stories. The peer revision provided each student with abundant feedback. The teacher provided a revision format during several minilessons. This process could be expanded to include more formal sessions using peer tutoring (see Greenwood et al., 2001). The revision strategy included four questions for students to ask themselves about their stories: (1) Does the story make sense? (2) What do I like about the story? (3) Does the story have characters, a setting, a problem, a resolution, and an ending? and (4) Is the capitalization, overall appearance, punctuation, and spelling correct? The students needed a significant amount of time to complete the assignment. Teacher intervention was necessary to ensure accomplishment. At the end of the week, the students wrote final drafts on the computer and created a class book. The book was given to another sixth-grade class as a gift.

A ninth-grade English teacher noted that her students were struggling with writing expository material. The teacher decided to use a think-aloud modeling procedure to teach report writing. As the teacher read to the students about the colonial tradition of Thanksgiving, the notetaking process was modeled on the overhead projector. After the reading and notetaking lesson, the teacher taught the five-paragraph essay strategy and gave the students a handout with the format of that strategy specified (see Figure 5.11, page 116). The format called for an introductory paragraph, three supporting paragraphs, and a concluding paragraph. The teacher then modeled essay writing by using the format to think aloud about a topic. The students were encouraged to make comments and suggestions as the outline was constructed on the overhead projector. If students were each assigned a role, this could be set up as cooperative learning (Johnson & Johnson, 1989). Finally, the teacher talked with students about the accuracy and logic of the outline.

After the outlining process on the topic of Thanksgiving, the teacher used the overhead projector again and wrote a report on it in concert with student participation. At another time, the students worked together in table groups and wrote reports about famous people in colonial history, such as Pocahontas, John Smith, and Miles Standish. For 20 minutes each day over the course of a week, each group completed five tasks: (1) reading

FIGURE 5.11 *Five-Paragraph Essay Format*

together while taking notes on orange paper, (2) preparing an outline on pink paper, (3) preparing a first draft on yellow paper, (4) editing the first draft, and (5) entering a final draft into the computer at the end of the week. During the next week, the groups shared their reports with the rest of the class. The students' writing quality was good compared to work done before they had been exposed to the essay strategy and the writing-as-a-process strategy.

## Summary

Explicit teaching of learning strategies can assist students in overcoming challenges they face in school. If a student has difficulty understanding a concept or rule or has been unable to devise a strategy, the teacher should provide explicit instruction to help the student succeed.

This chapter includes examples of how strategies can be embedded in sheltered content lessons. It offers specific lesson descriptions and classroom examples to demonstrate various types learning strategies. It includes guidelines for selecting learning strategies and planning lessons to teach learning strategies. Various methods for teaching specific learning strategies to promote learning skill are also explained. Strategies are essential for developing academic proficiency but are only a part of a quality instruction program for English-language learners. Chapter 6 will present another important approach to working with English-language learners: making curriculum adaptations.

## Activities

1. Thomas and six other students in the tenth grade are struggling with reading and writing tasks in their history class. What type of information needs to be gathered about these students (see Chapter 1)? If the teacher is currently involving students in role-plays and utilizing video and other concrete examples of historical events, what options does the teacher have to improve their reading and writing?

2. What particular guidelines are important for a strategy intended for use by students with intermediate fluency in English?

3. List the parts of a minilesson intended to teach a strategy explicitly. Why is each part important?

## References

Archer, A. (1990). *Effective instruction.* Reston, VA: Council for Exceptional Children.

Baca, L., & Almanza, E. (1996). *Language minority students with disabilities.* Reston, VA: Council for Exceptional Children.

Baca, L., & Cervantes, H. (1998). *The bilingual special education interface* (2nd ed.). Columbus, OH: Merrill.

Bos, C. (1988). Process-oriented writing: Instructional implications for mildly handicapped students. *Exceptional Children, 54,* 521–527.

Carnine, D., Silbert, J., & Kameenui, E. (1997). *Direct instruction reading* (3rd ed.). Columbus, OH: Merrill.

Chamot, A. U., & O'Malley, J. M. (1994). *The CALLA handbook: Implementing the cognitive academic language learning approach.* Reading, MA: Addison-Wesley.

Deno, S. L. (1985). Curriculum based measurement: The emerging alternative. *Exceptional Children, 52,* 219–232.

Deschler, D., & Schumaker, J. (1994). Strategy mastery by at-risk students: Not a simple matter. *The Elementary School Journal, 94,* 153–167.

DuCharme, C., Earl, J., & Poplin, M. (1989). The author model: The constructivist view of the writing process. *Learning Disability Quarterly, 12,* 237–242.

Echevarria, J. (1995). Interactive reading instruction: A comparison of proximal and distal effects of instructional conversations. *Exceptional Children, 61,* 536–552.

Ellis, E. S., & Graves, A. (1990). Teaching rural students with learning disabilities a paraphrasing strategy to increase comprehension of main ideas. *Rural Special Education Quarterly, 10*(2), 2–10.

Englert, C. S., Garmon, A., Mariage, T., Rozendal, M., Tarrant, K., & Urba, J. (1995). The early literacy project: Connecting across the literacy curriculum. *Learning Disability Quarterly, 18,* 253–277.

Espin, C. A., Scierka, B. J., Skare, S., & Halverson, N. (1999). Criterion-related validity of curriculum-based measures in writing for secondary students. *Reading and Writing Quarterly, 14,* 5–27.

Flores, B., Rueda, R., & Porter, B. (1986). Examining assumptions and instructional practices related to the acquisition of literacy with bilingual special education students. In A. Willig & H. Greenberg (Eds.), *Bilingualism and learning disabilities* (pp. 149–165). New York: American Library.

Gaffney, J. S., & Anderson, R. C. (1991). Two-tiered scaffolding: Congruent processes of teaching and learning. In E. H. Hiebert (Ed.), *Literacy for a diverse society* (pp. 184–198). New York: Teachers College Press.

García, E. (1993). *Education of linguistically and culturally diverse students: Effective instructional practices* (Educational Practice Report: 1). Santa Cruz, CA: National Center for Research on Cultural Diversity and Second Language Learning.

Gersten, R. M., & Baker, S. (2000). What we know about effective instructional practices for English-language learners. *Exceptional Children, 66,* 456–470.

Gersten, R., Brengelman, S., & Jiménez, R. (1994). Effective instruction for culturally and linguistically diverse students: A reconceptualization. *Focus on Exceptional Children, 27,* 1–16.

Gersten, R. M., & Jiménez, R. T. (1994). A delicate balance: Enhancing literacy instruction for students of English as a second language. *The Reading Teacher, 47*(6), 438–449.

Gersten, R. M., Taylor, R., & Graves, A. W. (1999). Direct instruction and diversity. In R. Stevens (Ed.), *Teaching in American schools: A tribute to Barak Rosenshine.* Upper Saddle River, NJ: Merrill/Prentice Hall.

Gersten, R., Taylor, R., & Graves, A. (1997). Direct instruction and diversity. In R. Stevens (Ed.), *Teaching in America: Essays in honor of Barak Rosenshine.* Columbus, OH: Merrill/Prentice Hall.

Goldenberg, C. (1992–93). Instructional conversations: Promoting comprehension through discussion. *The Reading Teacher, 46,* 316–326.

Graham S., & Harris, K. (1993). Self-regulated strategy development: Helping students with learning problems develop as writers. *Elementary School Journal, 94,* 169–181.

Graves, A. W. (1995). Teaching students who are culturally and linguistically diverse. *Teacher Educator's Journal, 15*(3), 32–40.

Graves, A. W. (1986). The effects of direct instruction and metacomprehension training on finding main ideas. *Learning Disabilties Research, 1*(2), 90–100.

Graves, A. W. (1998). Instructional strategies and techniques for students who are learning English. In R. Gersten & R. Jiménez (Eds.), *Promoting learning for culturally and linguistically diverse students: Classroom applications from contemporary research.* Belmont, CA: Wadsworth.

Graves, A., & Hauge, R. (1993). Using cues and prompts to improve story writing. *Teaching Exceptional Children, 25*(4), 38–41.

Graves, A. W., & Levin, J. R. (1989). Comparison of monitoring and mnemonic text-processing strategies in learning disabled students. *Learning Disability Quarterly, 12*, 232–236.

Graves, A., & Montague, M. (1991). Using story grammar cueing to improve the writing of student with learning disabilities. *Learning Disabilities Research and Practice, 6*, 246–251.

Graves, A., Montague, M., & Wong, Y. (1990). The effects of procedural facilitation on story composition of learning disabled students. *Learning Disabilities Research, 5*(4), 88–93.

Graves, A., Plasencia-Peinado, J., & Deno, S. (2002). *Multiple language settings: A study of first-grade instruction and outcomes.* Paper presented at the Pacific Coast Research Conference, La Jolla, CA.

Graves, A., Semmel, M., & Gerber, M. (1994). The effects of story prompts on the narrative production of students with and without learning disabilities. *Learning Disability Quarterly, 17*, 154–164.

Graves, A., Valles, E., & Rueda, R. (2000). Variations in interactive writing instruction: A study of four bilingual special education settings. *Learning Disabilities Research and Practice, 15*, 1–10.

Graves, D. (1983). *Writing: Teachers and children at work.* Portsmouth, NH: Heinemann.

Greenwood, C. R., Arreaga-Mayer, C., Utley, C. A., Gavin, K. M., & Terry, B. J. (2001). Class-wide peer tutoring learning management system: Applications with elementary-level English language learners. *Remedial and Special Education, 22*, 34–47.

Haager, D., Gersten, R., Baker, S., & Graves, A. (2002). The English-Language Learner Classroom Observation Instrument: Observations of beginning reading instruction in urban schools. In S. R. Vaughn & K. L. Briggs (Eds.), *Reading in the classroom: Systems for observing teaching and learning.* Baltimore, MD: Brookes.

Herrell, A. L. (2000). *Fifty strategies for teaching English language learners.* Upper Saddle River, NJ: Prentice-Hall.

Jiménez, R. T., García, G. E., & Pearson, P. D. (1995). Three children, two languages, and stragic reading: Case studies in bilingual/monolingual reading. *American Educational Research Journal, 32*, 67–97.

Jiménez, R. T., García, G. E., & Pearson, E. P. (1996). The reading strategies of bilingual Latina/o students who are successful English readers: Opportunities and obstacles. *Reading Research Quarterly, 31*, 90–112.

Jiménez, R. T., & Gersten, R. (1999). Lessons and dilemmas derived from the literacy instruction of two Latina/o teachers. *American Education Research Journal, 36*, 111–123.

Johnson, D. W., & Johnson, R. T. (1989). Cooperative learning: What special educators need to know. *The Pointer, 33*, 5–10.

Kaminsky, R. R., & Good, R. (1996). Toward a technology for assessing basic early literacy skills. *School Psychology Review, 25*, 215–227.

Klingner, J. K., & Vaughn, S. (1996). Reciprocal teaching of reading comprehension strategies for students with learning disabilities who use English as a second language. *Elementary School Journal, 96*, 275–293.

Lee, J. F. (1986). Background knowledge and L2 reading. *Modern Language Journal, 70*, 350–354.

Lenz, B. K., Schumaker, J. B., & Deshler, D.

D. (1991, March). *Planning in the face of academic diversity: Whose questions should we be answering?* Paper presented at the conference of the American Educational Research Association, Chicago.

Lucas, T., & Katz, A. (1994). Reframing the debate: The roles of native languages in English-only programs for language minority students. *TESOL Quarterly, 28,* 537–562.

Miller, R. (1999). *Helping Mexican and Mexican-American students in the schools of the East Side Union High School District* (Report No. RC-022-140). San Jose, CA: Office of Educational Research and Improvement, U.S. Department of Education. (ERIC Document Reproduction Service No. 435522)

Ortiz, A., & Graves, A. W. (2001). English language learners with literacy-related learning disabilities. *International Dyslexia Association Commemorative Booklet Series, 52,* 31–36.

Peyton, J. K., Jones, C., Vincent, A., & Greenblatt, L. (1994). Implementing writing workshop with ESOL students: Visions and realities. *TESOL Quarterly, 28(3),* 469–488.

Pritchard, R. (1990). The effects of cultural schemata on reading processing strategies. *Reading Research Quarterly, 25,* 273–295.

Rapp, W. H. (1997). Success with a student with limited English proficiency: One teacher's experience. *Multiple Voices for Ethnically Diverse Exceptional Learners, 2,* 21–37.

Reyes, M. de la Luz. (1992). Challenging venerable assumptions: Literacy instruction for linguistically different students. *Harvard Educational Review, 64(4),* 427–446.

Ruiz, N. T. (1995a). The social construction of ability and disability I: Profile types of Latino children identified as language learning disabled. *Journal of Learning Disabilities, 28,* 476–490.

Ruiz, N. T. (1995b). The social construction of ability and disability II: Optimal and at-risk lessons in a bilingual special education classroom. *Journal of Learning Disabilities, 28,* 491–502.

Scanlon, D., Deshler, D. D., & Schumaker, J. B. (1996). Can a strategy be taught and learned in secondary inclusive classrooms? *Learning Disabilities Research and Practice, 11(1),* 41–57.

Short, D. (1994). Expanding middle school horizons: Integrating language, culture, and social studies. *TESOL Quarterly, 28(3),* 581–608.

Stokes, S. M. (1989). LD students and language experience. *Journal of Language Experience, 10(2),* 19–23. (Language Experience Special Interest Group)

Vaughn, S., Gersten, R., & Chard, D. (2000). The underlying message in LD intervention research: Findings from research syntheses. *Exceptional Children, 67,* 99–114.

Yang, N. D. (1999). The relationship between English as a foreign language learners' beliefs and learning strategy use. *System 27,* 515–535. Available online: <www.elsevier.com/locate/system>.

Zaragoza, N., & Vaughn, S. (1993). The effects of process writing instruction on three second-grade students with different achievement profiles. *Learning Disabilities Research and Practice, 7,* 184–193.

# 6

## *Curriculum Adaptations*

- *Marta* speaks primarily Spanish with her family and friends, but she is in an English-only fourth-grade class. She reads at the second-grade level in English. How would you adapt instruction so as to improve Marta's reading ability?
- *Tuan,* whose native language is Vietnamese, is a fairly proficient writer and reader in English. However, his grades are poor in science and social studies. What adaptations for content vocabulary may improve his performance? What types of assignment modifications might the teacher try?
- *Ming,* a native Cantonese speaker, is good in math, but she is a very poor reader. What text adaptations may assist her in content area subjects?

A great challenge for teachers is making curriculum accessible to students with a native language other than English (Bell, 2000; Cheng, 1995; Lucas & Katz, 1994; Short, 1994; Faltis & Arias, 1993; Chang, 1992; Fradd, 1987). Expository content area texts are difficult because often the texts do not follow a predictable structure, such as that of a narrative, that is, a beginning, a middle, and an end to the story (Goodwin, 1991). Teachers need appropriate texts and materials for English-language learners (ELLs). Textbooks can be difficult semantically and syntactically for students learning English (Moran, Stobbe, Baron, Miller, & Moir, 2000; Lucas & Katz, 1994; Short, 1992, 1989).

This chapter builds on previous chapters, particularly Chapter 3 (Sheltered Instruction in Content Areas). This chapter will present information that adds to the strategies and techniques already presented in the book. It is divided into sections that help teachers to (1) demonstrate sensitivity to cultural and linguistic diversity, (2) provide relevant background knowledge, (3) analyze material into content knowledge and academic proficiency, (4) include language development and content vocabulary development activities, (5) modify texts, (6) modify assignments, (7) study resource guides, and (8) facilitate curriculum adaptations. This chapter includes lesson examples adapted for English-language learners in elementary and secondary classrooms (see Echevarria, 1998; Graves, 1998).

## Demonstrating Sensitivity to Cultural and Linguistic Diversity

Having a culturally and linguistically appropriate curriculum is essential (Gaye, 1993). Culturally relevant literature is available for most cultural groups. When culturally relevant literature is used in the classroom, students perform better. (For full review, see Baca and Almanza [1991] and Lynch and Hansen [1998].) Modifying and adapting lessons to include culturally relevant information and examples enhances student motivation (Cotterall, 1999; Banks, 1991).

Making lessons culturally relevant is described as *culturally and linguistically responsive teaching* (Graves, 1995). For example, a social studies unit was adapted to include a significant amount of information on the cultural diversity in America at the time of the Revolution (Short, 1994). This unit illustrated to recent immigrant students how culturally diverse the United States has been since its inception. Books emphasizing the historical contributions of African Americans, Asian Americans, Latinos, and Native Americans throughout history are recommended. When teachers use familiar current events as examples when defining historical terms such as *protest*, they are using responsive teaching. For example, newspaper clippings and pictures about the events in Los Angeles after the first Rodney King verdict might be shown as a modern example of protest.

Respecting and using students' native languages is integral to responsive teaching (Cummins, 1999; De Houwer, 1999). Native-language instruction has linguistic, cultural, cognitive-academic, and affective-psychological benefits to learning a new language (Baca & Cervantes, 1998). Hornberger and Micheau (1993) discuss the benefits of the biliterate approach to transferring background knowledge to the topic at hand. In one example, the teacher presents key vocabulary in social studies classes in both English and Spanish. In a lesson on the Pilgrims and Thanksgiving, the teacher discusses vocabulary words and uses the overhead projector to diagram his thoughts in both English and Spanish.

While the importance of native-language support was discussed in Chapter 4 from a psychological and self-esteem building perspective, the intent of this chapter is to demonstrate that lessons can be adapted to include short segments of native language to clarify meaning for students. Students' ability to retrieve words in a known language facilitates their progress in a new language (Jiménez, García, & Pearson, 1995; Franklin & Thompson, 1994 ). For example, when learning about the solar system, many of the words in English are similar to those in Spanish: *Mercurio* is Mercury, *Marte* is Mars, and *planetas* are planets. These are good examples of words that can be used in implementing the cognate strategy presented in Chapter 5.

## Providing Adequate Background Knowledge

Helping learners retrieve relevant background knowledge facilitates understanding of the lesson content and increases the likelihood of learning and retention. In addition to native-language support, other ways of providing and using background knowledge are listed in Figure 6.1. (page 124). Teachers who have students brainstorm at the beginning of a lesson encourage

FIGURE 6.1    *Phases for Providing Adequate Background Knowledge*

Phase 1:    Brainstorm with the whole group.

Phase 2:    Provide direct experiences, read sources, watch videos, and provide information-gathering opportunities.

Phase 3:    Provide a forum for using background knowledge and for adding knowledge gained (choosing a topic and preparing a report).

them to share what they already know about a topic, which facilitates learning (Fouzder & Marwick, 1999). Another way a teacher can enhance background knowledge is to provide students with direct experience through videotapes, Internet information, and field trips. Once students have a personal store of knowledge in a content area, the teacher can assist them in connecting new knowledge to what is already known (Buxton, 1999).

In one lesson, a science teacher presented a month-long unit on marine biology in phases. In phase 1, the teacher first focused on oceans by asking students to brainstorm about their own relevant experiences. Students who lived near the ocean were asked to talk about what they had observed. Their comments were written down by the teacher on the overhead projector and then copied and distributed. In the second phase, the teacher provided opportunities for students to develop knowledge of and experiences with the ocean by planning a field trip to a marine biology center by the ocean. When students returned to school after the trip, they were again asked to talk and write about what they had observed. Their comments and observations were again written down by the teacher on acetate and copied for all to study. The students also watched videotapes, the teacher read a few books aloud, and the students found library books and websites about ocean life.

In the final phase, students chose an ocean animal about which they were each to write notes on cards, write a report, draw a picture, and make a map. One student chose the sea turtle. He found a few books on sea turtles in the library, wrote notes on cards, transferred the information to a final draft on the computer, drew a picture of a sea turtle, and made a map of places in the world where sea turtles are most prevalent. On one of the final days of the marine biology unit, the students were putting the finishing touches on their projects and presenting them. The students, who were largely ELL, seemed to enjoy particularly drawing and coloring their animals and making the maps. Each presented his or her animal report to the class and chose a spot for it to be displayed in the class.

## *Categorizing Materials as Either Content Knowledge or Academic Proficiency*

In each subject area, teachers should be concerned with at least two important curricular strands: (1) determining the content knowledge the students must master in subject areas (information about) the solar system, the American Revolution, the chemical composition of colors, the names of the characters in a given literary work, and so forth and (2) determining the background academic skills necessary for students to learn and study content knowledge effectively.

### Content Knowledge

Gonzales (1994) suggests teachers develop an annual plan by reviewing textbooks, curriculum guides, and teacher manuals to determine the essential content for the specific grade level and course. Planning involves linking critical concepts and ideas into meaningful, connected units that build upon each other. When the most important concepts have been determined, the nonessential details can be eliminated.

Interdisciplinary curricula and thematic units provide students valuable links between subjects and are considered highly valuable for students (Englert et al., 1995; García, 1993). For example, in a fifth-grade American history course, the teacher might first analyze the content by constructing a timeline to span the entire year of study and then determining the relevant information to be covered. The teacher should focus particularly on how pieces of history fit together and how patterns in history repeat themselves.

To include interdisciplinary curricula, the teacher can rely on information shared by students in cooperative groups or in classroom exchanges. Hence, grade-level teams of teachers plan thematic interdisciplinary content and draw up examples that can be included across subjects enhance learning. For example, a team of teachers in a coastal Southern California community developed a thematic unit on coastal Native Americans. In this unit, students simultaneously studied tribal life and history in their social studies class, oceanography in science class, whale and dolphin counting and recordkeeping in math class, and *The Island of the Blue Dolphins* (O'Dell, 1970) in English class.

After essential content knowledge is determined and unit lesson planning is complete, teachers need to focus on determining the prerequisite or background knowledge the students need to understand the course content (Henze & Lucas, 1993). For example, when faced with a science unit on energy, teachers must first determine the experience level the students have with the concepts and content to be taught (such as heat or friction). Next, the teacher must determine the experiences that need to be provided in order to equip students for understanding the content of the course. A teacher could use class experiments or projects, videotapes, or library visits (see Figure 6.1) to provide this information. During the unit, field trips to electrical power plants or to a solar heat pump company might help students with background knowledge. The teacher can adapt the curriculum to provide students with experiences to enhance and formulate background knowledge. Students should also be encouraged to discuss and write about their own thoughts and reactions to experiences provided in the class. Class journals can provide a forum for students to express their ideas.

## Academic Proficiency Skills

Talking, listening, reading, writing, thinking, and studying are academic proficiency skills necessary for success in school (Graves, 1987). Teachers can divide the objectives for each lesson into three categories: language skills, content skills, and thinking/study skills (Short, 1994). For example, in a lesson on the Declaration of Independence, the teacher might have language skills objectives such as listening for the main ideas and reading and writing an outline. Examples of content skills objectives for the same lesson might be identifing the principles of the Declaration of Independence and recognizing some main ideas in the Declaration of Independence. Examples of thinking/study skills objectives might be evaluating the main ideas of the Declaration of Independence and writing about the effects they might have on the American people.

Teachers can determine the type of academic background skills necessary by analyzing the tasks required of the students and studying scope and sequence of academic proficiency skills (Gersten, Woodward, & Darch, 1986). They can determine that certain skills are necessary for studying, reading, and understanding the aspects of the content area to be covered throughout the year. They can then conduct an informal assessment of students' skills in the content areas (Gattullo, 2000). After the initial informal assessment, teachers can determine which skills the students have and do not have. When determinations are made, the teacher designs a plan to teach and practice the skills gradually throughout the year. The adaptation of curriculum supplements the standard content curriculum with knowledge and skills important for students' successful completion of science, social studies, literature, or math.

When curriculum is supplemented explicitly by instructing students in academic background skills, Lightbown and Spada (1994) and Reyes (1992) contend that teachers are most successful when they follow through by insisting that students demonstrate correct use of what has been taught. For example, after a strategy for recognizing main ideas is taught and practiced, students should be able to identify a main idea in a social studies text. If the main idea is misidentified, the student must be corrected. Focusing on form tends to build superior skill use and tends not to undermine self-esteem when the teacher uses a nonthreatening manner (Lightbown & Spada, 1994; Reyes, 1992).

In many parts of the United States, students are required to take a variety of high-stakes tests, most of which are related to grade-level standards. Appropriate accommodations often assist students in the process. However, some practitioners contend that these accommodations do little for the overall outcomes of ELLs with disabilities (Destefano, Shriner, & Lloyd, 2001; Fuchs & Fuchs, 2001).

# Including Both Language Development and Content Vocabulary Development

Language and vocabulary development in content areas is imperative in curricular adaptations for students who are learning English (Benson & Lor, 1999; Henze & Lucas, 1993; Cummins, 1989). Students need adequate preparation for the content material. Students need opportunities to develop the English skills necessary for future use and for transfer to life skills.

## Language Development

*Language development* is defined as curricular modifications to evoke talking, reading, and writing at the students' current English-language level. As presented in Chapters 1 and 2, students' level of language development must be assessed and appropriate questions and activities developed to promote continued progress. Particularly when students are in the early stages of language development, teachers can ask questions that require students to raise their hands or put their thumbs up if they agree. Teachers can ask the class to answer yes or no in unison. Teachers can give each student two pictures, one of mammals and one of birds. The student is asked to hold up the appropriate picture when the teacher mentions a characteristic of a group or a particular animal. Alternatively, a teacher could simply write the words *mammal* and *bird* on the board and ask the students to answer with the correct word when a characteristic or animal is mentioned. Simple answers reinforce and build knowledge with minimal language requirements but allow students a safe environment for language development.

For students at the speech emergence and emergent literacy levels of language development, the teacher provides many opportunities for language use while simultaneously developing content knowledge. Language development activities can include student pairs or small student groups talking about issues or content, reading aloud or silently, writing group reports, or solving group problems. In the social studies lesson about coastal Native Americans, each cooperative group chose a coastal tribe. Each group then wrote and illustrated a report and presented the report to the class. The group worked out the plan for accomplishing all the tasks and assignments within the group. The negotiations, discussions, and actions taken by each group were socially relevant opportunities for language use and development.

A teacher can speed language development by providing a connection to native-language vocabulary (Perez, 1993). A seventh-grade English teacher helped students develop language knowledge by writing a key-word or words in English on the board accompanied by pictures or examples. Each day the teacher said, "¿Qué es estos?" or "¿Cómo se dice en Español?" These simple phrases elicited the Spanish words and allowed the students to determine if the new English vocabulary was related to Spanish or if cognates existed. This method also allowed students to continue language development in both languages.

In one lesson on poetry, the teacher wanted to teach the English words *alliteration* and *rhyme*. The Spanish words are *aliteración* and *rima*. The teacher wrote *rhyme = rima* on the board first, thinking the students would know the meaning of but be unfamiliar with the word in English. The students immediately responded by saying "Ah, rima." The looks on their faces and their heads nodding indicated they understood the word. The teacher said, "We see *rhyme* in this poem; I'll show you two words that rhyme—*love* and *dove*. Now, find two more words that rhyme." Students were able to talk among themselves and locate more examples of rhyming words. Their discussions and continued reading of the poem facilitated language development.

For the word *alliteration*, the teacher knew the students might not know the meaning of the English word or the Spanish word. When the teacher asked about the word, some of the students looked to each other and shrugged their shoulders. The teacher used a handheld computer to find the word in Spanish and wrote *aliteración = alliteration* on the board. (Some of the new handheld computers can translate up to 20 languages and can be invaluable tools for teacher working with students learning English.) The teacher asked one of the Spanish-speaking teachers for some examples of alliteration in Spanish to further prepare for the lesson.

The teacher was careful to define alliteration in concise and consistent language: "*Alliteration* means words in a row with the same beginning letter sound. Listen to examples in Spanish: 'La luna lumbra la loma y Tito toma té y tomales.' Now listen in English: 'Slippery slimy slivering snake.' Now listen again: 'Happy lovable dog.' This is not alliteration. Why? Yes, because these are not words in a row with the same beginning letter sound." The teacher carefully provided examples and nonexamples to clarify the concept. The teacher also used consistent wording. The teacher did not say "same beginning letter sounds" one time and "same beginning letters" another time. The students were encouraged to generate examples in Spanish. The teacher could recognize alliteration in Spanish without understanding all the words in the examples generated by the students. Students shared their examples and the teacher continued providing examples from the poem as students read in English. In the end, the teacher asked students to find more English examples of alliteration and rhyme in the poem.

## Vocabulary Development

Content area courses in science, social studies, literature, and math are built around relevant vocabulary. Often, a student cannot comprehend a lesson without knowing critical vocabulary. A form of vocabulary development uses short, explicit class segments when the teacher directly teaches key vocabulary (Gersten, Taylor, & Graves, 1999; Jiménez, García, & Pearson, 1995; Bos & Anders, 1990). The 5-minute segments consist of both teacher and student activity. The teacher says the vocabulary word and writes the word on the board. The student then repeats the word and writes the word on paper. Finally, the teacher defines the word and uses pictures, demonstrations, and examples relevant to the students. In one example situation (Short, 1994), the teacher said the vocabulary word *protest* and wrote it on the board. The students said and wrote the word. The teacher then showed pictures of the African Americans who marched with Martin Luther King, Jr., to protest segregation. The teacher used a more recent protest and showed pictures of the outdoor mall in Washington, DC, covered with quilts to protest the level of funding for AIDS research.

Jiménez, García, and Pearson (1995) point out that good bilingual readers are focused on increasing vocabulary knowledge. Particularly with new vocabulary, research shows that less is more (Gersten & Jiménez, 1994). When a teacher chooses vocabulary sparingly but teaches the vocabulary in depth, the vocabulary will likely be retained. A sixth-grade math teacher taught the vocabulary word *sort* in great depth (Graves, 1998). As part of a math unit on graphing, the word *sort* was critical to many word problems. To teach the word *sort,* the teacher used kitchen items, spoons, spatulas, and two buckets. The teacher started the lesson by telling students that today they would "sort" the shoes in the room and graph the number in each group. The teacher then said, "Let's learn what the word *sort* means," and wrote the word on the board. The teacher then said, "Watch. I am going to *sort* these. Let's see . . . This is a spoon so this goes here in bucket 1. This is a spatula so this goes here in bucket 2. This is a . . ." After a few examples, the teacher became playful and said, "This is a

FIGURE 6.2 *World Wide Web Sources and Adaptations*

### Language Arts
- Study skills and self-help: www.ucc.vt.edu
- Archer, A. (2001). *Rewards*. Sopris West: www.sopriswest.com
- Green, J. F. (2000). *Language!* Sopris West: www.sopriswest.com
- Teaching tips: www.teachingtips.com
- Collection of language arts websites: www.edufly.com
- Vocabulary worksheet factory: www.worksheet.factory.dem
- Read, Write and Type: www.ridoe.com
- Reading Mastery: www.macgrawhill.sra.com
- Corrective Reading: www.macgrawhill.sra.com
- Language Arts Lesson Plans—Comprehensive lesson plans for middle and high school: education.educ.indiana.edu/cas/ttforum/lesson.html#language
- What's the Word? Vocabulary-Building Product—A vocabulary-building product utilizing videos, flashcards, and workbooks to teach over 600 commonly tested words; use for test prep and basic vocabulary building for ages 13 to adult: www.whats-the-word.com

### Math
- Saxon Math: www.saxonmath.com/
- Touchmath: www.touchmath.com/learn.why.php
- Connecting the Concepts: macgrawhill.com/

### Science Adaptations
- www.sciencelessons.com/

### Social Studies Adaptations
- www.social studies lessons.com/
- Awesome Library—K–12 Social Studies Lesson Plans—Provides carefully reviewed K–12 education resources covering current events, ecology, economics, history, holidays, geology, government, learning community, lesson plans, multicultural, and multi-disciplinary: www.neat-schoolhouse.org/social.html

### Peer Tutoring
- Greenwood, C. R. (2001). Classwide Peer Tutoring—Learning Management System: www.lsi.ukans.edu/jg/cwpt-lms

### English as a Second Language (ESL) and Sheltered Content Instruction
- Center for Applied Linguistics—Resources on topics such as language learning, ESL, and sheltered content instruction. Includes links to national research centers and ERIC: www.cal.org/si
- Tips for mainstream classroom teachers of ESL students: members.aol.com/adrmoser/tips/tips.html
- ESL Directory—A good source of information for ESL and bilingual teachers, from The Mining Company: esl.miningco.com
- Internet TESL Journal—A monthy web magazine for ESL teachers and students; includes lesson plans, classroom handouts, links of interest, articles, research papers, and other materials of immediate practical use: www.aitech.ac.jp/~iteslj
- EslGames.com—Home page of Edutainment, a photocopy-free book on the subject of teaching with games; provides free samples, as well as an essay on why pop music should be integrated into the English curriculum: www.eslgames. com
- Welcome to ESL Research—Indexes ESL, TESOL, EFL journals, online journals, search engines, and databases for ESL and applied linguistics professionals: www. eslresearch. com
- Educational Research–Bilingual Education—A large collection of articles from the National Clearinghouse on Bilingual Education, with practical application for teachers and other personnel involved in educating linguistically and culturally diverse (LCD) students; encompasses program evaluations and language research relating to bilingual education: www.ncbe.gwu.edu/library/edres.htm
- Dr. Jill Mora's Four-by-Four ESL Model: coe.sdsu.edu/people/jmora/MoraModules/BiliteracyRoadMap.htm

spoon, so it goes in bucket 2 . . . Ooops. No, it goes in bucket 1 with the other spoons." The concept of sorting was demonstrated without actually defining the word *sort*. Thinking aloud made the process overt for the students. The teacher also provided both examples and nonexamples of correct sorting to clarify the concept. Following the demonstration, the students sorted on their own. Each student was given an envelope containing three 25-cent coupons and three 50-cent coupons. The students sorted the coupons in piles on their desks as the teacher monitored. The teacher spent about 10 minutes on one vocabulary word rather than the more traditional approach of writing five words on the board and defining each one at the beginning of the lesson. Using demonstrations, modeling, thinking aloud, and visual representations to teach *sort*, all the students comprehended.

## *Modifying Plans and Texts*

Often, the teacher modifies lesson plans to meet the needs of those students who are not moving at the predicted pace for the year. Web sources can provide teachers with abundant information for transforming curriculum and instructional practices (see Figure 6.2, page 132).

Teachers can modify difficult sections of text as follows: (1) using graphic depiction, (2) outlining the text, (3) rewriting the text, (4) using audiotapes, (5) providing live demonstrations, and (6) using alternate books. Short (1989) used an original text about truck farms in the Middle Atlantic states to make a dense, difficult-to-read section of text comprehensible (see Figure 6.3, page 132). The original text is referred to throughout this section.

### Graphic Depiction of the Text

Graphic depiction of the text improves student performance. Graphic depiction of a text appears to benefit English-language learners, students in general education, and students with learning and behavior challenges. Teachers of ELLs can effectively use graphic organizers and visual displays such as charts, graphs, Venn diagrams, maps, timelines, and clusters to modify difficult texts. For example, the segment on agriculture in the Middle Atlantic states (see Figure 6.4, page 133) can be illustrated by a visual depiction of the states, with pictures of crops grown in each state (see Figure 6.5, page 133). Photographs, drawings, videotapes, and the Internet (the World Wide Web) provide a number of visual representations useful for the topics covered.

Graphic organizers and visualization strategies are useful tools in helping students organize thoughts in a meaningful way that enables

FIGURE 6.3    *Original Text*

---

**Agriculture.** Farmers in the the Middle Atlantic States grow many kinds of crops. In much of the region, the soil is fertile, or rich in the things plants need for growth. There is usually plenty of sunshine and rain. Each state has become famous for certain crops. New York is well-known for apples. New Jersey tomatoes and blueberries, Delaware white sweet corn, Pennsylvania mushrooms, and Maryland grains and other well-known crops. Herds of dairy cattle and livestock for meat are also raised in Atlantic States. The region produces a great deal of food for millions of people who live there.

**Truck Farms.** New Jersey is famous for its truck farms, which grow large amounts of many different vegetables for sale. Truck farms usually sell their products to businesses in a nearby city. New Jersey truck farms are the best known, but truck farms are found in all the Middle Atlantic States.

Another way truck farmers sell their crops is at farmers' markets in cities. Sometimes a farmers' market is outside, on the street, or in a city park. A market may be in a railroad station or in the lobby of a skyscraper. At a farmers' market, city people and farmers can meet each other face to face.

---

*Source:* D. J. Short, Adapting materials for content-based language instruction, *ERIC/CLL News Bulletin, 13* (no. 1, 1989), 1, 4–8. Reproduced with permission.

them to recall information and to recap a theme or topic. One type of graphic organizer is a *web* or a *map*. Webs provide simple visualization strategies. In a *cluster,* the topic is written in a radiating pattern around the encircled word. When teaching a second-grade class about the parts of a story, the teacher writes the title in a big circle in the center and the story parts in smaller circles radiating from the center (see Figure 6.6, page 134). The teacher uses the graphic organizer after students read each new story. The parts of the story and the graphic organizer thus become ingrained in the students' thinking.

A *Venn diagram* is also a good example of a graphic organizer used to modify a text and to reduce important points to an easily observed, simple format. The Venn diagram concept, borrowed from set theory in mathematics, can be used to demonstrate differences and similarities between situations, characters, or other selected aspects of a work. The differences are listed in large left and right circle portions, and the similarities are listed in the intersection of the two circles. For example, in a science lesson on a comparison of mammals to birds, the intersection of two circles in a Venn diagram could be used to show visually that both mammals and birds require water, move independently, are warm blooded, and breathe oxygen. On the left-side circle, mammals are represented as animals who have hair or fur and have live births. On the right-side circle, birds are represented as animals who have feathers and lay eggs.

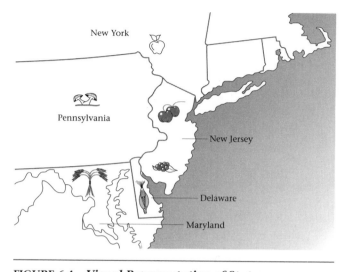

**FIGURE 6.4**  *Visual Representation of States*

*Source:* D. J. Short, Adapting materials for content-based language instruction, *ERIC/CLL News Bulletin, 13* (no. 1, 1989), 1, 4–8. Reproduced with permission.

## Outlining the Text

Several types of outlining can be effective for summarizing and emphasizing important information in a text. The traditional *framed outline* allows the student to see and prioritize key points, which facilitates understanding and memory. A framed outline has major chapter sections represented by roman numerals, main ideas by capital letters, and important details by numbers under each capital letter. For example, the framed outline for the text on agriculture in the Middle Atlantic states includes

**FIGURE 6.5**  *Pictures of Crops*

*Source:* D. J. Short, Adapting materials for content-based language instruction, *ERIC/CLL News Bulletin, 13* (no. 1, 1989), 1, 4–8. Reproduced with permission.

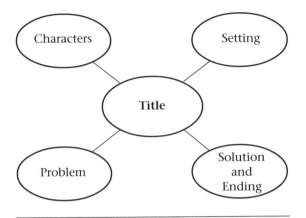

**FIGURE 6.6**    *Story Mapping*

agriculture, truck farms, and farmers' markets as roman numerals or main ideas (see Figure 6.7).

## Rewriting the Text

Rewriting curriculum is an effective text modification of curricular materials. Teachers of ELLs agree that most texts are written at or above grade level. As a result, many students do not read at the grade level for which the reading materials are intended. Written materials should be organized in small, sequential steps, avoiding long passages with dense groups of words. Short, simple sentences are preferable to long, complex sentences. Here is an example of a complex sentence from a science text: "Electrons have negative electric charges and orbit around the core, the nucleus, of an atom." The sentence can be improved by forming several new sentences: "Electrons have negative electric charges. They orbit around the atom. The core of the atom is called the nucleus."

If a text is rewritten, paragraphs must include a topic sentence and several supporting detail sentences. The rewritten text should maintain a specific format to promote easy reading. All sentences in the rewritten text should be direct and relevant to the subject. For example, the original text (see Figure 6.3) is a series of sentences, some of which do not relate to the topic. When the paragraph is rewritten (see Figure 6.8, page 136), there is a clear topic sentence: "Farmers grow many foods, or crops, in the Middle Atlantic states." The detail sentences follow and support the topic sentence. Key information can be listed with bullets or indented. The rewritten paragraphs are shorter and focus only on the central information.

FIGURE 6.7    *Framed Outline*

*Middle Atlantic States*
  I. Agriculture
     A. Many kinds of food crops
     B. State crops
        1. New York: apples
        2. New Jersey: tomatoes, blueberries
        3. Delaware: corn
        4. Pennsylvania: mushrooms
        5. Maryland: grains
     C. Cows for milk and meat
 II. Truck Farms
     A. Many truck farms in New Jersey
     B. Sell vegetables to stores in a city
III. Farmers' Markets
     A. Farmers sell crops in the city
        1. On a street
        2. In a park
        3. In a train station
        4. In a building
     B. Farmers and city people meet

*Source:* D. J. Short, Adapting materials for content-based language instruction, *ERIC/CLL News Bulletin, 13* (no. 1, 1989), 1, 4–8. Reproduced with permission.

When a text is rewritten, often the academic tasks that accompany the text must be modified. For example, when rewriting a section in a text, questions should be written to accompany the section. If the paragraph has been rewritten to reflect a main idea, the students can be asked to identify the main idea of the paragraph. For example, "What types of crops are grown by farmers in the Middle Atlantic states?" is a logical question to accompany the rewritten paragraph.

When modifying a text, the number of questions and the number of pages assigned can be modified to structure the activities for maximum success. Questions can be rewritten and presented one at a time, or students can use a *reading window* to frame one question at a time on the paper. A reading window is made by cutting an inch-high slot the width of a printed page in a sheet of cardboard.

Written directions in text or on handouts should be rewritten to conform to the lowest reading level in the class. If directions are convoluted, they should be rewritten and simplified. For the preceding text on agriculture, the original directions said, "Once you have read the passage below, determine what the author is trying to express. Mark the key words and

**FIGURE 6.8**   *Original Text, Rewritten*

---

*Agriculture in the Middle Atlantic States*
  Farmers grow many foods, or **crops**, in the Middle Atlantic States. The soil is good for plants. The plants have enough sunshine and rain to grow. Each state has one or two special crops:

> New York: apples
> New Jersey: tomatoes and blueberries
> Delaware: corn
> Pennsylvania: mushrooms
> Maryland: grains

  The farmers also raise cows. They get milk from some cows. They get meat from other cows.
  New Jersey has many **truck farms.** The farmers grow a lot of vegetables. They bring the vegetables to the city by truck. They sell the vegetables to stores in the city.
  Farmers also sell their crops at **farmers' markets.** Some markets are outside. They can be on streets or in city parks. Other markets are inside. They can be in train stations or in buildings. City people and farmers can meet each other at the markets.

---

*Source:* D. J. Short, Adapting materials for content-based language instruction, *ERIC/CLL News Bulletin, 13* (no. 1, 1989), 1, 4–8. Reproduced with permission.

---

the most important points." The directions were rewritten to say, "Read this paragraph. Underline one main idea. Circle three key words."

## Audiotaping Versions of the Text

Teachers can put sections or entire chapters on audiotape. Students with reading difficulties can listen to the tape and hear the material come alive (Bos, 1995). Students can also listen to the tape over and over again to reinforce learning. Teachers can ensure the information necessary for assignments and testing is recorded. Students can be assigned to help with the recording. Each week a group of students can be made responsible for recording the material.

## Providing Live Demonstrations

Live demonstrations can bring life to a text. In the agriculture example, if the teacher brings vegetables and fruits to class representing the various crops, the lesson will be more interesting. If the teacher shows a videotape on farming or picking crops, such as those in the lesson, the lesson may be more realistic.

In a class that was studing archeology, the teacher demonstrated how objects become buried deep underground. The teacher placed a quarter in a pie pan and blew dirt over it, just to cover the quarter. The teacher then put dried leaves over the dirt, followed by a sprinkling of rain. Finally, sand was put on top so the quarter was now underneath about an inch of natural products. This process was described in the text; however, most students did not have the reading skills or English proficiency to understand it. The demonstration made an impression on the students and the demonstration was later referred to when students were discussing other related topics.

## Using Alternate Books

Teachers can select alternate books with similar concepts but at an easier reading level. Alternate books are typically called *high interest–low vocabulary books* (see Figure 6.9). Alternate books focus on the same required curriculum material but are written to make reading automatic. The focus is on the curriculum rather than on the challenges of decoding the vocabulary and reading the text.

FIGURE 6.9    *Adapted and Multicultural Curriculum Resources for Grades One to Twelve*

*American Indian Baseline Essays.* (1993). Grades K–12. Portland Public Schools, 501 N. Dixon St., Portland, OR 97227.

*Colonialism in the Americas.* (1993). Grades 4–9. VIDEA, 407-620 View Street, Victoria, BC, Canada V8W 1J6.

*Cooperative Learning, Cooperative Lives.* (1987). Grades K–12, all subject areas, Lesson plans by Nancy Schniedewind & Ellen Davidson, Published by Wm. Brown Co.

*Hispanic Baseline Essays.* (1993). Grades K–12. Portland Public Schools, 501 N. Dixon St., Portland, OR 97227.

*Indian History & Culture Units.* Grades K–6. Bulletin No. 6474 & 0490, Wisconsin Department of Public Instruction, Drawer 179, Milwaukee, WI 53293.

*Mathematics for Consumers.* (1992). Kathleen Harmeyer, American Guidance Service, Inc., Circle Pines, MN.

*Math and Science: A Solution.* (1987). Grades 5–7. AIMS Education Foundation, P.O. Box 8120, Fresno, CA 93747-8120.

*Portraits of Asian-Pacific Americans, Portraits of Black Americans, Portraits of Mexican Americans, Portraits of Native Americans.* (1991). Good Apple, P.O. Box 299, Carthage, IL 62321-0299.

*Star Power.* (1991). Grades 6–adult (simulations of how inequality and oppression work). Simile II, P.O. Box 910, Del Mar, CA 92014.

*United States History.* (1990). Grades 7–8. New York City Schools, Instructional Publications Sales, 131 Livingston St., R. 515, Brooklyn, NY 11201.

Teachers in many different grades find that students with two sets of books progress faster. One set of books kept at school and one set at home aids the student in doing home reading and homework assignments.

## Modifying Assignments

If the student understands the information but is unable to express this knowledge in writing, he or she should be provided alternative forms of expression (Bos, 1995). Language proficiency level cannot be confused with a student's knowledge of the subject matter. Teachers are often quite knowledgeable about a variety of topics, but if asked to explain a concept, such as the three branches of the government, in a language other than English, most would be unable to communicate their knowledge. The same is true of English-language learners. Their language skills may restrict their expression of their actual understanding of a subject matter.

Alternate assignments include (1) simplifying objectives, (2) having students draw maps or pictorial representations, (3) using oral discussions in pairs or small groups, and (4) reducing the length and complexity of assignments. Students' performance improves if they use set formats for notetaking, writing activities, practice activities, homework, and progress checks. Examples of each type of modified assignment follow, based on the unit on consumerism described in Chapter 3.

### Using Simplified Objectives

A simplified lesson clearly specifies objectives and focuses on products and learning that directly relate to the objective. For example, a third-grade science chapter on the solar system could have the simple objectives of teaching students to say the names of the planets and having them construct a clay and wire model of the planets and their relationship to the sun. Information about miles from the sun, moons, gases, make-up of the surface of the planets, and so on will not be included in the objectives. The simplified objectives require fewer chapter questions and less reading in the chapter.

In the lesson from Chapter 3 on consumerism, the teacher simplified objectives recommended in the text. The original objectives were (1) to help students identify what health values to look for in products and services, (2) to learn how product labels can help consumers, (3) to learn how consumers can make informed decisions, and (4) to study how advertising can help consumers. Instead, the teacher offered these objectives each day: (1) "Today we will learn how to buy healthy products," (2) "Today we will learn how to buy wisely," (3) "Today we will learn how to read labels when we buy," and (4) "Today we will learn how to study advertisements before we buy." By focusing on one objective per day, reading loads were reduced and students were able to concentrate on one aspect of being a consumer without complicating their thinking.

## Asking Students to Draw

Requiring students to draw maps or pictures enhances learning and functions as an alternate form of expression for students struggling with English. For example, a high school science teacher asked students to draw a map of the water cycle during a lesson about condensation and evaporation. Drawing a map of the water cycle was an alternate way to find out what the students had learned. In another example, third-grade students were asked to draw a story map of *How the Children Stopped the Wars* (Wahl, 1969). The students drew the series of events and the characters from the story and placed the pictures in the appropriate order on a story board. The students drew the pictures even though their oral expression of the story line was still quite difficult.

In the unit on consumerism, students were asked to draw a model of the steps to take when making a purchase. In groups, students drew a person (1) looking for cheaper prices, (2) thinking about what healthy products to buy, (3) reading labels, and (4) comparing prices and health values before buying. Students illustrated a story about saving the family money and what the savings could be used to purchase.

## Creating Pairs and Small Groups

As presented in the language development section of this chapter, the teacher can provide many opportunities for language use while simultaneously developing content knowledge. Language development activities can include student pairs or small student groups, in which students talk about issues or content, read aloud or silently, write group reports, or solve group problems (Arreaga-Mayer, 1998). A middle school social studies teacher paired strong English-language learners with students weaker in English. When the teacher asked a question that required more than a one-word answer, the students were asked to talk to their partner about the answer. The teacher also created problem-solving activities and projects where students were placed in four-person cooperative groups. In the groups were usually two ELLs with strong skills and two who were not fluent. A cooperative group assignment required the students to construct an Old West boom town. Each group had access to wooden sticks, glue, colored paper, marking pens, crayons, and scissors. Students constructed the towns based on their knowledge of the gold rush and the types of businesses likely to be present at that time. Alternate group structures and alternate assignments can both be ideal for students struggling to learn English and content material.

In the unit on consumerism, the students who received sheltered instruction participated in hands-on activities with partners and in small groups. Students discussed items at the stations such as shampoo, soap, shoes, and socks. The students were to decide which items were the best buys and why. Students strong in English were sometimes paired with weaker students. Answers were written on workstation sheets cooperatively.

During other assignments in the unit on consumerism, students formed cooperative groups to score advertisements. For this activity the teacher established a 4-minute time limit. This allowed students to talk among themselves but provided structure for the activity. Students were able to complete more activities and have time to share results with each other when the teacher imposed time constraints.

## Modifying the Length and Difficulty of Assignments

Teachers can choose assignments carefully and make the assignments extremely useful to the students. Teachers can also try additional modifications to reduce the length and complexity of assignments. Here are some examples of ways to modify assignments:

- Use clear, simple wording.
- Shorten spelling tests by reducing the number of spelling words to include only the most functional.
- Offer an alternative to written assignments, such as clay models, posters, panoramas, or collections (such as posters of the steps to take when buying wisely).
- Require mastery of only key concepts. (For example, the glossary in the consumer unit can be modified to five terms.)
- Break down complex assignments into simpler, more meaningful parts.
- Give the students only one page of a workbook at a time so they are not overwhelmed.
- Make bright construction paper borders or reading windows (made from the faces of window envelopes) for the students to place around reading material or vocabulary words to keep their attention.
- Ask students to use a highlighter marker to identify key words, phrases, or sentences.
- Modify expectations based on students' needs and review expectations frequently (that is, determine how students are responding and decide to move on or to review material already covered).

# *Assigning Notetaking, Report Writing, Study Sheets and Homework, and Progress Checks*

Students benefit from regular academic practice activities modified for simplicity and ease of performance. The modified activities can lower anxiety for ELLs. Once a teacher knows which activities are important and how they should be modified, the teacher must require regular practice. The teacher might decide the important activities are notetaking, report writing, study sheets, homework, and progress checks. In each of these sections, examples from the consumerism unit from Chapter 3 are presented.

## Notetaking

When teachers teach a form of notetaking, students learn how it can be used in other academic and personal areas. For example, a middle school trained all the teachers to use a modified version of the Cornell notetaking system invented by Dr. Walter Pauk at Cornell University (see Schumm & Rddencich, 1992). The original version involved five simple stages for taking notes: record, reduce, recite, reflect, and review. The school modified the language of the system and made the notetaking strategy less complex by using familiar words. The modified version had four stages: write notes, write key words, remember, and study.

At the beginning of the year, each teacher in the school introduced the four-stage notetaking strategy. The students were taught to divide each notebook page into two columns by drawing a vertical line down the paper about 2 inches from the left margin. The left column was to remain blank while students wrote notes in the right column. During the next class, the notes in the right column were used to recall key points and the points were written in the left column adjacent to the notes. After the keywords were written, the students covered the right column with a piece of paper and looked only at the key words to trigger their memories. The students reviewed the material each night until a test was given. This notetaking strategy can help all students organize their schoolwork.

In the unit on consumers, students could use this notetaking format first to define terms, placing the words in the left column and the definitions in the right column. Student could then proceed to list key points about wise consumers on the right side, with keywords to remind them about each of the points. For example, in the right column a student might enter: "Consumers can use ads to get important information but should be wary of false advertising." To the left, the students might write: "Use of advertising." Students could be encouraged to take notes from the notes the teacher wrote on the overhead projector throughout the unit.

Students could also work together in pairs to read and make notes about the content.

## Report Writing

Report writing is an example of a writing activity teachers might use in social studies, science, literature, or math classes. For example, a teacher might provide a model for essay or report writing (see Chapter 5, Figure 5.11, page 116). Teachers should follow the previously specified guidelines for writing assignments. Students will benefit from completing an outline, a rough draft, a revised and edited draft, and a final draft. Students may also benefit from working in pairs and in cooperative groups the first few times a report is written. As students gain confidence, depending on their language skills, they may benefit from working on their own.

In the consumer unit, instead of being tested at the end, students might be asked to write a report about being a good consumer. The teacher could provide a format for the report, including an introductory paragraph, three detail paragraphs, and a conclusion paragraph. If students are encouraged to write their reports in pairs, they can outline the report and then actually compose the report together. Student pairs can exchange their work with other student pairs for peer editing and review. They can take turns writing sections of the final draft, or they can take turns inputting it on the computer for a perfect final copy. Students are encouraged to provide pictures or illustrations of their key points.

## Study Sheets and Homework

Teachers of English-language learners can modify study sheets, worksheets, and homework assignments to reduce their difficulty yet maximize their comprehensibility and applicability. For example, the number of science terms on a study sheet can be reduced or the assignment due date can be extended. Written materials and assignments are most effective if they are simply worded and directly related to the material taught in the class. Short words and simple sentences are best for directions. Study sheets are most appropriate when they reduce the covered material to the basic elements. Redundancy is maximized when students repeat information on the same study sheet. Anxiety can be reduced if students use the same types of study sheets for all units. When teachers clearly state expectations and instructions, student learning and efficiency are maximized.

Homework provides students with opportunities to practice skills and learn material. Homework in its best form requires students to complete tasks or use information already mastered in the classroom. Students benefit from the home practice of concepts, vocabulary, or writing activities with which they feel comfortable. Good homework assignments reduce the possibility students will become frustrated with tasks requiring unfamiliar language or concepts. Unfamiliar directions or tasks are inappropriate for all types of written assignments. Students may build an aversion to written assignments of any kind if they do not understand an assignment.

In the consumer unit, the teacher provided study sheets to be used during various activities or done as homework. For example, students had worksheets to fill in as they analyzed advertisements and products. The worksheets were simple and had redundant questions—for example, "Look at this advertisement and write the important information. Also, write the information that is not important." The study sheet for products said, "Look at these two types of shoes. Which ones are the best buy? How do you know?" Students were encouraged to take study sheets home with their notes. A typical homework assignment was, "What kind of toothpaste does your family buy? How much did it cost? Was it the best buy? How do you know?" Students could use study sheets from class to complete homework. All of this information could be used to study for tests.

## Progress Checks

Teachers need to know the progress of each student in order to modify and change curriculum objectives. Outcome-based accountability is essential in establishing improvements in both English-language knowledge and content knowledge. Progress must be checked several times a week. Progress checks can range from informal study sheets and short writing assignments ("quick writes") to formal quizzes or tests and Writer's Workshop–style writing assignments. Interviews with students can also be useful as progress checks. Students' perceptions of their own work and abilities is often quite revealing. Individual portfolios and journals allow teachers to keep a chronological assessment of their students' daily work. Teachers are the best observers of student performance in the classroom. Modifications of assignments are necessary if students are performing below appropriate levels for individual language development and content mastery.

In the consumer unit, all of the papers and assignments a student had completed were placed in a folder with his or her name on it. On the inside cover of each folder was a grid that listed all of the assignments and homework. The teacher graded each assignment and placed either a check or a grade on the grid beside each listing. Students were also required to include notes taken, tests taken, and reports written in their folders. All of these activities were marked on the grid so students and parents could see what had been completed at a glance. Then, both students and parents could review the students' work in greater depth as they looked through the folder. The teacher gained valuable information about the level of performance of each learner through this progress monitoring system.

## Using Study Resource Guides

Study resource guides can maximize the use of visual aids and other materials. In a study of 69 sheltered classes and 26 co-taught classes (Goodwin, 1991), teachers expressed the need for more materials and visual aids appropriate for English-as-a-second-language instruction. Photographs, slides, sketches, and videotapes are effective supplementary materials. Providing concrete, hands-on experiences serves to increase students' understanding of the subject matter.

Most districts provide a list of resources for teachers to use in supplementing the curriculum. Figure 6.9 (page 137) shows examples of multicultural curriculum resources for teachers of grades one to twelve. Options for supplementing the core curriculum are often included in resource guides. Rather than researching topics and spending time looking for materials, a teacher might find supplemental material listed in a district guide. For example, on the topic of the War for Independence, the district resource guide may provide suggestions for activities such as a colonial newspaper, a list of relevant movies (such as *Crossing the Delaware* or *A Fireball in the Night*), or a list of reading selections (for example, *Paul Revere's Ride*, by Henry Wadsworth Longfellow, or *I'm Deborah Sampson: A Soldier in the War of the Revolution*, by Patricia Clapp).

## Developing Methods to Facilitate Curriculum Adaptations

Teachers can develop methods to facilitate curriculum adaptations that avoid excessive consumption of time. These might include having students rewrite text, highlighting main points for the class, or encouraging cooperative efforts with other teachers.

### Rewriting by Students

One way to facilitate curricular adaptation is to have students rewrite texts as part of course assignments. Students can write paragraphs in their own words. For example, cooperative groups of four students could rewrite a certain section of the text using specified guidelines for proper paragraph formation. Or teachers could require students to rewrite sections individually. In still another way, teachers could use a language experience approach to facilitate curricular adaptation. The whole class or small student groups could decide through discussion how to rewrite sections of the text. The teacher might then write what the students suggest on the board. Over time, a text could be essentially rewritten into more comprehensible language by students.

## Highlighting Main Points

A similar method could be used to highlight the main points of a text. The students could use highlighting markers to focus on and mark the most salient aspects of the chapter. Teachers could give the text to the students and have them highlight as they read. Students could focus on and highlight main ideas and two supporting details for each main idea in a section or a chapter. The students could accomplish the task individually, in small groups, or as a whole-class activity. Students could also be asked to compare and contrast individual highlighting and reach a consensus on what should be highlighted before submitting the activity for a grade.

## Encouraging Cooperative Efforts among Teachers

In order to maximize outcomes and minimize effort, a cooperative project is possible where each teacher is assigned to modify a number of chapters in the textbook using agreed-upon guidelines. The modified chapters are compiled and distributed. The project could be at grade level, a schoolwide project, or a districtwide project.

Schools improve the performances of students if they encourage similar curricular modifications. Schools that adopt schoolwide plans for study methods, assignment calendars, homework, and report writing increase students' chances for success. Redundancy in assignments and school policies strengthens the overall consistency and effectiveness of a school.

## *Summary*

This chapter emphasized the critical information regarding curricular adaptations that concern teaching content subjects to secondary students who are not native speakers of English. Teachers face tremendous challenges in guiding students to listen, speak, read, and write in English while teaching them content knowledge. These two tasks are intertwined, and curriculum adaptations for students who are learning English require teachers to adapt content, analyze content material, teach academic proficiency, rewrite curriculum, modify assignments, and maximize visual aids and resources.

## Activities

1. Choose a lesson plan and adapt it in these two ways:

   **a.** To demonstrate sensitivity to cultural and linguistic diversity
   **b.** To provide background knowledge necessary for better understanding

2. Use the lesson plan and analyze the material. Write objectives for essential content, content vocabulary, and areas of academic language proficiency development.

3. Using the same lesson plan, outline five possible text or assignment modifications to accommodate students who are ELLs.

4. List several options teachers may use for obtaining assistance in curriculum adaptation.

## References

Arreaga-Mayer, C. (1998). Language sensitive peer mediated instruction for language minority studies in the intermediate elementary grades. In R. Gersten & R. Jiménez (Eds.), *Promoting learning for culturally and linguistically diverse students: Classroom applications from contemporary research*. Belmont, CA: Wadsworth.

Baca, L. M., & Almanza, E. (1991). *Language minority students with disabilities*. Reston, VA: Council for Exceptional Children.

Baca, L., & Cervantes, H. (1998). *The bilingual special education interface* (2nd ed.). Boston: Merrill.

Banks, J. A. (1991). A curriculum for empowerment, action, and change. In C. E. Sleeter (Ed.), *Empowerment through multicultural education* (pp. 125–141). Albany, NY: State University of New York.

Bell, J. S. (2000). Literacy challenges for language learners in job-training programs. *The Canadian Modern Language Review, 57*, 173–200.

Benson, P., & Lor, W. (1999). Conceptions of language and language learning. *System 27*, 459–472. Available online: <www.elsevier.com/locate/system>.

Bos, C. (1995). *Accommodations for students with special needs who are learning English*. Paper presented at the First Congress on Disabilities, Mexico City, Mexico.

Bos, C. S., & Anders, P. L. (1990). Effects of interactive vocabulary instruction on the vocabulary learning and reading comprehension of junior-high learning disabled students. *Learning Disability Quarterly, 13*(1), 31–42.

Buxton, C. A. (1999). *The emergence of a language of instruction for successful model based elementary science learning: Lessons from a bilingual classroom* (Report No. FL026069). Boulder, CO: National Science Foundation. (ERIC Document Reproduction Service No. ED436957)

Chang, J. M. (1992). Current programs serving Chinese-American students in learning disabilities resource issues. In *Proceedings of the Third National Research Symposium on Limited English Proficient Issues: Focus on Middle and High School Issues* (pp. 713–736). Washington, DC: U.S. Department of Education, Office of Bilingual Education and Minority Language Affairs.

Cheng, L. L. (1995). ESL strategies for API population. In L. L. Cheng (Ed.), *Integrating language and learning for inclusion: An Asian-Pacific focus*. San Diego, CA: Singular.

Clapp, P. (1977). *I'm Deborah Sampson: A soldier in the Revolutionary War.* New York: Lothrop, Lee, & Shepard.

Cloud, N. (1993). Language, culture and disability: Implications for instruction and teacher preparation. *Teacher Education and Special Education, 16,* 60–72.

Cotterall, S. (1999). Key variables in language learning: What do learners believe about themselves? *System, 27,* 493–513. Available online: <www.elsevier.com/locate/system>.

Cummins, J. (1989). A theoretical framework for bilingual special education. *Exceptional Children, 56,* 111–128.

Cummins, J. (1999). The ethics of doublethink: Language rights and the bilingual education debate. *TESOL,* Autumn, 13–17.

De Houwer, A. (1999). *Two or more languages in early childhood: Some general points and practical recommendations* (Report No. EDO-FL-99-03). Washington, DC: ERIC Clearinghouse on Languages and Linguistics. (ERIC Document Reproduction Service No. ED433697)

Destefano, L., Shriner, J. G., & Lloyd, C. A. (2001). Teacher decision making in participation of students with disabilities in large-scale assessment. *Exceptional Children, 68,* 7–22.

DuCharme, C., Earl, J., & Poplin, M. (1989). The author model: The constructivist view of the writing process. *Learning Disability Quarterly, 12,* 237–242.

Echevarria, J. (1998). Curriculum adaptations for students who are learning English. In R. Gersten & R. Jiménez (Eds.), *Promoting learning for culturally and linguistically diverse students: Classroom applications from contemporary research.* Belmont, CA: Wadsworth.

Englert, C. S., Garmon, A., Mariage, T., Rozendal, M., Tarrant, K., & Urba, J. (1995). The early literacy project: Connecting across the literacy curriculum. *Learning Disability Quarterly, 18,* 253–277.

Englert, C. S., & Mariage, T. V. (1992).

Shared understandings: Structuring the writing experience through dialogue. In D. Carnine & E. Kameenui (Eds.), *Higher order thinking* (pp. 107–136). Austin, TX: Pro-Ed.

Faltis, C. J., & Arias, M. B. (1993). Speakers of languages other than English in the secondary school: Accomplishments and struggles. *Peabody Journal of Education: Trends in Bilingual Education at the Secondary School Level, 69(1),* 6–29.

Faltis, C. J., & Hudelson, S. (1994). Learning English as an additional language in K–12 schools. *TESOL Quarterly, 28(3),* 457–468.

Figueroa, R. A. (1989). Psychological testing of linguistic-minority students: Knowledge gaps and regulations. *Exceptional Children, 56(2),* 111–119.

Flores, B., Rueda, R., & Porter, B. (1986). Examining assumptions and instructional practices related to the acquisition of literacy with bilingual special education students. In A. Willig & H. Greenberg (Eds.), *Bilingualism and learning disabilities* (pp. 149–165). New York: American Library.

Fouzder, N. B., & Markwick, A. J. W. (1999). A practical project to help bilingual students to develop their knowledge of science and English language. *School Science Review, 80,* 65–74.

Fradd, S. H. (1987). Accommodating the needs of limited English proficient students in regular classrooms. In S. Fadd & W. Tinkunoff (Eds.), *Bilingual education and special education: A guide for administrators* (pp. 133–182). Boston: College-Hill.

Franklin, E., & Thompson, J. (1994). Describing students' collected works: Understanding American Indian children. *TESOL Quarterly, 28(3),* 489–506.

Fuchs, L. S., & Fuchs, D. (2001). Helping teachers formulate sound test accommodation decisions for students with learning disabilities. *Learning Disabilities Practice, 16,* 174–181.

Garcia, E. (1993). Project THEME: Collaboration for school improvement at the middle school for language minority students. In *Proceedings of the Third National Research Symposium on Limited English Proficient Issues: Focus on Middle and High School Issues* (pp. 323–350). Washington, DC: U.S. Department of Education, Office of Bilingual Education and Minority Language Affairs.

Gattullo, F. (2000). Formative assessment in ELT primary (elementary) classrooms: An Italian case study. *Language Testing, 17*, 278–288.

Gay, G. (1993). Building cultural bridges: A bold proposal for teacher education. *Education and Urban Society, 25*, 285–299.

Gersten, R., Brengelman, S., & Jiménez, R. (1994). Effective instruction for culturally and linguistically diverse students: A reconceptualization. *Focus on Exceptional Children, 27*, 1–16.

Gersten, R., & Jiménez, R. (1994). A delicate balance: Enhancing literature instruction for students of English as a second language. *The Reading Teacher, 47*, 438–449.

Gersten, R., Taylor, R., & Graves, A. (1999). Direct instruction and diversity. In R. Stevens (Ed.), *Teaching in America: Essays in honor of Barak Rosenshine.* Columbus, OH: Merrill/Prentice Hall.

Gersten, R., Woodward, J., & Darch, C. (1986). Direct instruction: A research-based approach for curriculum design and teaching. *Exceptional Children, 53* (1), 17–36.

Goldenberg, C. (1992–93). Instructional conversations: Promoting comprehension through discussion. *The Reading Teacher, 46*, 316–326.

Gonzales, L. (1994). *Sheltered instruction handbook.* Carlsbad, CA: Gonzales & Gonzales.

Goodwin, J. (1991). *Asian remedial plan: A study of sheltered and co-taught classes in new instructional model secondary schools.* ERIC Document Number 344 956.

Gorski, P. C. (2001). *Multicultural education and the Internet: Intersections and integrations.* Boston: McGraw-Hill.

Graves, A. W. (1987). Improving comprehension skills. *Teaching Exceptional Children, 19*(2), 58–67.

Graves, A. W. (1995). Teaching students who are culturally and linguistically diverse. *Teacher Educator's Journal, 15*(3), 32–40.

Graves, A. W. (1998). Instructional strategies and techniques for students who are learning English. In R. Gersten & R. Jiménez (Eds.), *Promoting learning for culturally and linguistically diverse students: Classroom applications from contemporary research.* Belmont, CA: Wadsworth.

Henderson, R. W., & Landesman, E. M. (1992). *Mathematics and middle school students of Mexican descent: The effects of thematically integrated instruction* (Research Report: 5). Santa Cruz, CA: National Center for Research on Cultural Diversity and Second Language Learning.

Henze, R. C., & Lucas, T. (1993). Shaping instruction to promote the success of language minority students: An analysis of four high school classes. *Peabody Journal of Education: Trends in Biligual Education at the Secondary School Level, 69*(1), 54–81.

Hornberger, N., & Michaeu, C. (1993). Getting far enough to like it: Biliteracy in the middle school. *Peabody Journal of Education: Trends in Bilingual Education at the Secondary School Level, 69*, 54–81.

Jiménez, R. T., García, G. E., & Pearson, P. D. (1995). Three children, two languages, and strategic reading: Case studies in biligual/monolingual reading. *American Educational Research Journal, 32*, 67–97.

Krashen, S. D. (1985). *The input hypothesis: Issues and implications.* New York: Longman.

Lightbown, P. M., & Spada, N. (1994). An innovative program for primary ESL students in Quebec. *TESOL Quarterly, 28*, 563–578.

Lim, H. J. L., & Watson, D. (1993). Whole language content classes for second-language learners. *The Reading Teacher, 46*, 384–395.

Lucas, T., & Katz, A. (1994). Reframing the debate: The roles of native languages in English-only programs for language minority students. *TESOL Quarterly, 28*, 537–562.

McLaughlin, B. (1992). *Babes and bathwaters: How to teach vocabulary.* Working papers of the Bilingual Research Group, University of California, Santa Cruz.

Meskill, C., & Mossop, J. (2001). Electronic test in ESOL classrooms. *TESOL Quarterly, 585–592.*

Meskill, C., Mossop, J., & Bates, R. (1999). Bilingualism, cognitive flexibility, and electronic literacy. *Bilingual Research Journal, 23*, 1–10.

Moran, C., Stobbe, J., Baron, W., Miller, J., & Moir, E. (2000). *Keys to the classroom.* Thousand Oaks, CA: Corwin Press.

O'Dell, S. (1970). *Island of the blue dolphins.* New York: Bantam/Doubleday.

Palincsar, A. S. (1986). The role of dialogue in providing scaffolded instruction. In J. Levin & M. Pressley (Eds.), *Educational Psychologist, 21* (Special issue on learning strategies), 73–98.

Pease-Alvarez, L., & Winsler, A. (1994). Cuando el maestro no habla Espanol: Children's bilingual language practices in the classroom. *TESOL Quarterly, 28*(3), 507–536.

Perez, B. (1993). Biliteracy practices and issues in secondary schools. *Peabody Journal of Education: Trends in Bilingual Education at the Secondary School Level, 69*(1), 117–135.

Peyton, J. K., Jones, C., Vincent, A., & Greenblatt, L. (1994). Implementing writing workshop with ESOL students: Visions and realities. *TESOL Quarterly, 28*(3), 469–488.

Pierce, L. V. (August, 1988). *Facilitating transition to the mainstream: Sheltered English vocabulary development.* Washington, DC: National Clearinghouse for Bilingual Education.

Reyes, M. de la Luz (1992). Challenging venerable assumptions: Literacy instruction for linguistically different students. *Harvard Educational Review, 62*(4), 427–446.

Ruiz, N. T. (1995a). The social construction of ability and disability I: Profile types of Latino children identified as language learning disabled. *Journal of Learning Disabilities, 28*, 476–490.

Ruiz, N. T. (1995b). The social construction of ability and disability II: Optimal and at-risk lessons in a bilingual special education classroom. *Journal of Learning Disabilities, 28*, 491–502.

Schumm, J. S., & Rddencich, M. (1992). *School power: Strategies for succeeding in school.* Minneapolis, MN: Free Spirit Publishing.

Short, D. J. (1989). Adapting material for content-based language instruction. *ERIC/Clearing House on Languages and Linguistics news Bulletin, 13*(1): 1, 4–8.

Short, D. J. (1992). Adapting material and developing lesson plans. In P. Richard-Amato & M. Snow (Eds.), *The multicultural classroom.* New York: Longman.

Short, D. (1994). Expanding middle school horizons: Integrating language, culture, and social studies. *TESOL Quarterly, 28*(3), 581–608.

Slowinski, J. (1999). *Using the web to access online education periodicals* (Report No. EDO-IR-1999-08). Syracuse, NY: ERIC Clearinghouse on Information and Technology. (ERIC Document Reproduction Service No. ED40584)

Wahl, J. (1969). *How the children stopped the wars.* Berkeley, CA: Tricycle Press.

# Adjusting Discourse to Enhance Learning

- *Mr. Nishimoto* wants to improve the quality of class discussions. What practices can he begin using to improve student participation?
- At times, *Ms. Cooper* is frustrated when the students don't seem to understand what she is saying. What adjustments can she make to increase student comprehension?
- *Mrs. Roggeman* is a sheltered history teacher. What are some key ways that her discourse will be different from that of the mainstream history teacher?
- *Mr. Pa'u* believes that students comprehend text best in a small-group, interactive format. What are some important elements for getting the most out of such a format?

As we have discussed in previous chapters, students learning English must have ample opportunity to use the target language, to hear and see comprehensible English, and to read, write, and speak the new language within the context of subject matter learning. But there is one important caveat to this: The language, or discourse, must be meaningful. It is not only the quantity of exposure to language that affects learning but the quality, as well (Wong-Fillmore & Valadez, 1986).

In this chapter, we will discuss ways to incorporate meaningful discourse into sheltered lessons. We believe that substantiative student-to-student and teacher-to-student interaction is an essential component of effective sheltered instruction.

Research has shown that in most classrooms, not just those for bilingual or English-language learners (ELLs), students are severely limited in their opportunities to use language in a variety of ways (Cazden, 1986; Goodlad, 1984; Sirotnik, 1983). In a study of bilingual education and English immersion programs, it was reported that each program type reflected traditional transmission or recitation teaching, which is dominated by teacher talk. When students are given a chance to respond, their responses typically are limited to simple information-recall statements. The study concluded that teachers tend to offer a "passive language-learning environment, limiting student opportunities to produce language and develop more complex language and thinking skills" (Ramirez, Yuen, Ramey, & Pasta, 1991).

In secondary schools, where content is dense, students need opportunities to grapple with concepts by discussing topics in meaningful and productive ways. How are English-language learners going to practice and experiment with the new language if not in the classroom? There needs to be abundant opportunity for meaningful, original student contributions embedded in instruction throughout the day, providing opportunities to express, interpret, and negotiate meaning in the target language. ELLs need to be guided and "apprenticed" into more academic ways of communicating (Bartolome, 1998). The emphasis on standards-based instruction and accountability requires that ELLs be taught in a language-rich environment wherein students interact with important ideas and discuss lesson content. The structure of content classes needs to be altered so that instead of teachers talking and students listening, students are interacting in their collaborative investigation of a body of knowledge (Diaz, 1989).

Two ways to accomplish the goal of creating classrooms where meaningful discourse takes place will be presented. The first is to use language that is more comprehensible for English-language learners, which encourages increased participation. The second is to create opportunities explicitly for meaningful interaction through instructional conversations.

## *The Discourse of Sheltered Instruction*

In making adjustments for English-language learners, Pritzos (1992) cites modifications teachers can make to their speech to enhance comprehension. Many of these modifications are specifically addressed in the chapters on sheltered instruction (Chapter 3) and on curriculum adaptations (Chapter 6). These modifications have been shown to improve student achievement (Echevarria, Short, & Powers, in preparation), and they are consistently recommended in the literature. Such modifications include the following:

1. Sentence length and complexity of sentence structure (syntax) should be controlled.
2. Speech should be at a natural but slower rate than normal, and enunciation should be clear.
3. Use of idioms should be avoided, or meanings should be made clear.
4. High-frequency vocabulary should be chosen when possible, and vocabulary range should be controlled.
5. Full referents should be used rather than pronouns.
6. Emphasis should be placed on key words, phrases, and concepts by intonation or by using pauses to set them apart from surrounding material.
7. The same words and phrases should be repeated several times instead of using a variety of expressions.
8. Direct rather than indirect questions should be used.
9. Instructions should convey one idea or action each and should be presented in correct, temporal sequence.
10. Repetition, restatements, and redundant grammatical structures should be used.

How should these features be integrated into lessons? In a study comparing the language used in a mainstream science class and a sheltered science class (Pritzos, 1992), the following transcripts were included, which show a sheltered science teacher using several strategies that he did not use with mainstream students.

### Mainstream Class

**Teacher:**   Dustin, read Chris's answer for me.

**Student:**   An insulator holds electricity in, and a conductor lets energy flow through.

**Teacher:**   Very good. An insulator does not allow electricity to pass through. And a conductor allows electricity to pass through. Write OK beside the answer if they've done that, and then pass it back to them.

### Sheltered Class

**Teacher:**   I won't tell ya' any names 'cause I've seen a whole bunch of students—where the student writes this: Says, "A conductor conducts things." *(Writes on board)* Does that tell me anything? Does that tell me about this word?

**Student:**   Yeah.

**Teacher:**   It's in here *(points to the word* conductor*)*. No *(shakes head).* So I would say: "Conductors . . ." We said—and they told me "pass through" (writes on board). Eh, now . . . better answer. So we say, "A conductor allows things to pass through *(points to written words).* Insulator does not allow things to pass through *(points to* insulator, pass through *and shakes head)* or stops things." And in this case it stops electricity. Conductor allows electricity to pass through *(points to* conductor*)*. Now, look at your paper and at your partner's paper. Did they write something that tells you "Things pass through is a conductor, does not pass through is an insulator"? If they wrote that, then write OK. If they had that idea, write OK.

Although the two excerpts are comparable in content, in the sheltered class, the teacher makes several modifications to increase student understanding. For example, the teacher writes the words *conductor, conducts things, insulator,* and *passes through* on the board and refers to these terms with gestures at least seven times, providing visual clues to supplement his speech. In addition, he uses some metalinguistic analysis when he asks the students whether it is appropriate to use *conduct* to define *conductor.* In the mainstream class, the teacher says, "A conductor allows electricity to pass through." In the sheltered class, he initially uses the hypernym *thing* ("A conductor allows things to pass through") and then later uses the word *electricity.* Pritzos points out that this strategy could be used to lessen the cognitive load of the definition, allowing more attention to be placed on the ideas *insulator, conductor, pass through,* and *not pass through.* Further, when *electricity* is introduced, the teacher overtly identifies *things* as *electricity* for clarification and then restates the definition for *conductor* using the word *electricity.*

Another strategy for increasing comprehensibility is to paraphrase. The teacher first says "does not allow things to pass through" and then paraphrases with the synonymous phrase "or stops things." Other kinds of strategies that teachers in this study employed were reducing the rate of speech and more careful pronunciation when addressing the sheltered classes.

In another example, we transcribed discourse from the consumerism unit presented in Chapter 3. First, is the transcript of a portion of a typical lesson found in a mainstream class, and then is the transcript of the sheltered teacher teaching the same portion of the lesson.

### Mainstream Lesson

*Teacher:*   Look at the piece of clothing at the bottom. It says *(he reads),* "This shirt is flame-resistant," which means what?

*Student:*   Could not burn.

*Student:*   Won't catch fire.

*Teacher:*   It will not burn, won't catch fire. Right. *(Continues reading.)* "To retain the flame-resistant properties"—what does it mean "to retain"?

*Student:*   *(unintelligible)*

*Teacher:*   To keep it. All right. "In order to keep this shirt flame-resistant *(he reads),* wash with detergent only." All right *(he reads).* "Do not use soap or bleach. Tumble dry. One hundred percent polyester." Now, why does it say, "Do not use soap or bleach"?

*Student:*   'Cause it'll take off the . . .

*Teacher:*   It'll take off the what?

*Students:*   *(fragmented responses)*

*Teacher:*   It'll take off the flame-resistant quality. If you wash it with soap or bleach, then the shirt's just gonna be like any old shirt, any regular shirt, so when you put a match to it, will it catch fire?

*Student:*   No.

*Teacher:*   Yes. 'Cause you've ruined it then. It's no longer flame resistant. So the government says you gotta tell the consumer what kind of shirt it is and how to take care of it. If you look at any piece of clothing: shirt—it doesn't come on off on your underwear or your socks—but on your pants, your shirts, um, your skirts, anything. There's always going to be a tag on these that says what it is made of and how you're going to take care of it. OK. And that's for your protection so that you won't buy something and then treat it wrong. So labeling is important. All right. Let's review. I'll go back to the antiseptic. What did we say *indications* meant? *Indications?* Raise your hands; raise your hands. Robert?

**Student:**   What's it for?

**Teacher:**   What is it for, when do you use this? OK. What do directions, what is that for, Victor?

**Student:**   How to use . . .

**Teacher:**   How to use. OK, so *indications* is when you use it *(holds one finger up)*, *directions* is how you use it *(holds another finger up)*, and *warnings* is what?

**Students:**   *(various mumbled responses)*

**Teacher:**   How you don't use it. This is what you don't do.

Close inspection of this teacher's discourse patterns indicate some behaviors that do not facilitate learning or English acquisition. The first inappropriate behavior is complete teacher dominance. He talks for lengthy periods of time, with students often losing interest judging by their looking away, engaging in quiet conversations with each other, and being inattentive. He does not give students much opportunity to interact with him or with other students.

The second inappropriate behavior is cutting students off and answering his own question, even when he does ask for student input. The first time this happens, a student says, "'Cause it'll take off the . . ." and the teacher responds, "It'll take off the what?" Prompting the student to finish the sentence is a good teaching strategy; some researchers believe a brisk instructional pace is desirable. However, this teacher consistently cuts students off and answers questions himself, stifling student participation. A more productive behavior for English-language learners would be for the teacher to wait for the student to think of the word. Alternately, he could direct the students to the text for the word. Instead, he waits each time a mere split second before answering the question himself.

The third inappropriate behavior is not providing opportunities for elaborated responses. He tends to ask for single-word answers, or when he does ask a question that requires a complete sentence, rather than validating students' responses by saying "Tell me what you mean" or "So you're saying . . . ?" he moves ahead with the lesson. He asks questions but does not listen to the students' answers or try to encourage them to elaborate.

Here is the same lesson using a sheltered approach.

### Sheltered Instruction

**Teacher:**   Most clothing must have labels that tell what kind of cloth was used in it, right? Look at the material in the picture down there *(points to picture in text).* What does it say, the tag right there?

*Student:*  The, the, the . . .

*Teacher:*  The tag right there.

*Student:*  Flame-resis . . .

*Teacher:*  Resistant.

*Student:*  Flame-resistant. To retain the flame-resistant properties, wash with detergent only. Do not use soap or bleach. Use warm water. Tumble dry.

*Teacher:*  One hundred percent.

*Student:*  Polyester.

*Teacher:*  Now, most clothes carry labels, right *(pointing to the neck of her sweater),* explaining how to take care of it, like dry clean, machine wash, right? It tells you how to clean it. Why does this product have to be washed with a detergent and no soap or bleach?

*Student:*  Because clothes . . .

*Teacher:*  Why can't you use something else?

*Students:*  *(Several students mumble answers.)*

*Student:*  *(says in Spanish)* Because it will make it small.

*Teacher:*  It may shrink, or *(gestures to a student)* it may not be . . . what does it say?

*Student:*  It's not going to be able to be resistant to fire.

*Teacher:*  Exactly. It's flame resistant, right? So if you use something else, it won't be flame resistant any more. How about the, uh, look at the antiseptic (holds hands up to form a container), the picture above the shirt, the antiseptic?

*Student:*  Read it?

*Teacher:*  Antiseptic. *(Teacher reads.)* And other health products you buy without a prescription often have usage and warning labels. What can you learn from this label? Read this label, quietly please, and tell me what you can learn from the label. Read the label on that antiseptic.

*(Students read silently.)*

*Teacher:*  What can you learn from this label?

*Student:*  It kills—oh, I know.

*Teacher:*  Steve?

*Student:*  It kills germs.

*Student:*  Yeah, it kills germs.

**Teacher:** It kills germs. You use it for wounds, right? What else?

**Students:** *(various enthusiastic responses)*

**Teacher:** One person at a time. OK, hold on. Veronica was saying something.

**Student:** It tells you in the directions that you could use it, that like that, 'cause if you use it in another thing, it could hurt you.

**Teacher:** It could hurt you. OK, what else? Ricardo?

**Student:** If you put it in your mouth. Don't put it in your mouth or your ears or your eyes.

**Teacher:** Very good. Don't put it in your mouth, ears, and eyes. OK, for how many days should you use it? No more than what?

**Student:** No more than ten days.

**Student:** Ten days.

**Teacher:** So don't use it—you have to follow what it says so don't use it more than ten days. Now, the next activity you're going to do . . .

*(The teacher explained that they would be doing an activity in which they would read labels for information.)*

The sheltered lesson differs from mainstream instruction in two distinct ways: (1) the balance of teacher to student talk and (2) the level of student participation. The sheltered teacher asked questions, waited for student responses, and restated or elaborated the responses. The transcript shows a more even balance between teacher talk and student talk. The videotape reveals substantially more student participation in the sheltered lesson, with students enthusiastically responding to questions, while during the effective instruction lesson, students were more passive. Further, the sheltered teacher used the text as a referent during the lesson, pointing to terms and illustrations.

The teacher effectively implemented components of sheltered instruction to enhance comprehension of the subject matter while delivering whole-group instruction. Small-group instruction can provide even more individualized engagement in meaningful discourse. One such interactive approach is the use of instructional conversations.

# The Discourse of
# Instructional Conversations

*Instructional conversations (ICs)* use a small-group format (five to seven students) to create opportunities for students to engage in thoughtful, reflective, and sometimes provocative discussions about ideas, texts, and concepts (Goldenberg, 1992–93; Tharp & Gallimore, 1988). As the teacher seeks to improve comprehension and develop language, ICs provide a forum for developing new understandings and constructing meaning from the text. Together, the group discusses possible interpretations or predictions and constructs meaning and ideas jointly. IC is less a direct transmission of knowledge and understanding from teacher to student and more an opportunity for students and teachers to reach jointly new levels of understanding. During an IC, both teacher and students are responsive to one another, with no one person dominating the discussion, although the teacher does serve as the primary facilitator.

ICs might be particularly effective for culturally and linguistically diverse populations, since these students are often deprived of adequate language opportunities both in terms of the amount and the quality of language used in the classroom. Observations of classrooms with ELLs reveal that teachers dominate the linguistic exchanges, leaving students with little or no opportunity to use language to express their ideas in meaningful ways (Ramirez, Yuen, Ramey, & Pasta, 1991). The goal of ICs is to create rich language opportunities for students during which they can think, reflect, express ideas, and argue positions as they develop new understandings around a text.

Most of the work with ICs has been with students who have characteristics that are associated with poor academic performance and school failure: poor families, immigrant status, or limited English proficiency. Research conducted with ICs has shown several positive effects. Echevarria (1995b) found that students, even those labeled language and learning disabled, used higher levels of discourse and had greater participation during IC lessons than during those taking a more conventional basal approach. Further, ICs promoted higher understanding of concepts than a recitation or basal-like comprehension lesson (Saunders & Goldenberg, 1999). Most of the IC students understood the literal details of the story as well or better than the control group but also displayed a more complex conceptualization of friendship, which was the theme of the story. ICs have also been used with students in special education who responded positively to the holistic and thematic approach, although some adaptations were required with this population (Echevarria & McDonough, 1995).

## *Theoretical Background*

The theoretical roots of IC can be found in the writings of L. S. Vygotsky (1978, 1962). Vygotsky's theory places great importance on the role of social context and verbal scaffolding. Vygotsky calls *language* a vehicle of intellectual development, and he suggests that a great deal of development is *scaffolded* by a more competent person. Based on this theory, Tharp and Gallimore (1988) have criticized recitation script—the typical discourse used in schools—as "a series of unrelated teacher questions that require convergent factual answers and student display of (presumably) known information. Recitation questioning requires predictable, correct answers" (p. 14). Exclusive reliance on recitation is particularly limiting to ELLs whose home experiences might not include the language of school or the level of emergent literacy experiences that middle-class children receive. Tharp and Gallimore assert that children of poverty, as well as many ethnic minorities who do not perform well in school, need language and literacy development conversations in school. ICs provide such opportunities.

Thus, the role of the teacher in an IC lesson is one of facilitator, assisting students in joint activity, helping them construct meaning from texts, and promoting their understanding of ideas and concepts they otherwise would not understand on their own. In other words, an IC is more than a good discussion. An IC involves movement in understanding so that by the end of the IC, students should have a greater understanding of the theme or concept than when it began.

A growing number of educators and researchers, particularly those specializing in culturally and linguistically diverse populations, recognize the importance of an interactive approach to teaching—interaction that provides the necessary scaffolding. Cummins (1989), for instance, advocates instruction that consists of genuine dialogue between the student and teacher, as well as student-to-student collaborative talk. The teacher's role is one of facilitator, encouraging students to use meaningful language without focusing on the correctness of form. Development of higher-level cognitive skills, rather than factual recall, is the goal. All of these features are found within an IC.

In an effort to create a model for conducting ICs in a tangible, systematic way, 10 elements that characterize an IC were developed (see Figure 7.1, page 160) (Goldenberg, 1992–93; Goldenberg & Gallimore, 1991). These elements provide a framework for teachers in planning and implementing ICs in their classrooms:

**1.** *Thematic focuze* teacher selects a theme or idea to serve as a starting point to focus the discussion and has a general plan for how the theme will unfold, including how to "chunk" the text to permit optimal exploration of the theme. The purpose of a thematic focus is for the teacher to have a particular goal in mind that will lead the students to some new understanding. Teachers should ask themselves, "To what extent am I engaging the students in a discussion that is moving somewhere?"

To assure that the theme is carried throughout the lesson, some IC teachers have written questions on detachable flags and affixed them to the pages of the book. For example, when the theme is courage, the

FIGURE 7.1   *Features of an Instructional Conversation (IC)*

1. Thematic focus
2. Activation and use of background knowledge and relevant schemata
3. Direct teaching
4. Promotion of more complex language and expression
5. Elicitation of bases for statements or positions
6. Fewer "known-answer" questions
7. Being responsive to student contributions
8. Connected discourse
9. A challenging but nonthreatening atmosphere
10. General participation, including self-selected turns

teacher might have a question posted on the page for reference, such as "In what ways do you think the main character showed courage here?" With this strategy, the teacher is reminded to link the discussion to the theme consistently, enhancing the students' understanding of the concept or the theme. The theme has been described as the glue that holds the lesson together, and without it, the lesson may be fragmented. In every IC lesson, there should be a larger point or issue that drives the direction of the lesson rather than a simple series of questions and answers that are often disconnected.

In order to have an interesting discussion, the theme should be something that is relevant to the students. For instance, in a textbook story about a girl who is disinterested in reading but gets turned on to books when she goes with her brother to the library and hears the librarian reading aloud to a group, obvious themes might be reading or learning to like something. Or the teacher might select a theme about caring for or being cared for by siblings. This might lead to a lively discussion of students' own experiences. By the time the teacher explains that they are going to read a story about a girl who is in the care of her older brother, so she has to accompany him to the library, they will be eager to hear about the character's experience. A rather mundane story from a basal reader comes to life when the students can read it from this thematic perspective. If they can relate to the situation, their interest will be held during the lesson, as the theme or concept is woven through it.

*2. Activation and use of background knowledge and relevant schemata.* The teacher either "hooks into" or provides students with pertinent background knowledge and relevant schemata necessary for understanding a text. Background knowledge and schemata are then woven into the discussion that follows.

IC provides a format for activating prior knowledge or building requisite knowledge through discussion. As discussed in Chapters 4, 5, and 6, English-language learners bring to the classroom their own set of experiences and knowledge, as well as their unique view of the world. ICs explicitly capitalize on what the students bring. A lesson about a pioneer girl making friends with some Native Americans might seem irrelevant to the lives of urban middle school students, but if the teacher draws upon the students' experiences with friends, these experiences can then be tied to the character and to her new friends.

If students have a rudimentary understanding of a concept or idea, it can be used to move them to greater levels of understanding. Even if they have no prior exposure to a topic or idea, students will explore what they do not know and their thoughts and ideas will be validated through the IC discussion. Simply put, IC provides a bridge between their knowledge and experiences and other new concepts.

Teachers elicit students' prior knowledge and learning by asking questions such as these:

- What have you experienced that is similar to the character's experience?
- How do you think the settlers felt?
- How would a situation like this be handled in your native country?
- If you were the character, what would you do?
- Would your parents allow you to do that?

Questions such as these that relate the text to the students' experiences are skillfully presented throughout the discussion, providing a continuous link between the students and the story.

**3.** *Direct teaching.* When necessary, the teacher provides direct teaching of a skill or concept. When a student does not understand a vocabulary word, concept, decoding skills, or process, the teacher provides specific, direct instruction. For instance, "Add the numbers in this column and then the numbers in that column." As the student progresses and becomes more independent, the teacher adjusts the amount and type of assistance provided, perhaps asking questions such as, "Where do you think you could start?" Within the context of an IC, direct teaching may be simply defining a term and moving on, or it may require more in-depth teaching of a skill or concept.

**4.** *Promotion of more complex language and expression.* The teacher encourages more extended student contributions by using a variety of elicitation techniques. For example, the teacher invites students to expand ("Tell me more about . . ."), asks direct questions ("What do you mean by . . . ?"), offers restatements ("In other words, . . ."), and makes frequent pauses.

As mentioned previously, there is abundant evidence that teachers tend to dominate lessons linguistically, without being aware of the need to elicit elaborated student utterances and genuine student responses. Such opportunities are created by using comments like "Tell me more about that" or "Tell me what you mean by that." If the student gives a one-word answer, the teacher may ask, "Why do you think that?" or "What basis do you have for that?" After asking the question or making a request for elaboration, the teacher then remains quiet—even for an extended period. With practice using these strategies, the students become acutely aware that the expectation is for them to fill in and that the teacher is not going to jump in and paraphrase or finish the thought for them.

Increasing wait-time gives students the opportunity to formulate their ideas. As one special education teacher using ICs explained:

> I found that my expectations of what the students could produce and the kinds of ideas that they could come up with are very different than they used to be. . . . Allowing them wait-time and asking them to explain why they feel the way they do and to relate it to something we've read, . . . I'm more willing to give them more opportunities to speak and explain themselves in a variety of situations.

5. *Elicitation of bases for statements or positions.* The teacher promotes students' use of text, pictures, and reasoning to support an argument or position. Without overwhelming students, the teacher probes for the bases of students' statements by asking "How do you know?" or "What makes you think that?" or "Show us where it says . . ."

6. *Fewer "known-answer" questions.* Much of the discussion centers on questions and answers for which there might be more than one correct answer. A teacher mentioned that when she is not getting the responses she wants from the students, she does a self-evaluation. She usually finds that her questions are of the type that elicit a yes-no response or a predictable answer. The kinds of questions that generate a good discussion are those for which there may be more than one correct answer. *Open-ended* or *prompting questions* encourage students to think, express opinions, and construct meaning. Here are some examples of open-ended questions:

- By looking at the page, what do you think the chapter will be about?
- What can you learn from reading this label?
- How are these plants different?
- Why would the colonists do that?
- What else can you tell me about that?
- On what basis would you group these objects?
- Why might that be?
- What makes you think this might be different?

These questions call for opinions, inferences, or predictions. However, teachers have reported that asking such questions consistently is difficult, since literal recall questions are easier to formulate. Nevertheless, higher-order questioning is critical in encouraging students to really think about the material and to give more elaborated responses to questions.

7. *Being responsive to student contributions.* While having an initial plan and maintaining the focus and coherence of the discussion, the teacher is also responsive to students' statements and the opportunities they provide.

In an eighth-grade language arts class with a group of ELLs who were labeled learning disabled, the teacher was discussing a story about a young man reading a magazine on the bus (Echevarria, 1995a). The students read the next part of the story as a group. It described how some men speaking Russian boarded the bus and how when the main character, Mike, reached his stop, he exited the bus and said a quick greeting in Russian to the men. The story explicitly stated that Mike's brother-in-law spoke Russian, which is how Mike learned the phrase. The next part of the story describes how Mike realizes that the men have gotten off the bus at the next stop and are running after him, firing a gun. He quickly escapes from the men and arrives safely at his second-story apartment. Some time later, he hears noise outside, looks out the window, and sees that the men have found where he lives. The teacher pauses in the reading and asks, "How do you suppose the men found out where Mike lived?" The correct answer was that they got his address from the subscription label on his magazine, which he'd left on the bus. However, one student said that the Russians probably asked other Russian people in the neighborhood who Mike was. The teacher reported later that she was tempted to skip over the student's response, which seemed to at best implausible and at worst "out in left field." Instead, she was responsive to the student's contribution and probed to clarify his point. She said, "Tell me more about that. How would they do that?" The Latino student explained that in their predominately Latino community, everyone knows where the few Samoan families live, and if anyone wanted any information about a Samoan-speaking person, everyone would know where to go. By being responsive and encouraging the student to elaborate and clarify his meaning, the teacher said she learned an important lesson: that there are connections between students' seemingly "off the wall" comments and the point being discussed, which will be clear if only students are given the encouragement to explain their ideas.

8. *Connected discourse.* The discussion is characterized by multiple, interactive, connected turns. Succeeding utterances build upon and extend previous ones. As with any good conversation, each person in the discussion

makes contributions, often building on what the other person has said. Students are encouraged to express their agreement and disagreement with what the others say.

**9.** *A challenging but nonthreatening atmosphere.* The teacher creates a *zone of proximal development,* which means that he or she provides the amount of assistance the students need until they are able to function independently. A challenging atmosphere is balanced by a positive affective climate. The teacher is more collaborator than evaluator and creates an atmosphere that challenges students and allows them to negotiate and construct the meaning of the text.

The teacher conducting an IC strives to engage students in a good conversation but does not lose sight of the instructional intent of ICs. It is not enough simply to have an interesting discussion. The discussion needs to be linked to the instructional goal of the sheltered lesson. Students should be engaged intellectually in ways they might not be otherwise. In a videotape of ICs (Echevarria & Silver, 1995), the teacher pushes the students to go farther in their thinking by asking questions such as "How could that be? Why would that be?" "What gives you the idea that the buffalo could be the woman?" "How can you just accept that? Would that happen in our lives?" or "How would they show us that?" Without intimidating the students, she challenges them to think about and discuss the story at higher levels of understanding.

**10.** *General participation, including self-selected turns.* The teacher encourages general participation by all students. He or she does not hold exclusive rights to determine who talks, and students are encouraged to volunteer or otherwise influence the selection of speaking turns. The teacher functions more as a facilitator, encouraging students to contribute to the discussion spontaneously without having to be granted permission to speak.

Typically, quality interaction does not naturally happen once the teacher begins using an IC approach. The students have to overcome the conditioning of schooling, where most instruction, even discussions, usually consists of the teacher initiating a question or topic and the students anticipating what the teacher is looking for, volunteering a response only when they think they have the right answer and otherwise waiting to be called upon. Often students who are not called on disengage and are not involved in the discussion. With practice using ICs, students begin to realize that the teacher is genuinely interested in their ideas and opinions and will give them the time they need to formulate and express their thoughts.

An example of the type of discourse used during an IC can be seen in the following transcription of a lesson with Latino fifth-graders, where the teacher encouraged meaningful discourse by guiding students' thinking (Echevarria & Silver, 1995):

*Teacher:* There was a word that came up: *respect.* You said he had *respect.* Why did he have respect for her instantly like that?

*Student:* Cause he . . .

*Student:* Love.

*Teacher:* He had love? How did he have that instant love for her?

*Student:* 'Cause she came from the buffalo nation.

*Student:* She, she was nice. She dressed not like them.

*Student:* She dressed . . .

*Student:* Differently.

*Teacher:* But he still felt this love and respect for this different, this person from a different kind of a culture?

*Several:* Yes, uh-huh.

*Teacher:* How can that be? Why would that be? *(Students remained quiet.)*

*Teacher:* You know, what that brings me to is that Rolando brought up his idea about the author's purpose—why this is going on. Okay. And I'd like you to remind us what you said about the author's purpose, Rolando, and we're gonna check out what we think about that, okay? What was it that you thought might be the author's purpose?

*Student:* That, like, 'cause the man, he fell in love with the woman, and the woman's a buffalo and the man likes hunting buffalo, he might kill her. And the author's purpose means never to kill buffalo 'cause they're a great part of nature.

*Teacher:* What do you guys think about that? Why would you agree? Why do you think that's a good idea?

*Student:* 'Cause they're almost 'stint.

*Students:* They're not very much.

*Teacher:* Okay. So not killing them, what would that serve?

*Student:* That would make more and then the buffalos make little ones and they're an endangered species and soon they, they won't be endangered species anymore.

*Teacher:* Okay. That would be a good author's purpose. Any other author's purpose that is a possibility? . . . Cynthia brought up a different idea in her prediction. It wasn't about killing buffalo—do you remember? Could you tell us what you said?

*Student:* It's like, killing a buffalo is like killing a beautiful woman.

The teacher provided assistance to the students, guiding them to higher levels of understanding. The students undoubtedly couldn't have reached this level of discussion on their own, but with the assistance of a skilled teacher, they came to understand some complex ideas.

## *Summary*

The classroom needs to be a place where ELLs have an opportunity to practice using academic language in meaningful ways. But how does a teacher encourage meaningful discourse with students whose English proficiency is limited? One way is to make sure the message is understandable to English-language learners. Another way is to structure sheltered lessons so that they promote opportunities for students to think through ideas and concepts and express themselves in elaborated ways. Instructional conversations provide a format for the teacher to scaffold student learning, providing the support they need to reach independent functioning. The teacher takes students from where they are and verbally guides them to a new level of understanding where they can function independently (Vygotsky, 1978). The interaction between the students and teacher is meaningful and purposeful, as it moves the student to a level of independent thinking and expression through collaborative interaction and inquiry.

## *Activities*

1. Using a textbook from any subject area, select a short passage to teach. Write a brief outline of how you might teach the passage. In a small group, role-play teaching the lesson, focusing on using discourse that encourages linguistically balanced student-teacher interaction. Be sure to develop questions that allow students to use complete sentences, as well as other features that encourage meaningful discourse by students.

2. Select a videotape of any teaching situation (for instance, a commercial demonstration videotape or footage of students practice teaching). Transcribe a segment of the lesson and discuss the aspects of sheltered discourse discussed in the chapter, including teacher talk versus student talk, elaborated speech versus phrases and single-word answers, and the use of wait-time.

3. As a group or with a partner, brainstorm practical ways that you can begin to use more meaningful discourse in working with English-language learners.

## *References*

Bartolome, L. (1998). *The misteaching of academic discourses: The politics of language in the classroom.* Oxford: Westview Press.

Cazden, C. (1988). *Classroom discourse: The language of teaching and learning.* Portsmouth, NH: Heinemann.

Cummins, J. (1989). A theoretical framework for bilingual special education. *Exceptional Children, 56*(2), 111–128.

Diaz, D. (1989). *Language across the curriculum and ESL students: Composition research and 'sheltered' courses.* (ERIC Document Reproduction Service No. ED 326 057).

Echevarria, J. (1995a). *Instructional conversations: Understanding through discussion. Facilitator's guide.* Santa Cruz, CA: National Center for Research on Cultural Diversity and Second Language Learning.

Echevarria, J. (1995b). Interactive reading instruction: A comparison of proximal and distal effects of instructional conversations. *Exceptional Children 61*(6), 536–552.

Echevarria, J., & McDonough, R. (1995). An alternative reading approach: Instructional conversations in a bilingual special education setting. *Learning Disabilities Research and Practice, 10*(2), 108–119.

Echevarria, J., Short, D., & Powers, K. (in preparation). *Using sheltered instruction to improve the achievement of English language learners.* Manuscript submitted for publication.

Echevarria, J. (Producer & Writer), & Silver, J. (Producer & Director) (1995). [Videotape]. *Instructional conversations: Understanding through discussion.* Santa Cruz, CA: National Center for Research on Cultural Diversity and Second Language Learning.

Goldenberg, C. (1992–93). Instructional conversations: Promoting comprehension through discussion. *The Reading Teacher, 46*(4), 316–326.

Goldenberg, S. & Gallimore, R. (1991). Changing teaching takes more than a one-shot workshop. *Educational Leadership, 49*(3), 69–72.

Goodlad, J. (1984). *A place called school: Prospects for the future.* New York: McGraw-Hill.

Pritzos, S. (1992). *Teacher communication in regular and sheltered science classes.* Unpublished Master's Thesis.

Ramirez, J., Yuen, S., Ramey, D., & Pasta, D. (1991). *Executive summary: Final report: Longitudinal study of structured English immersion strategy, early-exit and late-exit transitional bilingual education programs for language-minority children.* (Contract No. 300-87-0156). Submitted to the U.S. Department of Education. San Mateo: Aguirre International.

Saunders, W., & Goldenberg, C. (1999). The effects of instructional conversations and literature logs on limited and fluent English proficient students' story comprehension and thematic understanding. *The Elementary School Journal, 99,* 277–301. Also published as Research Report No. 6, Center for Research on Education, Diversity & Excellence, University of California, Santa Cruz. Available online: <www.cal.org/crede/pubs/research/RR6.pdf>.

Saunders, W., Goldenberg, C., & Hamann, J. (1992). Instructional conversation begets instructional conversations. *Teaching and Teacher Education, 8*(2), 199–218.

Sirotnik, K. (1983). What you see is what you get—consistency, persistency and mediocrity in classrooms. *Harvard Educational Review, 53,* 16–31.

Tharp, R., & Gallimore, R. (1988). *Rousing minds to life.* Cambridge: Cambridge University Press.

Vygotsky, L. S. (1962). *Thought and language* (E. Hanfmann & G. Vaker, Trans.). Cambridge, MA: Massachusetts Institute of Technology Press.

Vygotsky, L. S. (1978). *Mind in society: The development of higher psychological processes.* (M. Cole, V. John-Steiner, & E. Souberman, Eds. & Trans.). Cambridge, MA: Harvard University Press.

Wilgosh, L. (1984). Learned helplessness in normally achieving and learning disabled girls. *Mental Retardation and*

*Learning Disabilities Bulletin, 12*(2), 64–70.

Wong-Fillmore, L., & Valadez, C. (1986). Teaching bilingual learners. In M. C. Wittrock (Ed.), *Handbook of research on teaching* (pp. 648–685). New York: Macmillan.

# 8

## *Self-Evaluation and Collaborative Implementation*

- A group of teachers want to meet once a week to discuss and refine their teaching. What four features would enhance the process?
- *Ms. Mason* videotapes herself teaching and later watches the tapes. What are the benefits to such a practice?
- *Mr. Rojas* has students from 13 different language backgrounds in one of his science classes, 8 of whom are performing poorly. He speaks only Spanish and English. What can he do to increase student success?

One of the most important ways that teachers can improve their teaching with English language learners (ELLs) is through ongoing professional development. Many teachers find themselves unprepared to work effectively with ELLs because they did not receive adequate training in their teacher education program. Some districts offer inservice programs for working with ELLs, but in many schools the influx of these students is a relatively recent occurrence and professional development has lagged behind the need. Often, mainstream teachers lack sufficient preparation in second-language teaching methodology or experience in supporting second-language development while those teachers who are English as a second language (ESL) trained may not have the content background to meet the increasing demands of standards-based content area curricula.

Although adequate teacher preparation and support are critical, they are in short supply. As one study revealed, "As in sheltered content classes, one of the most profound challenges that mainstream content-area teachers face in meeting the needs of ELLs is the lack of ongoing support for working with such diverse student populations" (Bunch et al., 2001, p. 24). The need for sustained professional development is receiving more attention, however (Jaramillo, 1998).

This chapter is designed to assist readers in using the information presented throughout this book to enhance their teaching. It may be used as a text in teacher preparation courses or as a tool for continued professional development. In the previous seven chapters, we have presented information based on research in the areas of second-language instruction, multicultural education, and special education. Also, we have provided examples from classroom observations and our own suggestions for teaching English-language learners. In implementing the practices about which we have written, we encourage readers to engage in self-evaluation, goal setting, and collaboration with other school personnel.

To underscore the importance of these efforts, recent research suggests that well-prepared teachers have a greater impact on student achievement than the influences of student background factors such as poverty, language, and minority status (Darling-Hammond, 2000). Darling-Hammond

(1998) has reviewed the kinds of knowledge teachers need to prepare students for standards-based instruction and offers these guidelines:

- Teachers need to understand the subject matter deeply and flexibly.
- Teachers need to know about learning (teaching strategies, decision-making strategies about the content to cover and the best way to do so, assessment strategies, language acquisition theory).
- Teachers need to know about curriculum resources and technologies.
- Teachers need to know about collaboration—their collaboration with other teachers, students collaborating together, and collaboration with parents.
- Teachers need to be able to analyze and reflect on their practice, to assess the effects of their teaching, and to refine and improve their instruction.

## *Self-Evaluation and Goal Setting*

The purpose of this section is to provide a framework (see Figure 8.1, pages 172–174) to assist teachers in self-evaluation and goal setting as they relate to students learning English. Teachers can rate themselves on a scale of 1 to 5 on each item on the framework (5 = outstanding, 4 = very good, 3 = marginal, 2 = needs improvement, 1 = not being addressed).

As a result of these ratings, teachers can set personal goals, focusing on areas that need improvement. This process provides teachers with an opportunity for reflective teaching. Teachers are able to continually extend their knowledge, work at perfecting their technique, and analyze the merits of both older and newer pedagogical approaches.

In Chapter 1, we described the four students who represent four types of English language learners: Sonia, Krishna, Pon, and Luisa. Think of them as you use the framework and decide which of your students are similar to the learners described here:

> *Sonia* is a tenth-grader who was born in Guatemala. She moved to Southern California in the second grade. She was a good student in Guatemala and learned to read and write in Spanish. When she began school in the United States, she was placed in a bilingual classroom, where she received native-language support before transitioning into English instruction. Now in high school, she is performing at or above grade level in mainstream classes and has communication and literacy skills in her native language, as well. Because Sonia can speak, read, and write well in both languages, her English teacher is considering referring her to the gifted program at her school.

FIGURE 8.1   *Framework for Self-Assessment and Goal Setting*

| Step | Factors |
|---|---|
| 1. **Conduct Assessment** <br> Informal assessment and planning for instruction including annual and monthly goals | a. Native-language knowledge and home experience <br> b. English-language knowledge <br> c. School experience <br> d. Home experience <br> e. Academic background <br> f. Learning and behavior patterns |
| 2. **Consider Theories across Disciplines** <br> Practice reflects language and learning theories | a. Reviewing—check previous day's work and reteach if necessary—connect to background knowledge <br> b. Objectives stated clearly <br> c. Presenting new content/skills appropriate to grade level <br> d. Presenting a variety of delivery modes including modeling, demonstration, and visual representations <br> e. Ample student practice including frequent questions, verbal encouragement, and feedback <br> f. Ample independent practice including higher-order skills such as problem solving, hypothesizing, organizing, synthesizing, categorizing, evaluating, and self-monitoring <br> g. Weekly and monthly reviews |
| 3. **Use Sheltered Instruction** <br> Some features are unique and others differ in the degree to which they are used | a. Clearly defined content and language objectives <br> b. Supplementary materials used to a high degree, making the lesson clear and meaningful, and providing concrete examples <br> c. Content adapted to students' level <br> d. Speech appropriate to students' level <br> e. Sufficient wait-time <br> f. Link learning to students' experience <br> g. Select and teach key vocabulary |

**FIGURE 8.1** *Continued*

| Step | Factors |
|------|---------|
| **4. Consider Affective Issues** | **a.** Provide constructivist activities in reading and writing<br>**b.** Provide ample practice and careful corrections<br>**c.** Focus on relevant background knowledge<br>**d.** Actively involve learners<br>**e.** Use alternative grouping<br>**f.** Focus on content and activities that are meaningful to students<br>**g.** Provide native-language support<br>**h.** Create roles in the classroom for family and community members<br>**i.** Hold high expectations for *all* learners<br>**j.** Be responsive to cultural and personal diversity |
| **5. Use Learning Strategies** | **a.** Define a *learning strategy* and delineate types of learning strategies<br>**b.** Provide guidelines for selecting learning strategies<br>**c.** Describe lesson formats when teaching learning strategies<br>**d.** Identify presentation methods used to teach learning strategies<br>**e.** Embed specific strategies in reading, writing, and content areas |
| **6. Use Curriculum Adaptations** | **a.** Demonstrate sensitivity to cultural and linguistic diversity<br>**b.** Provide relevant background knowledge<br>**c.** Analyze material into content knowledge and academic proficiency<br>**d.** Include activities for language development and content vocabulary development<br>**e.** Modify text<br>**f.** Modify assignments<br>**g.** Study resource guides<br>**h.** Facilitate curriculum adaptations |

*(continued)*

FIGURE 8.1 *Continued*

| Step | Factors |
|------|---------|
| 7. **Use Interactive Approaches** | a. Thematic focus<br>b. Activate and use background knowledge<br>c. Direct teaching<br>d. Promote complex language and expression<br>e. Require students to support stated positions with sources<br>f. Ask many questions for which there are no single right answers<br>g. Encourage student elaborations<br>h. Encourage student dialogue about topics<br>i. Provide a challenging but non-threatening atmosphere<br>j. Encourage equal participation and open forum discussions |
| 8. **Engage in Self-Evaluation and Goal Setting** | a. Score yourself on a scale of 1 to 5 on the previous steps<br>b. Set goals by focusing on those areas that have the lowest scores |
| 9. **Collaborate with School Personnel to Encourage Schoolwide Change** | a. Meet in peer work groups<br>b. Exchange lessons and discuss steps 1 to 8<br>c. Plan that each teacher will share successes and challenges<br>d. Videotape lessons and analyze according to steps 1 to 8<br>e. Plan a unit together and brainstorm applications from steps and factors above |

*Krishna* is a recent immigrant who attends middle school. He has grade-level academic ability in his native language but speaks very little English. Since he has lived all his 13 years outside the United States, certain cultural knowledge presents difficulties for him. Krishna is quite shy and does not seek help readily. He has excellent social and academic language skills in his primary language and has already studied English for a few years, but his proficiency is quite limited. His history of learning and behavior at school, at home, and in the community is positive. He is described as a good citizen and a student who demonstrates appropriate behavior in most settings.

*Pon* is a fourth-grader who mainly speaks Khmer (Cambodian) and is one of two Cambodians in a rural school district. He is a nonreader in English and struggles with even the simplest words. His spoken English is quite limited when he interacts with students and the teacher in class. The members of his family are not literate and have not been able to provide literacy experiences for him at home. He has behavior problems in school. He often defies the teacher and engages in surreptitious or antisocial activities (fights, stealing, and so forth).

Born in an urban U.S. city, *Luisa* is a friendly 15-year-old who sits quietly in class, as if she understands everything. When written assignments are given, she writes down the assignment and begins to work. Her writing, however, is illegible and her spelling is extremely poor. Spanish is her first language, although her family speaks a mix of English and Spanish at home. She writes in English in a knowledge-telling mode without recognizable structure in her sentences or in her paragraphs. Luisa can converse quite well in both languages but for some reason has not made academic progress in either language. Although she is popular at school, she is at risk for dropping out because of consistent underachievement.

These are the types of learners who need the instructional practices presented in this book. The framework provided in Figure 8.1 is a series of nine steps that can assist a teacher in evaluating current instructional practices and setting goals that will produce change for both teacher and students.

Step 1 on the framework is taken from Chapter 1 (see Figure 1.2, page 6). It illustrates areas needing both assessment and instructional planning: native-language knowledge, English-language knowledge, school experience and academic background, and learning and behavior patterns. Instructional planning starts after assessment of the student and can be developed with all of the factors discussed in Chapters 1 to 7 in mind.

Step 2 on the framework is derived from Chapter 2. We concluded in this chapter that teachers make instructional choices that reflect particular theoretical perspectives. In Step 2, we have listed some factors that are sometimes referred to as *effective instruction*. Theorists agree that students learn more if a teacher reviews previous work and relevant content before beginning a lesson. This includes assisting students in focusing on relevant background knowledge. After this, the teacher makes a goal statement in language understandable to the learners. As the teacher begins the lesson, new content and skills are at an appropriate grade level for the learner and the teacher is careful to use many different approaches, including modeling, presenting concrete objects when possible, setting up group work, and encouraging opportunities for active learning. Practice takes place with the teacher present, and much independent practice in groups, with partners, or by individuals is important for maximum learning. As the students become more independent, the teacher assigns critical-thinking and higher-order applications of the content.

Step 3 on the framework recommends sheltered instruction, which uses specific strategies and techniques for making the content understandable for ELLs developing their English language proficiency. The model of sheltered instruction instantiated in the SIOP model provides concrete examples of the features of sheltered instruction that can enhance and expand a teacher's instructional practice (Echevarria, Vogt, & Short, 2000). Some of the features of the SIOP include clearly defined content and language objectives, adaptation of content to students' level, use of speech that is appropriate for students' level, linking new learning to students' background experiences, providing sufficient wait-time for students' responses, consistent use of scaffolding, and assessing students' comprehension and learning of objectives. The SIOP has been shown to significantly improve the writing skills of students whose teachers implemented the model over time.

Step 4 encourages teachers to focus on affective issues. Teachers can organize and manage their classrooms in such a way as to enhance the self-concept and self-esteem of each learner. The infrastructure of all units of instruction must have a foundation in which these affective issues are consistently part of the way in which lessons are configured. By allowing students to construct their own meaning through reading and writing and to practice whatever they are learning so they become successful, the teacher focuses on factors that enhance the self-concept and self-esteem of the learner. This is a focus on affective issues. Other ways to facilitate high self-esteem and self-concept as they relate to school are to focus on relevant background knowledge, actively involve learners, use alternative grouping, focus on content and activities that are meaningful to students, provide native-language support, create roles in the classroom for family and community members, hold high expectations for all learners, and be responsive to cultural and personal diversity. Students who receive these opportunities are likely to perform at a higher level in school and to like school better than students who do not have these opportunities.

Step 5 calls on teachers to use learning-strategy instruction when students do not appear to generate necessary learning strategies on their own. This instruction should always be a supplementary segment during a class or period. Such instruction might continue across many days until students understand and can apply the strategy, but the instruction should not continue longer than 15 or 20 minutes on any one day. Teachers carefully select learning strategies to teach students based on the individual or group needs of those students. The teachers present the strategy in a concise format so that students are sure to learn it. Teachers are careful to embed the strategy into a meaningful lesson. Teachers move from a segment on teaching a learning strategy into an instructional segment in which students participate actively in problem solving, conversations, or learning-centered work. In this way, the segment is sandwiched in between meaningful content instruction.

Step 6 calls for the use of curriculum adaptations. When using sheltered instruction, curriculum adaptations and use of curriculum that is sensitive to cultural and linguistic diversity is critical. In addition, curriculum must be adapted to include relevant background knowledge and relevant academic proficiency skills instruction. Language development as well as content vocabulary development should be part of most lessons. Texts and assignments can be modified. Resource guides can provide adaptations that have already been prepared to save teachers effort. Teachers are advised to delegate tasks because adaptations can be very time consuming.

Step 7 encourages teachers to use interaction and discourse patterns that provide students with opportunities to use and practice English, the target language. Again, teachers can focus on themes that are meaningful to students and provide recurrent vocabulary and concepts that encourage students to participate in discussions. Discussions can tap into background knowledge to motivate and interest students. One model of interaction is instructional conversations (ICs). The crux of the instructional conversations approach is the teacher's ability to elicit complex language from students, including the framing of postulates, arguments, elaborations, and dialogue. Teachers provide a nonthreatening atmosphere that challenges all students and often encourages open-forum discussions.

Step 8 has teachers rate each of the factors in the previous steps and decide which areas are strongest and which need improvement. Teachers select a lesson, think about which types of learners are in the class, and then rate each of the factors. Priority should be given to setting goals in the areas that received scores of 1, 2, or 3. Teachers can plan which goals to address and how those goals will be met. They should then make a list of each of the areas that needs additional work in a prioritized fashion. This provides teachers with a plan of action for change.

However, teachers should not operate alone. Reflection is much more powerful and effective when teachers share in the process and work together to bring change. In addition, students benefit more when many teachers at a school site engage in similar approaches. Students have an opportunity to learn more content and perform better in school when teachers have a common philosophy. The next section is written to elaborate on Step 9, "Collaborate with school personnel and peers."

## Collaboration with School Personnel and Peers

Because few systematic and sustained forms of professional development are available for sheltered instruction teachers (Short, 2000), we advocate a schoolwide system that allows for planning time, collaboration, discussion, and reflection. For change to occur at a school level, teachers need time to meet together and to have opportunities for self-evaluation, setting goals, and discussing common problems (Saunders et al., 2001; Short & Echevarria, 1999; Gersten, Morvant, & Brengelman, 1995; Fradd, 1993).

Students learning to be teachers can also benefit from collaboration with peers, which allows for planning time, collaboration, discussion, and reflection. Four features tend to enhance this process: meeting time with skilled consultants, meetings organized around perceived needs or areas of concern, evaluations of lesson delivery and student achievement, and videotaping of lessons to allow for analysis and review (Goldenberg & Gallimore, 1991).

Mastery of the factors presented in this book requires systematic implementation and practice. Although many features of sheltered instruction are not necessarily new, they seem more complex when teachers are striving to achieve consistently effective lessons with a heterogeneous group of students. The collaborative group can share readings on sheltered instruction, garnering ideas to put into practice. Teachers in the group can assist one another in planning specific lessons, or the group can develop a comprehensive curriculum plan for the whole year.

The SIOP model discussed in Chapter 3 was used for three years to train and coach middle school teachers in implementing effective sheltered lessons in their classes in four urban school districts, two on the East Coast and two on the West Coast (Short & Echevarria, 1999). The English-language learners in the classes ranged in English proficiency levels from beginning to advanced and represented a number of native-language groups. The teachers and researchers met monthly to discuss successes and challenges of implementing the SIOP, and each summer, a three-day summer institute was held. Also, teachers were videotaped three times per year, and the videotaped lessons were often used for analysis and discussion at the meetings. The project helped teachers expand their knowledge base and refine their practice in several of the aforementioned areas reviewed by Darling-Hammond (1998).

The process of videotaping a lesson, analyzing it, and discussing it with colleagues creates a context for reflection, prompting thought about what goes on in the lesson and toward what end. A group of teachers involved in the process suggested that meetings take place once a week but at least once a month to monitor progress and stay on track. As one put it, "It forces you to think about what you're doing. Teachers tend to zip through the lesson, the week, and the year without really reflecting."

Teachers in the group learn from one another by sharing concerns or describing areas in which they are struggling. The group can offer assistance by validating the positive aspects of lessons and constructively pointing out areas that need improvement. Much more can be accomplished by peers viewing videotapes of lessons than by a teacher doing it alone. Most teachers find the work group supportive, offering constructive comments when needed and compliments on positive outcomes. Teachers consistently say that hearing the ideas of others helps: "Sometimes you know something was wrong or didn't work but you couldn't think of how to do it differently."

A forum in which teachers can share areas of need and elicit ideas from one another has proven beneficial in sustaining ongoing movement toward change (Saunders & Goldenberg, 1996). The evaluation of classroom lesson delivery should be as much a part of the learning process as is the evaluation of student achievement (Gonzales, 1994). The process of meeting together, discussing readings, and analyzing videotaped lessons assists teachers to better conceptualize and implement sheltered techniques. As group members grapple with implementing specific features of sheltered instruction and share activities that are particularly effective, they become more conscious of what it is they are doing every day in the classroom.

Videotaping teachers' lessons and providing opportunities for them to review and analyze their efforts is indispensable. It is one thing for teachers to plan to improve a particular aspect of their teaching, but it is quite another to see exactly how the lesson unfolds. Videotape offers a completely objective set of eyes that capture not only the teacher's role in the lesson but also the students' participation levels and reactions to the lesson. A high school teacher commented, "It is more than seeing [the lesson] in your mind; you're a little more removed from the lesson itself and can give it an objective look." That objectivity reveals the parts of the lesson that went well and identifies things that could have been done differently. Visuals that were particularly helpful in illustrating a point or an activity that was fun and instructive will surely warrant being repeated. Some parts of the lesson may need to be altered—maybe too much time was spent on a certain part and the students lost interest—while other parts may need to be left out altogether. In the process of teaching, it is nearly impossible to deliver the lesson and to monitor constantly the effectiveness of every aspect at the same time.

Sheltered lessons are most effective when teachers pay attention to their teaching behaviors: rate of speech, use of idioms, body language to create context, and other components (see Chapter 3). Videotape allows teachers to monitor behaviors such as using gestures (frequency and timing), talking too fast, using idioms, and enunciation. One teacher said, "I never realized I said 'um' and 'okay' and 'you guys' too much." Another teacher acknowledged that she used gestures quite effectively, while a colleague noticed that he used idioms, which he had not realized previously. For example, he repeated several times "You've got that down pat" and "Keep your shirt on" in addition to saying "This is a kick-back activity" and "Don't blow this question off."

Videotape can yield valuable information regarding student behavior, as well. It becomes clear when students are bored with an activity or when there is too much teacher talk—they disengage, talk among themselves, put their heads down, and so forth—as well as when they are particularly stimulated by an activity or discussion. Perhaps the students did not comprehend something, but at the time the teacher was unaware and forged ahead. Later viewing can show what teacher behaviors lead to the confusion: Did the teacher use only verbal explanation without any visuals? Was the pace too fast? Was there sufficient guided practice? Such information helps in planning future lessons, knowing areas that need modification. In terms of behavior management, one teacher realized from watching the videotape that every time she turned to write on the blackboard, one student began fooling around, punching the student next to him. Based on this information, she began using an easel on which she could write while facing the group. A fifth-grade teacher commented, "There are so many things you're not aware of because you're focusing on the moment. You need to step back and see what's going on."

While there is no question that videotaping may be the single-most effective way for teachers to self-analyze and improve their teaching, it is also difficult for many teachers to be videotaped, particularly if colleagues will be viewing the tape. One teacher commented, "I hated it. I was petrified. I couldn't sleep. But it did really help. I saw my kids in a different way. They loved it." Another said, "It takes a lot of guts to face yourself. I hate hearing myself on tape or seeing myself on video."

Frequently, the idea of seeing oneself on videotape is more difficult than actually doing it. Teachers overwhelmingly endorse the value of analyzing videotape and often tape themselves for their own benefit.

## *Summary*

Experience has shown a tendency for teachers to assume that sheltered instruction is not much different from what they already do. This chapter has provided a systematic way in which teachers can evaluate the extent to which they are using the information in this book when teaching English-language learners. An important element of teaching ELLs is for teachers to engage in refection, goal setting, and collaboration with others who can lend support, contribute fresh ideas, and assist in analyzing ways to improve students' comprehension.

## Activities

1. With a teacher or on your own, select any ELL who has been placed in special education and write a summary of the available information according to Step 1 (Assessment) of the Framework for Self-Assesssment and Goal Setting (Figure 8.1, pages 172–174). Next, write recommendations regarding the assessment process. Were all the factors considered in the assessment?

2. Meet with a group of three to six colleagues and plan a sheltered lesson. Teach the lesson, and then meet again to discuss the successes and challenges of the lesson. Provide a self-assessment and goal-setting description of your teaching.

3. Bring any lesson plan (from a curriculum guide or a teacher-made plan) to class. Adapt the plan using the information from Steps 3, 4, 5, and 6 of the Framework for Self-Assessment and Goal Setting (Figure 8.1).

## References

Bunch, G., Abram, P., Lotan, R., & Valdes, G. (2001). Beyond sheltered instruction: Rethinking conditions for academic language development. *TESOL Journal, 10*(2/3), 28–33.

Darling-Hammond, L. (2000). Teacher quality and student achievement: A Review of state policy evidence. *Education Policy Analysis Archives, 9,* 1.

Darling-Hammond, L. (1998). Teacher learning that supports student learning. *Educational Leadership, 55,* 6–11.

Echevarria, J., Vogt, M., & Short, D. (2000). *Making content comprehensible for English language learners: The SIOP model.* Boston: Allyn and Bacon.

Fradd, S. H. (1993). *Creating the team to assist culturally and linguistically diverse students.* Tucon, AZ: Communication Skill Builders.

Gersten, R., Morvant, M., & Brengelman, S. (1995). Close to the classroom is close to the bone: Coaching as a means to translate research into classroom practice. *Exceptional Children, 62,* 52–67.

Goldenberg C., & Gallimore, R. (1991). Changing teaching takes more than a one-shot workshop. *Educational leadership, 49*(3), 69–72.

Gonzales, L. (1994). *Sheltered instruction handbook.* Carlsbad, CA: Gonzales & Gonzales.

Graves, A., Landers, M., Lokerson, J., Luchow, J., & Horvath, M. (1993). The development of a competency list for teachers of students with learning disabilites. *Learning Disabilities Research and Practice, 8,* 188–199.

Jaramillo, A. (1998). Professional development from the inside out. *TESOL Journal,* 12–18.

Saunders, B., O'Brien, G., Hasenstab, K., Marcelletti, D., Saldivar, T., & Goldenberg, C. (2001). Getting the most out of site-based professional development. In P. Schmidt & P. Mosenthal (Eds.), *Reconceptualizing literacy in the new age of pluralism and multiculturalism* (pp. 289–320). Greenwich, CT: IAP.

Saunders, W., & Goldenberg, C. (1996). Four primary teachers work to define constructivism and teacher-directed learning: Implications for teacher assessment. *The Elementary School Journal 97*(2), 139–161.

Saunders, W., Goldenberg, C., & Hamann, J. (1992). Instructional conversations beget instructional conversations. *Teaching and Teacher Education, 8*(2), 199–218.

Short, D. (2000). What principals should know about sheltered instruction for English language learners. *NASSP Bulletin, 84*, 17–27.

Short, D., & Echevarria, J. (1999). *The sheltered instruction observation protocol: A tool for teacher-researcher collaboration and professional development.* Santa Cruz, CA: Center for Research on Education, Diversity and Excellence.

# *Index*